Narrative Therapy

A NORTON PROFESSIONAL BOOK

Narrative Therapy

THE SOCIAL CONSTRUCTION
OF PREFERRED REALITIES

Jill Freedman and Gene Combs

Evanston Family Therapy Center, Evanston, Illinois

W.W. NORTON & COMPANY • *NEW YORK* • *LONDON*

For information about permission to reproduce selections
from this book, write to
Permissions, W.W. Norton Company, Inc., 500 Fifth Avenue,
New York, NY 10110

Library of Congress Catologing-in-Publication Data
Freedman, Jill, M.S.W.
    Narrative therapy : the social construction of preferred realities / Jill
Freedman and Gene Combs.
        p.   cm
    "A Norton Professional Book."
    Includes bibliographical references and index.
    ISBN 0-393-70207-3
    1. Storytelling --Therapeutic use.   2. Metaphor--Therapeutic use.
3. Constructivism (Psychology)   4. Postmodernism--Psychological
aspects.   I. Combs, Gene.   II. Title.
RC489.S74F74   1996
616.89'165--dc20   95-53127   CIP

W.W. Norton & Company, Inc., 500 Fifth Avenue, New York, NY 10110
                    http://web.wwnorton.com
W.W. Norton & Company Ltd., 10 Coptic Street, London WC1A 1PU

2 3 4 5 6 7 8 9 0

To Cheryl White, who has made it possible for so many of us to join together in what's becoming a world-wide community.

And to Steve Freedman, without whose help in a thousand and one details of day-to-day life this book wouldn't exist.

Contents

Foreword

The original vision for this foreword was of a weaving made of many voices—voices of therapists who have studied narrative ideas and used them in their work and voices of people who have consulted with narrative therapists and experienced the ideas in practice. To this end, one Saturday seven of us—Diane Chisman, S. Michele Cohen, Cheryl Davis, Liz Gray, Ann Kogen, Al Ross, and Dina Shulman—met and talked for two hours about our experiences. Later, we (AR and DS) set out to review a videotape of the conversation and excerpt parts of it, which we planned to then intersperse with our reflections. Because each individual story was so rich and varied, this proved to be an impossible task. Around the same time, I (DS) began discussing the book with my dear friend, who was seeing Jill in therapy. She had inhaled the book, and was bursting with news of how it had changed her life's journey. I told Al about our discussions and suggested that each of the three of us could write our stories and pass them along in a way that would closely approximate our original vision. So, here we go—first my friend who has chosen not to publish her name, then me, Dina, a fairly recent social work school graduate, and then Al, an experienced clinician.

I

At the age of 23 I began to have full-blown panic attacks. They were hell. It wasn't for another two years that I would come to connect them as a symptom from childhood sexual abuse. And it was 12 years later that I came to know the extent to which my father brutally abused me—sexually, physically, and emotionally. I can't say what facet of my life has suffered most from this assault. The eras of torture, then turmoil, have since bled together. But I can say, with full clarity, that the astoundingly long search for help was, sadly, more often than not abusive in and of itself.

The culmination of a lifetime of hard work and dedication brought me to the pinnacle of my career in the performing arts. The slow and arduous climb upwards in my professional life was, conversely, mirrored by a halting feeling of being sucked into the abyss of the negativity of abuse. While, at the same time, I was made senior vice president of creative affairs of a prestigious producing organization, I was on my twelfth therapist. Repeatedly rejecting the growing urgency with which each therapist recommended hospitalization and more drugs became exhausting and overwhelming. And the financial burden was crushing. The loss of everything I had worked for — a lifelong dream — seemed imminent. I became emotionally paralyzed, incapacitated, and, finally, suicidal thoughts that were spawned by a captious three-page psychological evaluation some seven years prior, ballooned to an unmanagable level, leaving me no room to see *anything* positive.

The abuse of a process inundated with confusion and frustration and cloaked in a shroud of mystery had left me feeling re-traumatized. I sat helplessly in the darkness of the past abuse while a list of "experts" sat in judgment about what was "wrong" with me. I was infused with pain. This had BECOME the era of turmoil.

Desperate to gain some perspective, I retreated to the home of a friend who had proven to be unrelenting in her support for my search for help. On my first day of this "emotional shut-down," I received a call from Dina Shulman, another friend, who had often spoken passionately of her work as a therapist. I had, for some time, been awestruck by the degree to which she genuinely felt compassion for her clients and the respect she paid her colleagues and mentors within the narrative community. She gently implored me to consider making an appointment with Jill Freedman, with the explanation that "it would be different this time." I did. It was. And the impact of the therapy that followed led to a marked turning point.

The process by which Jill Freedman has worked with me to dismantle the steely layers of the foreboding darkness has been at once compelling, challenging, and enlightening, never threatening or mysterious. I feel as though I have been sitting on a path that has become overgrown with briar and thorns, closing me in and torturously leaving me witness to my shrinking options. And Jill now stands around me and whacks down the brush so that I can see which path *I* want to take. She has opened up the options and so the opportunities become mine for the choosing. She checks in with me as if to say, "Is there someplace we should be going?" And if I'm stuck, she might say, "Do you think that we could go here . . . or there?" And I feel free to say yes or no. At times I may sit down on this journey to tell a story or just rest quietly, because it can be tiresome. And I am continuously amazed and grateful that she is with me for every beat. Eye to eye.

I have begun to start the healing process.

I am now trying to see how the abuse could be separate from me. Make no mistake, this is an extraction. I am *pulling* the darkness of the abuse OUT of ME.

I often have noted that, with each small step towards healing, I felt a revulsion to the response that this is a "good thing," as nothing in the devastating wake of child abuse can be considered "good." So we (I and my team of Jill and Dina) have adopted the paths of "white direction,"[1] which works *against* the abuse, and "black direction," which works *for* the abuse. Slowly and cautiously I have come to recognize that if I am to rise above this venomous obstacle, I need to commit to the white direction. "White tools" have become the symbol of that direction. For me, they are music, crayons, candles, and, not least, the willingness to receive love and support from those anxious to give it . . . no matter how hard it is to accept. I have slowly entrusted my "black tools" to my friend Dina, to whom I am indebted for reasons that are obvious, but that, as yet, go unspeakable in our earthly terms.

I am most astonished simply by my awakening to the fact that therapy can actually be *therapeutic*. And with a somewhat sad touch of facetious levity, I offer you . . . "Who knew?"

The seed of my commitment to the "white direction" was planted when I read this book. And it is consistently nurtured with the constant patience, understanding, and graceful compassion of my teammates, the likes of which I continue to absorb with touching disbelief.

I hope that this book will inspire many to see the "white direction" and find the hope that someone cares and that someone will strive to see the diamond in the rough. That beneath the toxicity of problems and intense pain, lies a sparkling uniqueness that will emerge as a meaningful and striking contribution to the fabric of our existence. With this, we can begin to clear away the brush and see the vastness of the possibilities that lie beyond the path.

---

[1]It is with a sense of worry and grief that I address the issue that the use of my metaphors of black and white may mistakenly conjure an image of racism. My crayons (being the most important tool in my healing) recreate for me that autumnal jubilance of childhood, that hope of a new scholastic and personal beginning . . . the coveted, brand new, *box of 64*. My black crayon denotes, quite simply, the darkness that I lived in during the nights of the abuse. To date, I have only colored the concept of healing once. It was immediately following my reading of this book, and it is denoted by a rainbow, symbolizing *all colors* and *choices*. Objects tend to reflect the color that is within them when white light is shed upon them. Since I have just drunk up the writings of Michael White I rededicate my term "white direction" in deference to the values he embodies.

II

When I thought about contributing to this foreword, I found obstacles standing in my way. I kept thinking, "Who am I to be writing this foreword? I'm not an expert in the field. I'm still in a training program. How can I possibly summarize the importance of this book and narrative ideas in general?" And then one day as I was reading this book (actually waiting to get a haircut), I realized that I was being seduced by the dominant discourse of what a foreword should be. If stories constitute our lives and are the basis of narrative therapy, then wouldn't it be great if I could just tell the story of how this book, and narrative ideas in general, have affected my life?

I think of myself as one of the lucky ones. I was introduced to narrative therapy as an intern in my second year of graduate school. During that year, I began to feel my way through the different theories I was learning in school while at the same time learning about narrative therapy at my internship. I struggled with finding my personal theory and kept finding myself attracted to these narrative ideas — mainly by the way I felt when using them. However, in the beginning, I found that just using some of these techniques seemed to fall short, and I found myself interested in finding out more about the ideas that constitute their foundation. I then began to read literature written by Michael White, David Epston, Jill Freedman, and Gene Combs, while also attending conferences where I found the ideas intriguing.

As a new therapist, I almost felt like an imposter — someone who is supposed to have "the secret" and can solve all problems and answer all questions. I found this to be an unattainable quest and an overwhelming burden. However, when using narrative therapy, I found this burden to be lifted, and I could just be myself. Coming from a "not-knowing" position made me feel more comfortable and ethical by learning from the clients how their stories unfolded. In the beginning, this transparency seemed scary. How can I share with my clients that I don't have all the answers? And yet, it was such a great feeling being able to collaborate with them as a team rather than feeling alone in the process. This idea of a team also seemed to bring the client-therapist relationship to a new level which seemed to bring on never-ending possibilities.

One of my biggest struggles in practicing therapy was being sucked into the pain of all the problems. Narrative therapy shed new light on this struggle. It taught me that "problems are problems and people are people." Externalizing problems led me to see my clients as who they are. I could see them as problems or I could see them as stories. Problems entrench you with pain, while stories allow for possibilities. During the training program, I was encouraged to look at stories from a journalistic point of view, researching the story from different angles. Each story is like a mystery, and my job is to help define the plot and counterplot. The client, then, is allowed to choose which is preferred.

Reading this book helped to define my reasons for choosing narrative therapy. When reading literature of a pathologizing nature, I found myself once again awash with pain and pessimism. Reading this book left me with a feeling of optimism. The possibilities seemed endless and each chapter helped enormously in my work, reinforcing what I am learning. Jill and Gene's vast clinical experience, ample case examples, and style of writing allow for easy accessibility.

I cannot possibly write about all the ways that narrative has affected my professional and personal life. I am grateful to Jill and Gene, whose program has allowed me to immerse myself in learning. Contributing to this foreword has given me the opportunity to reflect on my own evolution. As in narrative therapy, when one gets a chance to refect on one's own life, choices multiply, instilling excitment at the realization that the preferred outcomes are within one's grasp.

Dina Shulman

III

I struggled hard through my training, some 24 years ago, to understand and accept the commonly held truths about therapy as my own — I wanted to be a "good" therapist. I, like Jill and Gene, attempted to find meaning from a variety of different schools of thought, searching for a "theoretical home." In the background — terribly muted by the louder voices of "systems theory," "psychodynamic theory," and a myriad of other "radical approaches" that I had hoped would provide me with the theoretical nucleus I had been looking for — were quieter voices I could barely make out. These faint voices, I believe, were originally responsible for leading me into this field in the first place.

These voices spoke to me of respect for the notion that people are people and problems are problems; they told me that problems never define the person's entire being; they reminded me that being connected to those around us, living or dead, is vital; and they coached me in terms of being a collaborator, not an expert, in people's lives, with about as much need to learn and as much expertise as they have.

As time progressed, I realized that the ideas and beliefs I was learning through school and supervision rarely reflected "my" ideas and beliefs about people. The more I strove to be a "good clinician" the less I felt I was a good "me." Hence, I felt oppressed by many of the popular versions of psychotherapeutic knowledge. The quiet, but persistent voices kept reminding me that I really "knew" very little about people and why they did the things they did. These voices reassured me that "knowing" was not the stuff good therapists were made of. But I had no way of finding a legitimate path that would allow me to follow the curiosity and wonderment generated in response to these different voices until I attended a conference where I heard Jill and Gene verbalize *their* wonderment and excitement for narrative therapy. I heard echos of my "own" voices in the words of this workshop. I sat in awe with goose bumps and tears in my eyes as a new story appeared on the horizon.

As this story has developed, I have become less concerned about how to explain my work in culturally dominant language and freer to explore new territories of experience. As this shift has taken on momentum, I have found myself curious about the lives "problems" themselves have developed over time, and, further, how the social context impacts the lives of these problems and their relationships with the people sitting in my office. And I find that I have many questions about these people and their possibilities. I have given myself permission to ask questions about things that previously I thought I had to have the answers for.

What happened next constituted what was perhaps the most enriching experience of my professional life. I found that as I relinquished responsibility for maintaining and practicing expert knowledge, the people I questioned in fact had answers, wonderfully imaginative answers that spoke precisely about their lives and their experiences of who they were— their truths. I realized that every person I ever worked with had expert knowledge about his or her own life or "story."

These experiences have begun to resonate with the voices I have come to acknowledge as the knowledge of my own lived experience. Silenced by a culture entrenched in science and technology, this "knowledge" had had little influence in the work I did as a therapist, or my life as a whole. But as I began to travel the landscape called narrative therapy, I discovered paths long grown over, which led me to my "theoretical home."

The plot has begun to thicken as I have re-remembered old stories and even older voices that I lost contact with many years ago when I began my training as a therapist. I am reconnecting to ways of being that are congruent with who I believe I am and who I choose to be.

I believe that what has happened for me as a therapist is exactly what happens for those I have the privilege of working with in my office. Whether it has to do with ways of being a therapist, or ways of being a male, or ways of being a Caucasian, etc., I now have a language that is productive for examining the real effects of particular narratives in my life. I now possess tools for evaluating the value of these narratives for myself, not relying on other factors within our culture to make those evaluations for me. I have given myself permission to retain or discard those narratives I wish to. Finally, I have found a community of others who reinforce and fortify these developments. With them, I continue to find the courage and support to go up against the continued barrages of the culturally dominant voices.

I am moved to express the many ways Jill and Gene's words and teachings have deeply impacted my life. They have played so many roles in the uncovering of my own "truths" and the identification of narratives which reflect a growing sense of peace in my work as a therapist. They have acted as teachers and co-visors (I like this word as compared to super-visors). Their co-vision has opened space for my own vision, never shadowed by their super-vision. They have been co-workers, as we've struggled to find ways of expanding our work into the community where we live. And last but certainly not least, they have become friends. Their voices have become part of the choir that keeps me connected to new, exciting, and preferred developments in my work and in my life. With eloquence and vibrance, this book beautifully describes the body of work that is becoming known as narrative therapy. It was their introduction to narrative therapy five years ago, very much like the thoughts and ideas expressed within these pages, that opened me up to a new world of possibilities. It is my hope that for you, the reader of this book, an adventure somewhat akin to the one I've had (and will continue to have for years to come), will begin as you introduce yourself to the ideas, beliefs, and practices that constitute narrative therapy.

Jill and Gene, in this book, will talk about "spreading the word." I am intensely grateful that they have chosen to spread the word of the work they have engaged themselves in. I could only wonder if both Jill and Gene have not experienced the effects of this work in ways which reflect the ways I and others have experienced the effects of this work. I am curious about the impact writing and publishing this book has had and will have on their ever-evolving stories. I am truly honored to be one of those invited to "spread the word" of my developments and I wonder what effects sharing my story will have as I continue my journey.

Alec Ross

Introduction

We have written this book in response to the many, many requests for an overview of the ideas, attitudes, and practices that have come to be known as "narrative therapy." In presenting as clear, unified, and accessible an overview as we can, our fervent wish is that you not take our presentation as *the* way to practice narrative therapy, but as an illustration of *some* ways.[1]

This book's primary focus is on the ways of working that have arisen among therapists who, inspired by the pioneering efforts of Michael White and David Epston, have organized their thinking through two metaphors: narrative and social construction. Seven of its ten chapters are devoted to specific clinical practices—describing each practice, locating it in relation to the ideas and attitudes that support it, and illustrating it with clinical examples.

However, as we will stress throughout the book, we do not recommend that people approach these practices as "techniques" or that they attempt to use the practices without a solid grounding in the worldview from which they spring. For this reason, Chapters 1 and 2 focus on historical, philosophical, and ideological aspects of the narrative/social constructionist worldview. In Chapter 1, we tell the story of our own development as particular therapists in a particular part of the world during a particular historical period. We hope that situating ourselves in this way will give you some idea about how to take our ideas and will encourage you to make the practices that you take from this book your own by adapting them to your particular circumstances and experiences. In Chapter 2, we try to give a clear, concise, and not-too-heady overview of the philosophical ideas that have shaped the "narrative" way of working.

---

[1] We should, perhaps, be writing about narrative therap*ies*—to reflect the many differences in practice that exist.

We encourage you to read the first two chapters before you wade into the clinical material. We believe that you will wade differently if you first understand the ideas and attitudes that the practices represent. However, some people prefer to try out practices and then learn about the supporting ideas. In that case, you might come back to the first two chapters after you explore the clinical work a bit.

Chapters 3 through 6 focus on practices that comprise the basics of our clinical work. In Chapter 3, we acquaint you with how we join people to acknowledge problem-saturated stories, how we listen in ways that begin to objectify problems and situate them in sociocultural contexts and open space for new stories, and how, when our listening alone isn't enough, we ask questions to bring forth openings for new, less problematic life narratives. In Chapter 4, we describe practices for expanding openings into substantial, multi-stranded, memorable stories that support preferred values, actions, and directions in people's lives. Chapter 5 reviews the joining-listening-deconstructing-reconstructing process that we have laid out in Chapters 3 and 4 in terms of the many kinds of questions we ask in that process. It includes a general schema and suggestions for what to ask when. Chapter 6 consists of three fairly lengthy transcripts of acutal conversations that we believe will give you a feel for the "reweaving" process in action.

Chapters 7, 8, and 9 describe various practices for "thickening" new narratives and circulating them within people's local culture. In Chapter 7, we describe that important body of practices that has grown up around the idea of "reflecting"—starting with "reflecting teams," but also looking at how therapists can reflect without teams and how people can be invited to reflect on their own and each others' preferred narratives as they emerge. Chapter 8 reviews ways of thickening preferred stories through such means as letters, documents, celebrations, and particular interviewing practices. Chapter 9 describes how new stories can be circulated in families, leagues, "communities of concern," and the like, so that ultimately the ripples from local changes in individual stories can overlap and spread to affect our larger society.

In Chapter 10, the final chapter, we open our lens again for a larger view, looking at ethics, especially at a particular ethics of relationship that guides us in the use of specific narrative practices.

When we teach, we try to make our workshops, classes and seminars interactive. That's not just because it's our preferred style. It's also because we've found that what emerges from the interaction is more than what we bring as teachers. So, in writing this book, you, the reader, were very much present for us. We wondered what you would wonder, what you would think, and what you would say at various points along the way. We would consider it a privilege to hear your ideas, questions, and reflections.

Acknowledgments

This book reflects the ideas and work of many, many people. Besides those cited throughout, much of what we've learned and written about comes from the wisdom of the people who have consulted with us. We offer them our heartfelt thanks and our solidarity.

Countless friends and colleagues have encouraged and supported us in this project in particular and in our work in general. We can only name a few here, but we are grateful to all, and do not intend the naming as an exclusionary process.

Michael White has been a constant source of inspiration, friendship, and encouragement for many years now. We had the great good fortune of meeting him just as he began teaching in this country, and the effects of his ideas and commitment have been nothing short of continually transformative in our lives and our work. We hope that we've been clear throughout the book about how much our ideas and practices draw from what he has shared with us.

David Epston has offered faithful encouragement and enthusiasm. His multiple faxes declaring, "Don't stop now!" spurred us on and made us smile. Although we have not had the fortune of spending as much time with David as with Michael, his ground-breaking ideas, his unflagging belief in those he works with, and his unique creative practices have been incredibly inspirational to us and influential in our work.

Cheryl White has believed in us, opened up opportunities for us, encouraged us, and inspired us with her tenacity, energy, and courage.

Jennifer Andrews and Dave Clark first alerted us to this new way of doing therapy — back before it had a name. They are always ready to talk about ideas, and have generously included us in many of the rich and collaborative learning experiences that seem to spring up around them wherever they put down roots.

Since the moment we met Sallyann Roth she has been available to us to talk enthusiastically and share ideas. We particularly want to thank her for caring enough about us to tell us when what we are doing isn't working.

Melissa and Griff Griffith have supported us in gentle and strong ways. It has been important for us to have friends who are also partners, both in this work and in life.

We've been lucky to have been included in a group that began to talk about narrative ideas and grew to include teaching together. The group now includes Jeff Zimmerman, Vicki Dickerson, Janet Adams-Westcott, John Neal, and Stephen Madigan. It is a continuing pleasure to learn, work, and play with these friends and colleagues, both in group projects and individually. We particularly thank Janet and Vicki for keeping us organized.

Kathy Weingarten, Dean Lobovits, Jenny Freeman, Rick Maisel, and Craig Smith have all shared their ideas and their support in ways that have been important to us.

We also have a local narrative community that shares ideas and projects. Many of our particular ways of thinking and working were shaped by conversations with this group. Virginia Simons has long been an important member of our community. Although she has recently moved, we all still consider her a member. Other members include Ann Kogen, Al Ross, Klaus Boettcher, Diane Chisman, Joyce Goodlatte, S. Michele Cohen, and Dina Shulman. We are indebted to these friends and colleagues for the many times they have stepped in to pick up the slack for us as we were writing this book.

John Walter and Jane Peller, besides providing encouragement and enthusiasm, have joined us in our work with families on several occasions, and compared and contrasted ideas with us on many others. Their "solution-focused" questions gave us a different, and usually complementary, perspective on our work.

John Rolland, Froma Walsh, and the faculty of the Chicago Center for Family Health have provided a context where our narrative voices could be heard among other family therapy voices. We appreciate the support and interest faculty members there have shown us, as well as the grace they have shown in understanding our lack of participation as we've been finishing this book.

I (JF) want to thank the members of the Illinois Association for Marriage and Family Therapy Gender and Minority Committee for our work together, particularly the labor we shared in studying white privilege and internalized racism. Special thanks go to Mary Shesgreen, Barbara Thomas, Fabiola Palacios, Vicky Whipple, Dave Arksey, Judith Doyle, Dolly Derstein, and Larry Frank.

I (GC) want to thank the members of the MFTC listserve. The conversations there, even those that I "lurk" on without participating in, have fed me throughout this project—both through their solid intellectual content and through the respectful and collaborative way of interacting that they exemplify.

We also want to thank Tom Dafforn for sending us papers and video-tapes and helping us to stay up to date with the many ways people are using these ideas.

We are indebted to Christie Turner, Sallyann Roth, Lois Shawver, and Herb Klar, each of whom read an earlier version of our manuscript and provided invaluable reflections, ideas, and suggestions. The book is significantly better for their participation.

In our first book we wrote, "Steve Freedman gave ready help and enthusiasm, beyond the call of brotherhood." He did it again, this time transcribing several of the most lengthy therapy transcripts in the book from videotapes in which the audio quality was not always high.

We would like to thank Rosie and Milton Freedman for their enthusiasm and their uncomplaining forbearance in not seeing us for long stretches of time while we were working on this project.

We also wish to thank those who have come to our workshops and seminars. Their thoughts and questions have been invaluable in refining our ideas and letting us know what this book should address and how we might most usefully address it.

Our editor and friend, Susan Munro, has been unfailingly supportive, helpful, patient, and enthusiastic. To say that we couldn't have done it without her is an understatement of monumental proportions.

Narrative Therapy

Shifting Paradigms: From Systems to Stories

Is this work better defined as a world-view? Perhaps, but even this is not enough. Perhaps it's an epistemology, a philosophy, a personal commitment, a politics, an ethics, a practice, a life, and so on.

> —*Michael White, 1995, p. 37*

There is properly no history; only biography.

> —*Ralph Waldo Emerson, 1830*

This book describes how we, two particular therapists within a community of therapists, are applying two metaphors—"narrative" and "social construction"—to organize our clinical work. Using the narrative metaphor leads us to think about people's lives as stories and to work with them to experience their life stories in ways that are meaningful and fulfilling. Using the metaphor of social construction leads us to consider the ways in which every person's social, interpersonal reality has been constructed through interaction with other human beings and human institutions and to focus on the influence of social realities on the meaning of people's lives.

A guiding metaphor, such as narrative, is no small matter. The metaphors through which we organize our work have a powerful influence on both what we perceive and what we do. Paul Rosenblatt (1994) has written a whole book explicating this phenomenon in the field of family therapy. He discusses such metaphors as "family as entity," "family as system," "communication," and "structure." In his discussion, he describes not only what each metaphor highlights, but also what it obscures when used to guide one's thinking and perceptions.

For instance, in using "structure" as a guiding metaphor, we tend to think of families as rather rigid, geometric arrangements of people. Such thinking has led to the development of useful ideas like "triangulation" and "boundaries." Therapists using "structure" as a guiding metaphor might concern themselves with rearranging, strengthening, or loosening existing structures. They would tend to approach problems and their resolution in some of the ways that carpenters, architects, or sculptors would. This can make for very clear, teachable, and effective approaches to therapy.

However, the "structure" metaphor can at times invite us to pay too little attention to the ever-shifting, ever-changing aspects of family relationships. It can freeze our perceptions in time and oversimplify complex interactions. It can invite us to treat people as objects, thus dehumanizing the therapeutic process. There are plusses and minuses for all organizing metaphors.

Because the metaphors that we use influence what we look, listen, and feel for in this way, we have thought carefully about the guiding metaphors we have choosen. Here we want to situate our choices in our experiences as therapists.

We (Combs & Freedman, 1994b) have joined a number of therapists and thinkers-about-therapy (e.g., Anderson & Goolishian, 1988, 1990a; Gergen, 1985; Hoffman, 1990; White & Epston, 1990; Zimmerman & Dickerson, 1994a) in choosing the metaphors of narrative and social construction rather than the metaphor of *systems*,[1] which has been at the heart of family therapy theory for several decades now, as a theoretical basis for therapy.

The "systems" metaphor has served the field well. It has given us useful ways to talk about the processes by which people connect in patterns that transcend individual bodies. Working with such processes and patterns of interconnection has been a distinguishing feature of family therapy. However, just as the idea of individual minds in individual bodies once limited our ability to conceptualize and work with mind as an interpersonal phenomenon in family systems, the idea of "family systems" now can limit our ability to think about the flow of ideas in our larger culture.

We think you will best understand the story of our fascination with the metaphors of "narrative" and "social construction" if we start by telling you a little about what our work was like before we encountered them, when "systems" was our guiding metaphor.

FIRST-ORDER CYBERNETICS

We (JF & GC) are most familiar with the systems metaphor through the cybernetic paradigm, which Gregory Bateson is generally credited

---

[1]For discussion of the metaphor of systems and the many ways this metaphor has been used in the therapy literature, see de Shazer (1991, chapter 2) and Auerswald (1987).

with introducing into our field. Norbert Wiener (1950) coined the word "cybernetics" to refer to an emerging body of knowledge about structure and flow in information-processing systems. He derived it from a Greek root (*kubernetes*[2]), which signifies the pilot of a boat. Thus, cybernetics, in his mind, was a science of guidance, of control through the kind of successive cycles of error correction that are involved in keeping a boat on course. In fact, much of the early work in cybernetics was done on guided missile systems during World War II. When we used the metaphor of cybernetics to "guide" our thinking, we tended to focus our attention on whether therapy was "on target" or not, that is, we tended to think of the help we offered as being help in controlling things so that a specific goal was reached.

Our work as beginning family therapists was solidly within the "strategic therapy" framework (Erickson & Rossi, 1979; Haley, 1963, 1973, 1976; Madanes, 1981, 1984; Watzlawick, Weakland, & Fisch, 1974), which drew many of its ideas from cybernetics. Our thinking as "strategic cybernetic systems" therapists focused on how families could become stuck in repetitive loops of unfulfilling behavior or in hierarchical structures that were improperly balanced, and on what therapists could do to interrupt those patterns and guide families into a healthy rather than an unhealthy stability.

Looking back, we now view our work from that time as guided not just by cybernetics but by "first-order cybernetics," and, from our present perspective, we would say that first-order cybernetic theories invite therapists to view families as machines (like thermostats, guided missiles, or computers). This sort of view presupposes that therapists are separate from and able to control families, that they can make detached, objective assessments of what is wrong and fix problems in a way analogous to the way a mechanic fixes a malfunctioning engine. At the time, we didn't notice or worry about the aspects of the work that now seem detached or mechanical to us. We were excited by having found a way to talk about people in interaction. Also, the practices developed by people like Jay Haley and the MRI team *worked*, and this in itself was very compelling.

When our work as therapists was guided by the metaphors of first-order cybernetics, we focused our initial efforts on eliciting a specific goal from each family. We believed that what often kept people from reaching their goals was that they were stuck in recurring patterns of behavior in which they tried harder and harder to apply the same ineffective "solution" again and again.

---

[2]This is the same Greek word from which we get our word "governor," whether that refers to the mechanical controller of the upper speed of an engine or the human who guides a state.

Once we had spotted a recurring pattern, we believed that it was our job to design a strategic intervention that would disrupt it and redirect family members to new behaviors through which they could achieve their goal, which we conceptualized as some sort of new and more satisfying homeostatic balance. We also believed that it was our job to convince the family to carry out the intervention we had designed, much in the way that it is a physician's job to convince his[3] patient to take a medicine that he prescribes. Most of the people who came to us seemed satisfied with what we did under the guidance of this model, and for a number of years we liked it too. But gradually we began to question certain of our practices.

Looking back, we now think that the notion of control toward a goal seemed to invite us to become ever more controlling toward the people we worked with, especially when we perceived that goals were not being reached. It seems that our work, when guided by the metaphor of "guidance," could at times invite people to behave in ever more mechanistically controlling ways toward themselves. We now believe that this model let us, as the designers of clever interventions, take too much credit for changes that occurred, while the people we worked with could easily experience themselves as passive recipients of external wisdom and give themselves too little credit. So, although people usually achieved their goals, it now seems to us that the therapy experience often did not enhance their sense of personal agency.

It wasn't unusual to hear therapists describe therapy sessions wholly in terms of a problem and what *they* did to solve it or a goal and what *they* did to achieve it. Sometimes it seemed that strategizing to reach a specific goal had constrained both the people we worked with and ourselves from noticing interesting and useful possibilities that lay outside the path toward the specified goal.

Lynn Hoffman (1988, p. 112), looking back on her own first-order cybernetics work, writes that when she was writing *Foundations of Family Therapy* (Hoffman, 1981), the picture she drew throughout the body of that work was of "family system as machine" and "therapist as repair person." She (1988, p. 111) writes, "Once you have such an entity, it is easy to see it in terms of dysfunction. . . . The assumption was that the therapist knew what a 'functional' family structure should be and should change the family accordingly." She (1988, p. 111) also writes of "a general tendency to objectify pathology" in American family therapy of the time, citing *DSM-III* and "dysfunctional family systems" as examples of objectified pathologies.

While we had thought that we were looking for people's strengths and

---

[3]Patriarchal associations are intended here.

resources, we would agree with Hoffman that first-order cybernetics gave us too many invitations to focus on what was dysfunctional in the lives of people who came to us for therapy. It also invited us to treat dysfunction as the focus of therapy. In making our assessments of what people needed to reach goals, we were unwittingly deciding what was wrong with them.

SECOND-ORDER CYBERNETICS

Over the time that Hoffman was writing her book, other people (e.g., Dell, 1980, 1985a; Keeney, 1983; Keeney & Sprenkle, 1982; Watzlawick, 1984) were beginning to think differently about systems, and in the book's prologue and epilogue she (Hoffman, 1988, p. 112) attempted "to point the way to a less control-oriented model, a model that did not place the therapist outside of, or above, the family." This new way of thinking came to be called "second-order cybernetics" or "cybernetics of cybernetics." It developed as people began to realize that therapists couldn't really stand outside of family systems to make "objective" assessments and adjustments. A therapist was, like it or not, part of the very system undergoing therapy, and therefore incapable of detached objectivity. People also began to realize that change was at least as important as stability, and to assert that therapists might more profitably focus on how cybernetic systems were always changing through time rather than on how they were always seeking homeostatic stability.

As the focus shifted from first- to second-order cybernetics, the metaphors therapists used began to change. Where we once talked about governors and thermostats and simple feedback loops, we started thinking in terms of biological and ecological systems (Bateson, 1972, 1979; Bogdan, 1984). Words like "coevolution" and "cocreation" crept into our language. Auerswald (1987, p. 321) called this new paradigm the *ecological systems* paradigm, and wrote that it defined "a family as a coevolutionary ecosystem located in evolutionary timespace." He saw this paradigm as profoundly different from the "family systems" paradigms that preceded it.

At about the same time that second-order cybernetic ideas were beginning to supplant first-order cybernetics in the literature, we went to study with Luigi Boscolo and Gianfranco Cecchin of the Milan Systemic Family Therapy team (Boscolo, Cecchin, Hoffman, & Penn, 1987; Selvini Palazzoli, Boscolo, Cecchin, & Prata, 1980). To us, the ideas that they were teaching then are the archetype of second-order cybernetics in family therapy.

The Milan team, working in relative isolation from mainstream North

American family therapy, had developed their own unique perspective on how to apply Gregory Bateson's ideas in the practice of family therapy. Instead of looking for patterns of behavior in families, they were looking for patterns of *meaning*. Their interviews focused on identifying a premise or "myth" that was shaping the meaning of family members' actions, around which they would brainstorm as a team to design an intervention, often a ritual, that they prescribed at the end of each session. In interviewing to find the family myth, they had developed a distinctive form of questioning, which they called "circular questioning" (Fleuridas, Nelson, & Rosenthal, 1986; Penn, 1982; Selvini Palazzoli, Boscolo, Cecchin, & Prata, 1980). Circular questions presupposed that family members were connected in ongoing relationships, that the actions and emotions of one person affected everyone else in recursive ways. Milan team members used these questions to bring forth information about how relationships worked in the family. This information was then used to develop hypotheses about a family which shaped the interventions.

It was circular questioning that first drew our attention to the Milan team. Our interest in strategic approaches to therapy had led us to intensive study of Milton Erickson's work, especially his work on hypnosis, through which we became very interested in indirect suggestion. We came across a paper (Schmidt & Trenkle, 1985) that discussed Milan-style circular questioning as a way of offering indirect hypnotic suggestions—suggestions that would influence one or more family members while seemingly speaking to another. Gunther Schmidt was using questions, which had always been a natural part of any clinical interview, to *give*, rather than to get, information. This was an exciting idea to us— still, you will note, a first-order-cybernetic, the-therapist-is-outside-of-and-guiding-the-system idea, but an exciting idea nonetheless.

By the time we actually went to study with Boscolo and Cecchin, they were focusing less on designing interventions and more on asking questions. There seemed to be something transformative about the process of circular questioning itself; families were changing as members listened to each other's answers. Asking questions seemed to foster an attitude of curiosity, of eagerness to learn more and more about family members' experiences of the world and of each other, that made it hard for therapists to feel as comfortable as they once had been in telling people how their worlds *should* be. As family members searched for answers to circular questions, they stepped into a reality that focused their attention on their interconnectedness, on how any single member's feelings and actions influenced and were influenced by the feelings and actions of the others. In such a reality, rather than looking to the therapist for suggestions, they thought about the information that had come forth about the family and each other. Looking back, we can see that these factors tended to soften or flatten the hierarchy between therapists and family members.

As participants in their supervision process, we encountered other innovations that Boscolo and Cecchin had developed. They were using behind-the-mirror teams in ways that we had not experienced before. Teams actually functioned as teams. Instead of just listening in as a supervisor thought out loud or called in advice to the therapist in the room, supervisees behind the mirror participated in brainstorming discussions. Although the goal of these discussions was to arrive at a single intervention or message, the often-repeated slogan, "Flirt with your hypotheses, but don't marry them" suggested that this goal was not in any way held to be the singular or final truth. This sort of collaborative team discussion de-emphasized the hierarchy that we were used to experiencing between supervisors and supervisees, giving supervisees more of a voice.

The team was divided into a T-team, which directly assisted the therapist, and an O-team, which observed all family, therapist, and T-team interactions, both in the therapy room and in the observation room. While the T-team met to discuss their hypotheses about the family, the O-team met separately to discuss hypotheses on three levels: family system, family/therapist system, and family/therapist/team system. After each therapy session, the teams met together and the O-team began by discussing the observations of its members at all three levels. The T-team then discussed the thinking behind its chosen intervention, and a more general discussion ensued that served to integrate ideas from all positions. Reflection on all these levels kept people aware that therapists could not be detached, "objective" observers. Throughout this process, Boscolo and Cecchin participated more as team members than as detached or hierarchically superior supervisors.

Participation in Milan-style team supervision was an education in the multi-leveled and multi-directional nature of interpersonal influence. Simple circular feedback loops were an inadequate map for charting the flow of information we experienced. Milan-style teamwork gave us direct experience of the value of diverse perspectives in a conversation. This experience was very generative.

Minimizing hierarchy, encouraging multiple viewpoints, and reflecting on team process in the way that the addition of the O-team made possible, when combined with the attitude of curiosity (Cecchin, 1987) and the focus on relationship that came from using circular questions, fostered rapid evolution in our clinical practice. The ideas of people from several Milan-inspired groups — Lynn Hoffman (1981, 1985, 1988, 1990, 1991), who worked first with a group at the Ackerman Institute, then as part of a team in Brattleboro, Vermont, Tom Andersen (1987, 1991a) and his colleagues in Tromsø, Norway, and Karl Tomm (1987a, 1987b, 1988) in Calgary, Canada—inspired and influenced us[4] as we struggled to integrate the "second-order cybernetic" ideas of Boscolo and Cecchin with our Ericksonian-strategic predisposition. It seems that people who began to use Milan-style teams in their own settings couldn't help but evolve new ways of thinking and working.

The metaphors guiding all these people initially tended toward Batesonian "ecology of ideas" (Bateson, 1972, 1979; Bogdan, 1984) notions.[5] These ways of thinking were interesting and useful in that they helped us perceive ourselves as co-participants in the same systems as family members. They also helped us focus on the kind of flow and change that is inherent in evolution, thus de-emphasizing the "stuckness" that sometimes goes hand-in-hand with metaphors of homeostasis.

When we were guided by ideas of coevolution, we placed more conscious emphasis on collaboration than we had in the past. Instead of designing rituals and strategizing to get people to carry them out, we asked people what sort of between-sessions activity would seem useful to them and used in-session time for cocreating rituals (Combs & Freedman, 1990). Experiencing ourselves as "in process" meant letting go of any sense of objectivity concerning specific long-term goals; if client-therapist outcomes were coevolving, we couldn't specify our ultimate destination at any moment in the present. At its best, letting go of our role as pilots steering toward a specific goal encouraged humility and moment-by-moment collaboration about whether therapy was moving in a satisfactory direction. At its worst, it invited a sense of helpless, aimless "co-drifting."

We did some of both. At times, we felt we were collaborating with people in genuinely new ways. There seemed to be more room for non-therapist voices and ideas in our conversations. We thought people were getting a greater sense of themselves as resourceful and creative beings than they had in our earlier way of doing therapy. At other times, we felt lost, out of contact, and less effective than we had ever been. It seemed that this coevolution stuff took more patience than we were used to exercising.

---

[4]We were also strongly influenced by the writings of Harlene Anderson, Harry Goolishian, and their colleagues (Anderson & Goolishian, 1988; Anderson, Goolishian, Pulliam, & Winderman, 1986; Anderson, Goolishian, & Winderman, 1986) at the Houston-Galveston Institute, who were developing related ideas.

[5]Many of the people we were influenced by were also strongly influenced by the ideas of Humberto Maturana (e.g., Maturana & Varela, 1987), whose guiding metaphors were based in biology and physiology. Perhaps because we never studied them closely enough, we never found these ideas particularly useful.

A DIFFERENT STORY

The story you have just read is "true," but it's not the whole story. We have been writing as if there were a clear and logical progression in our understanding, and as if our understanding were reflected in a clear and logical way in our practice. We have also been writing as if we were guided almost exclusively by the metaphor of cybernetic systems. Our experience as we lived through the times we have been recounting was, of course, much messier and richer than that.

In the story so far, we have mentioned Milton Erickson's influence on our development only tangentially. Erickson doesn't fit neatly into the story of our struggles to understand and apply the "systems" metaphor. He doesn't fit neatly into anyone's overarching theories about psychotherapy. Be that as it may, Erickson was a huge and ever-present source of inspiration for both of us.

Erickson's approach to therapy was pragmatic and anti-theoretical. Here is a typical quote from him (Erickson & Rossi, 1979, pp. 233–34) on the subject:

> Psychotherapists cannot depend upon general routines or standardized procedures to be applied indiscriminately to all their patients. Psychotherapy is not the mere application of truths and principles supposedly discovered by academicians in controlled laboratory experiments. Each psychotherapeutic encounter is unique and requires fresh creative effort on the part of both therapist and patient to discover the principles and means of acheiving a therapeutic outcome.

Erickson (1965/1980, p. 223) believed that a therapist's job was to understand the beliefs and experience of the people who came to consult him or her. The therapist's beliefs were not to be inflicted on others:

> The therapist's task should not be a proselytizing of the patient with his own beliefs and understandings. No patient can really understand the understandings of his therapist nor does he need them. What is needed is the development of a therapeutic situation permitting the patient to use his own thinking, his own understandings, his own emotions in the way that best fits him in his scheme of life.

We met in 1980 at an advanced workshop on Ericksonian hypnotherapy. (And we have been deeply entranced with each other ever since, but that's a different story.) Although we were ostensibly there to learn about hypnosis, we both agree that what we really wanted to learn was how to cultivate the kind of relationships that Erickson had with the people who came to consult him. We liked the way Erickson attended to and respected the experience of the people he worked with. He cultivated a kind of therapeutic relationship that de-emphasized the therapist's professional, theoretical ideas and put a benevolent spotlight on people's particular situations. We wanted to further our abilities to do the same.

Erickson showed a lively and interested appreciation for people. He fully and palpably believed that there was something unique and wonderful about every human being. When he asked a question, he would await its answer with an air of delighted expectation — with a twinkle in his eye, an encouraging grin, and great patience. You just knew that he knew that any person he asked was going to come up with a wonderful answer, something different from what anyone could have predicted.

Erickson saw people as resourceful. He believed that we are all lifelong learners, and that life is an adventure in which we never know what is around the next bend, but whatever it is, it's going to be interesting, and we can probably handle it, and we will learn and grow and enrich our lives by handling it.

It was through Erickson that we first became interested in the therapeutic use of stories. He was famous for his "teaching tales," and much of his therapeutic work involved expanding and enriching people's stories about themselves.[6] This was often accomplished by telling inspirational, evocative stories about experiences with other people or about his own life experience. The first book that we wrote together (Combs & Freedman, 1990) was inspired by Erickson's use of stories, symbols, and ceremonies.

To us, the most impressive illustration of Erickson's understanding of the importance of stories in shaping reality is the way that he wrote and rewrote his own life story as he lived it, giving positive meaning to what others might have experienced as adversity. His nearly lifelong struggle with polio and its aftereffects was a recurring theme in his teaching tales, and, instead of framing the effects of the polio as deficits, he storied them as assets. For instance, Sid Rosen (1982, pp. 226–227) documents a story Erickson told about his days as a medical professor. There was a student who became "very withdrawn and oversensitive" after losing a leg in an auto accident. Erickson arranged for a few other students to help him stall the elevator one morning, and here's what happened:

> On that Monday, with Jerry holding the elevator doors open and Tommy stationed at the head of the stairwell, I found the class all on the ground floor waiting for me at seven-thirty. . . . I said,

---

[6]What has come to be called his "February Man" approach (Erickson & Rossi, 1980, 1989) is probably the clearest and most famous example of this.

"What's the matter with your thumb, Sam? Is it weak? Push that elevator button."

He said, "I have been."

I said, "Maybe your thumb is so weak, you ought to use two thumbs."

He said, "I tried that too, but that damn janitor is so worried about getting his pail and mops down, he's probably holding the elevator doors open."

. . . Finally, at five minutes of eight I turned to the student with the artificial leg and said, "Let's us cripples hobble upstairs and leave the elevator for the able-bodied."

"Us cripples" started hobbling upstairs. Tommy signaled to Jerry; Sam pushed the button. The able-bodied waited for the elevator. Us cripples hobbled upstairs. At the end of the hour, that student was socializing again — with a new identity. He belonged to the professorial group: "Us cripples." I was a professor; I had a bad leg; he identified with me; I identified with him.

It strikes us that, in identifying with the medical student, Erickson was writing a new chapter in his personal narrative. He was constructing a society of professionally competent, outgoing, well-liked physicians who had the further distinction of being "crippled," and placing himself squarely in the middle of that society.

Toward the end of his life, when students began to worry aloud about Erickson's death, instead of joining them in their potentially pessimistic narratives, he told stories of the longevity and optimism of his parents. We believe that these stories served an inspirational purpose for Erickson's students and for Erickson himself, advancing the construction of the mindset that led him to say, "I have no intention of dying. In fact, that will be the last thing I do!" (Rosen, 1982, p. 167).

So, it was through Erickson that we first encountered the belief that people can continually and actively re-author their lives. While the story of our relationship with the systems metaphor is one of change leading to an eventual parting of the ways, the story of our relationship with the re-authoring metaphor is one of constancy. It is the central organizing idea of this book. Erickson's commitment to making therapy fit the person and his delight and appreciation for those he worked with are also aspects of his work we still aspire to carry on.

There are other ideas that we first encountered through Erickson that continue to shape our clinical practice. One is that there are many possible experiential realities. He wrote, "There are plenty of alternatives in any situation. . . . When you attend a session of group therapy, what on earth are you going to see? That [plenty of alternatives] is what you go there for" (Erickson & Rossi, 1981, p. 206).

Erickson utilized the principle of alternative experiential realities in his therapy and teaching. He told stories of the Tarahumara Indians, the Balinese people, and other people in other places to suggest (among others) the idea that one need not be limited by the belief system that one is born into. He said, "I had always been interested in anthropology, and I think anthropology should be something all psychotherapists should read and know about, because different ethnic groups have different ways of thinking about things" (Zeig, 1980, p. 119).

Another idea that we first encountered through Erickson and that continues to inform our practice is that our expreriential realities are constituted through language. Erickson was very aware of the constitutive power of language. Much of his work was built on the presupposition that particular language can lead to particularly altered states of consciousness. He often talked about the importance of choosing appropriate language in suggesting a more workable reality to a person who came to see him.

In summary, looking back on how Erickson has influenced our work, the things that stand out for us are his delight in and respect for people, his belief that we can constantly re-author our lives, his belief in multiple possible realities, and his emphasis on the constitutive power of language.

YET ANOTHER STORY

During the time that we were struggling to integrate our Ericksonian/ strategic ideas with the things we were learning from the Milan team, feminist family therapists (e.g., Avis, 1985; Carter, Papp, Silverstein, & Walters, 1984; Goldner, 1985a, 1985b; Hare-Mustin, 1978; Taggart, 1985) were beginning to offer a critique of the theory and practice that had guided our field since its inception. They drew our attention to how first- and even second-order systemic explanations and interventions were based on normative models of family functioning that assumed "separate-but-equal" power for men and women. They argued that such models ignored the larger social-historical-cultural context in which men had much more political, financial, and "moral" power than women.

In large part, it was this feminist critique that led us to question the paternalistic expertness of some of our Ericksonian/strategic practices and to strive to develop more collaborative ways of working with people who came to us for help. Even though Erickson valued people's own experiential realities, even though he deeply believed that everyone was surprisingly resourceful, he was still a white, male physician of a certain era. He was a benign and benevolent patriarch, but a patriarch nonetheless. While he usually handled people with velvet gloves, he spoke at times of having an iron fist in his velvet glove.

When we look back on our years of studying and striving to apply Erickson's ideas, there are things that, although they seemed important at points along the way, we no longer find so useful. One of these is the notion of trance.

For a while, trance was an organizing metaphor for us. We talked as if people were always in some sort of trance and as if what we did as hypnotherapists was to help them cultivate and utilize their abilities to enter appropriate trance states for each of the various situations of their lives. This meant that an important focus of our work was on "trance induction."

Although Erickson often spoke to people who were in "trance," interacting collaboratively with them, the style of hypnosis that became popular with second- and third-generation Ericksonians like us was one in which the therapist spoke at great length, offering strategically designed indirect suggestions to a person who sat very still and quiet with her eyes shut. As we applied the feminist critique to our work, we became more and more uneasy with doing so much of the talking in therapy. We did fewer and fewer extended trances.

Two other ideas that have become less important to us (we have already alluded to this in the discussion on cybernetics) are those of strategizing and of hierarchy. When we modeled ourselves on Erickson, we tended to feel that it was our duty to design clever strategies that would (benevolently) influence people to do things that would begin to move their lives in new directions. Even in its most responsible, benign, and well-intentioned form, that way of working is characterized by a oneupness and lack of collaboration that, in the light of the feminist critique, we no longer want to affiliate ourselves with.

Turning away from Erickson and back to the "systems" metaphor, the feminist critique has led us to believe that that metaphor — at least as it has evolved and been applied in family therapy — is as much a hindrance as a help. It invites our attention to rather small, rather tight, recursive feedback loops when, instead, we want to be paying more attention to ideas and practices at play in the larger cultural context. The "systems" metaphor tempts us to look within families for complementary circuits and for collaborative causation of problems, rather than to work with family members to identify the negative influence of certain values, institutions, and practices in the larger culture on their lives and relationships, and to invite them to pull together in opposing those values, institutions, and practices. It encourages a position of neutrality (Selvini Palazzoli, Boscolo, Cecchin, & Prata, 1980) or curiosity (Cecchin, 1987) rather than one of advocacy or passion for particular values and against others.

Looking back, it now seems to us that in our lost, impatient, and dissatisfied moments as Ericksonian/second-order cybernetic therapists, we were on the edge of a bigger shift in worldview than we had previously experienced. Up to this point, we had been working within and developing a more and more subtle understanding of "systems" as an organizing metaphor for our work. We were soon to encounter, as they used to say on The Monty Python Show, "something completely different!"

THE NARRATIVE METAPHOR
AND SOCIAL CONSTRUCTIONISM

To our way of thinking, this different thing is not simply a further evolution of systems theory, it is a discontinuous paradigm, a different language. In its broadest form this paradigm has been referred to by many labels; while "post-structuralism," "deconstructionism," "the interpretive turn," and "the new hermeneutics" have all been proposed, it seems to us that "postmodernism" is the most commonly used label at this moment for the worldview of which we speak.

We will attempt to acquaint you more thoroughly with these ideas in the next chapter, but before we do that, we would like to continue the story of how we, personally, made the shift to the worldview that supports these ideas. Perhaps the most important thing we met on our way to adopting a postmodern worldview was none of the labels or metaphors we have just listed, but a person — Michael White.[7]

When we met him, we were immediately attracted to White's work, to the kind of relationships he forged with the people who came to see him, and to the way he lives out his values both inside and outside the therapy context. He was showing the same sort of confidence, interest, and excitement about the people he worked with that had been so attractive to us in Erickson. At the same time, he was citing Michel Foucault (1975, 1977, 1980), who wrote about the objectification and subjugation of persons, and talking about helping people stand up to "the gaze" of the dominant culture. Now-middle-aged 60s activists, we had no idea what these ideas would look like when applied in therapy, but we sure wanted to find out!

When we first met him, White (1986b) was basing his practices in part on Gregory Bateson's (1972) notions of negative explanation, restraint, and double description. While White's take on Bateson was novel enough

---

[7]We are indebted to Jennifer Andrews and David Clark, who included us in Michael's first consultations in Chicago, and to Cheryl White, whom we also met at these early consultations. While Michael taught these ideas, Cheryl and he were living them.

to be intriguing, we were very familiar with Bateson's work, and that, along with his Erickson-like interpersonal style, helped us feel at home with White's ideas. But White's explanations for why he did what he did in therapy were changing rapidly, and we soon became swept up in those changes.

White, who insists that he has no familiarity whatsoever with Milton Erickson's work, writes (White & Epston, 1990, p. xvi) that he was encouraged to use the narrative metaphor, or "story analogy," by David Epston, who had encountered it in studying anthropology, and by Cheryl White, "who had enthusiasm for this analogy from her readings in feminism." Upon examining the narrative metaphor, he found that it offered a useful expansion and elaboration of the "interpretive method" that Bateson's work had introduced him to.[8] In *Narrative Means to Therapeutic Ends* (White & Epston, 1990), White reminds us how Bateson used the metaphor of "maps," saying that all our knowledge of the world is carried in the form of various mental maps of "external" or "objective" reality, and that different maps lead to different interpretations of "reality." No map includes every detail of the territory that it represents, and events that don't make it onto a map don't exist in that map's world of meaning.

He also reminds us of how important *time* was for Bateson:

> In arguing that all information is necessarily "news of difference," and that it is the perception of difference that triggers all new responses in living systems, he [Bateson] demonstrated how the mapping of events through *time* is essential for the perception of difference, for the detection of change. (White & Epston, 1990, p. 2)

An advantage that Michael White saw in the narrative metaphor was that a story is a map that extends through time. It combines both of Bateson's notions in one concept. When we first began to use the narrative metaphor in White's rather than Erickson's sense, we saw it as simply a useful extension of Bateson's thinking. However, as we continued to use it and began to explore its theoretical ramifications, we realized that it had brought on quite a large shift in our worldview.

In our work up to this time, interventions were aimed at specific problems and goals. Listening to White, we no longer tried to solve problems. Instead, we became interested in working with people to bring

---

[8]The "interpretive method" refers to ways of working developed by social scientists who believe that we have no direct access to knowledge about "objective" reality. In the absence of such knowledge, we must *interpret* the "news of difference" our sense organs bring us in order to make meaning of the world.

forth and "thicken" (Geertz, 1978) stories that did not support or sustain problems. We discovered that, as people began to inhabit and live out these alternative stories, the results went beyond solving problems. Within the new stories, people could live out new self-images, new possibilities for relationship, and new futures.

Scholars in the humanities and social sciences (e.g., E. Bruner, 1986b; J. Bruner, 1986; Geertz, 1983) had been using narrative as an organizing metaphor for a number of years before it began to be used in family therapy circles. For example, Jerome Bruner (1986, p. 8) writes,

> By the mid-1970's the social sciences had moved . . . toward a more interpretive posture: meaning became the central focus — how the world was interpreted, by what codes meaning was regulated, in what sense culture itself could be treated as a "text" [story] that participants "read" for their own guidance.

As we read and studied more widely about the stream of ideas from which David Epston, Cheryl White, and Michael White had taken the narrative metaphor, we found that another important current in the same stream was that of *social constructionism*.[9] While we will discuss social constructionism in more depth in Chapter 2, let us say here that its main premise is that the beliefs, values, institutions, customs, labels, laws, divisions of labor, and the like that make up our social realities are constructed by the members of a culture as they interact with one another from generation to generation and day to day. That is, societies construct the "lenses" through which their members interpret the world. The realities that each of us take for granted are the realities that our societies have surrounded us with since birth. These realities provide the beliefs, practices, words, and experiences from which we make up our lives, or, as we would say in postmodernist jargon, "constitute our selves."

When we use both narrative and social constructionism as guiding metaphors for our work, we see how the stories that circulate in society constitute our lives and those of the people we work with. We also notice how the stories of individual lives can influence the constitution of whole cultures — not just the stories of people like Gandhi or Martin Luther King, but also those of people like Pocahontas, Annie Oakley, Helen Keller, and Tina Turner, as well as the stories of "ordinary" people whose names we have never heard. As we work with the people who

---

[9]At this point, we are not sure whether we first encountered the term "social constructionism" in conversation with Harry Goolishian or in Lynn Hoffman's (1990) article, "Constructing Realities: An Art of Lenses." At any rate, we highly recommend both Hoffman's article and Kenneth Gergen's (1985) considerably earlier article, which have acquainted many people in psychotherapy circles with social constructionist ideas.

come to see us, we think about the interactions between the stories that they are living out in their personal lives and the stories that are circulating in their cultures — both their local culture and the larger culture. We think about how cultural stories are influencing the way they interpret their daily experience and how their daily actions are influencing the stories that circulate in society.

Adopting the metaphors of narrative and social construction as our guiding metaphors has affected how we think about other metaphors and how we use them. Early in our relationship with David Epston, he was discussing our first book (Combs & Freedman, 1990) with us. He wondered why we used the metaphor "resource" so often. It was Epston who first called our attention to how talking of resources evokes thoughts of mining. A resource to him seemed like a fixed thing inside of someone that you had to go in and get. He preferred the metaphor of "knowledge," as knowledge is something that develops and circulates among people.

Kathy Weingarten (1991, p. 289) writes,

In the social constructionist view, the experience of self exists in the ongoing interchange with others . . . the self continually creates itself through narratives that include other people who are reciprocally woven into these narratives.

This conception of self is at odds with the skin-bound container with fixed contents (resources) that we had previously conceptualized.

As we pondered the implications of this new "constitutionalist" (White, 1991, 1993) metaphor of self, my (JF) taken-for-granted reality was so shaken up that I became motion-sick. I literally became nauseated. I had always believed that "deep down" I was a good person no matter what I did. If we were really to adopt these new ways of thinking and perceiving — which we wanted to do because of the kinds of therapy they support — we would become responsible for continually constituting ourselves as the people we wanted to be. We would have to examine taken-for-granted stories in our local culture, the contexts we moved in, the relationships we cultivated, and the like, so as to constantly re-author and update our own stories. Morality and ethics would not be fixed things, but ongoing activities, requiring continuing maintenance and attention.

As we became accustomed to this idea, we realized that, in our work as therapists, in co-authoring projects with others, our stories have the potential not only to be helpful but also to be harmful. I (JF) am a white, Jewish woman of Eastern European descent. I (GC) am a white, Anglo-Saxon, ex-Baptist man who grew up in the mountains of the rural

South. We are educated, middle-aged members of the professional class. As such, we are in positions of privilege in many contexts, including the therapy room. We do not want to reproduce, in therapy, the oppression many people have experienced at the hands of the dominant culture. We know that we are blind to many of the ways this could happen, even though we continually look back and question our therapeutic practices with an eye to unmasking dangerous dominant stories that we live. We try to recognize and own that we do not fully understand the experience of other people, especially those from different cultures. An ongoing dilemma for us is how to be more accountable for the effects of our (mis)understandings and actions. [10]

Our experience of the process that we call therapy has shifted as we have taken on the narrative and social constructionist metaphors. We no longer organize our experiential worlds in terms of "information" and "pattern." Instead, we think in terms of "stories." Rather than "systems," we think about "culture" or "society." Instead of seeing ourselves as mechanics who are working to fix a broken machine or ecologists who are trying to understand and influence complex ecosystems, we experience ourselves as interested people — perhaps with an anthropological or biographical or journalistic bent — who are skilled at asking questions to bring forth the knowledge and experience that is carried in the stories of the people we work with. We think of ourselves as members of a subculture in collaborative social interaction with other people to construct new realities. We now work to help people notice the influence of restrictive cultural stories in their lives and to expand and enrich their own life narratives. We strive to find ways to spread the news of individual triumphs — to circulate individual success stories so that they can keep our culture growing and flowing in satisfying ways.

Our switch to these ways of thinking has been discontinuous, bumpy, and exciting. Because we are working in a therapy culture dominated by modernist ideas, there are always invitations to identify people by equating them with pathological labels. Because we are part of a community of people using narrative ideas in therapeutic practice, there are also invitations to take up these new ideas as monolithic truths. We hope that as you read on, you will take the stories we tell not as truth claims, but as preliminary reports and works in progress from an exciting new culture. We hope some of you will make your stories part of the stories of that culture.

---

[10]In Chapter 10 we write about some of the ways we have begun to address our privilege.

The Narrative Metaphor and Social Constructionism: A Postmodern Worldview

... stories matter. So ... do stories about stories.
— Clifford Geertz, 1986, p. 377

[Three umpires] are sitting around over a beer, and one says, "There's balls and there's strikes, and I call 'em the way they are." Another says, "There's balls and there's strikes, and I call 'em the way I see 'em." The third says, "There's balls and there's strikes, and they ain't *nothin'* until I call 'em."[1]

— Walter Truett Anderson,
1990, p. 75

We have envisioned this as a very clinical, practice-oriented book, and indeed, descriptions of clinical actions do make up most of it. Learning and applying narrative/social constructionist clinical practices can lead to a deeper experience of a narrative/social constructionist worldview, but without some understanding of that worldview it is difficult to use the ideas we present here effectively or appropriately. Therefore, this chapter is dedicated to narrative/social constructionist *attitudes*. (Chapter 10 revisits the worldview in terms of the ethics it is drawn from and the relationships it supports.)

Perhaps the most important feature of the worldview that informs narrative therapy is a certain attitude about reality. David Paré (1995, p. 3), describing three different stances regarding human knowledge of reality, writes that things have

---

[1]This constructivist joke addresses how realities are constituted through language. To become a social constructionist joke, it would have to be broadened to acknowledge that if an umpire "calls 'em" in ways that don't fit others' perceptions, she may be hit with tomatoes or fired. Isn't it just like postmodernists to deconstruct a joke?

. . . been evolving from a focus on the observed world as object, to a focus on the observing person as subject, to a focus on the place between subject and object, that is, the intersubjective domain where interpretation occurs in community with others.

To put that in different language, Paré says that three beliefs exist: (1) reality is knowable—its elements and workings can be accurately and replicably discovered, described, and used by human beings; (2) we are prisoners of our perceptions—attempts to describe reality tell us a lot about the person doing the describing, but not much about external reality; and (3) knowledge arises within communities of knowers—the realities we inhabit are those we negotiate with one another. Paré asserts that there has been a gradual, and as yet incomplete, evolution from the first to the third of these views over the course of this century.

We see a rough correlation between Paré's three views and the first-order cybernetic, second-order cybernetic, and narrative/social constructionist worldviews that we have encountered on our personal journey as therapists. Narrative therapy is based in Paré's third worldview.

Evolution notwithstanding, the first worldview, variously called "modernism," "positivism," "structuralism," or "old-fashioned common sense," that Paré describes is alive and well. In science, it is the worldview in which people believe it is possible to find essential, "objective" facts that can then be tied together into overarching, generally applicable theories that bring us closer and closer to an accurate understanding of the real universe. In the humanities, it is the kind of humanism that seeks to develop grand, sweeping, meta-narratives about the human condition and how to perfect it. When people are invested in this worldview they believe the ideas they are using are more than ideas. They believe they are representations of general truths about a basic, underlying reality that we all share.

In a science course I (JF) once took, the teacher described scientific theories as explanatory systems that periodically are overthrown for better ones. The criterion for the best theory, he said, is that it offers the simplest explanation for all the known phenomena. New theories gain prominence when new phenomena are discovered or when a simpler explanation is developed.[2] The teacher went on to say that our understanding of electricity is a theory, not a truth, but that when he's fixing a

---

[2]This description could either be a modernist or postmodernist one, depending on whether the premise was that each successive theory got closer to the truth or that new theories were new stories that became more popular through political/social constructionist processes (see Kuhn, 1970). I never was very good at science and I don't remember which perspective the explanation was couched in. For our purposes, the story is now a postmodern one.

broken television set he drops that distinction and, during that time, for him the theory is true. Otherwise, he explained, the task of fixing a television set becomes too confusing.

From a postmodern viewpoint, we see many of the enterprises in the mental health field as analogous to this teacher's way of fixing a television set. We see this happening when diagnosticians who use criteria like those in *DSM-IV* behave as if they possessed, instead of a research tool, a set of descriptions for real, homogeneous, mental disorders that holds true for all people across all contexts. Or when geneticists and pharmacologists, as well as the clinicians who rely on their studies, behave as if they are in possesion of "the truth" about the causes and cures for *DSM-IV* disorders. Or when people within the managed care movement seem to believe that it is possible to develop standardized methods that will produce predictable, effective results with all psychiatric "illnesses" in a specified number of sessions within specified intervals.

There are problems with these and similar projects. For one thing, people are not television sets. When they are approached as objects about which we know truths, their experience is often one of being dehumanized. They can feel like machines on an assembly line. Also, even though a pill or a procedure may make a person function better, she may think worse of herself — we have seen several people who slept better, had more energy, and cried less on antidepressant medication who at the same time viewed themselves as broken or defective because the medication was "required" for their functioning.[3] The "objectivity" of the modernist worldview, with its emphasis on facts, replicable procedures, and generally applicable rules, easily ignores the specific, localized meanings of individual people. When we treat people with this kind of "objectivity," we regard them as objects, thus inviting them into a relationship in which they are the passive, powerless recipients of our knowledge and expertise. Addressing this, Kenneth Gergen (1992, p. 57) writes,

. . . the postmodern argument is not against the various schools of therapy, only against their posture of authoritative truth.

Postmodernists believe that there are limits on the ability of human beings to measure and describe the universe in any precise, absolute, and universally applicable way. They differ from modernists in that exceptions interest them more than rules. They choose to look at specific, contextualized details more often than grand generalizations, difference

---

[3]We are not against medication. Neither are we against clinical research or the naming of problems. What we are against is using medication, research, findings, or diagnostic terminology in mechanized, routine, and/or dehumanizing ways.

rather than similarity. While modernist thinkers tend to be concerned with facts and rules, postmodernists are concerned with meaning. In their search for and examination of meaning, postmodernists find metaphors from the humanities more useful than the modernist metaphors of nineteenth-century physical science. As Clifford Geertz (1983, p. 23) puts it,

. . . the instruments of reasoning are changing and society is less and less represented as an elaborate machine or quasi-organism and more as a serious game, a side-walk drama, or a behavioral text.

A POSTMODERN VIEW OF REALITY[4]

Adopting a postmodern, narrative, social constructionist worldview offers useful ideas about how power, knowlege, and "truth" are negotiated in families and larger cultural aggregations. It is more important to approach people and their problems with attitudes supported by these ideas than it is to use any particular "narrative technique." For this reason, we want to acquaint you with four ideas that relate to this worldview before we describe the practices that have come to be associated with the worldview. The ideas are:

1. Realities are socially constructed.
2. Realities are constituted through language.
3. Realities are organized and maintained through narrative.
4. There are no essential truths.

Realities Are Socially Constructed

Imagine two survivors of some ecological disaster coming together to start a new society. Imagine that they are a man and a woman who come from very different cultures. Even if they share no language, no religion, and no presuppositions about how labor is to be divided, or what place work, play, communal ritual, and private contemplation have in a good

---

[4]Among scholars there is much argument about exactly what constitutes a postmodern worldview. As we are clinicians and not scholars, the distinctions we discuss here are those that seem most relevant to our preferred therapy practices.

society, if culture of any sort is to continue, they must begin to coordinate their activities. As they do this, some agreed-upon habits and distinctions will emerge: certain substances will be treated as food, certain places found or erected to serve as shelter, each will begin to assume certain routine daily tasks, and they will almost certainly develop a shared language.

Between the two founding members of the emerging society, the habits and distinctions that arise will remain "tenuous, easily changeable, almost playful, even while they attain a measure of objectivity by the mere fact of their formation" (Berger & Luckmann, 1966, p. 58). They will always be able to remember, "This is how we decided to do this," or "It works better if I assume this role." They will carry some awareness that other possibilities exist. However, even in their generation, institutions such as "childcare," "farming," and "building" will have begun to emerge.

For the children of the founding generation, "This is how we decided . . . " will be more like "This is how our elders do it," and by the third generation it will be "This is how it's done." Mothers and farmers and builders will be treated as always-having-existed types of people. The rough-and-ready procedures for building houses and planting crops that our original two survivors pieced together will be more-or-less codified as the *rules* for how to build a house or plant corn. In all likelihood laws will have been written about where, when, and how buildings may be built or crops may be planted. It is hard not to imagine that customs governing the proper rites for starting a family or harvesting a crop will have come to be, and that certain individuals will be identified as the proper people to perform those rites. Institutions like women's societies and masons' guilds will have begun to emerge.

By the fourth generation of our imaginary society, "This is how it is done" will have become "This is the way the world is; this is reality." As Berger and Luckmann (1966, p. 60) put it, "An institutional world . . . is experienced as an objective reality."

The preceding thought experiment is a paraphrase of one given by Peter Berger and Thomas Luckmann, who, in their now-classic work, *The Social Construction of Reality*, describe how ideas, practices, beliefs, and the like come to have reality status in a given social group.

A central tenet of the postmodern worldview in which we base our approach to therapy is that beliefs, laws, social customs, habits of dress and diet—all the things that make up the psychological fabric of "reality"—arise through social interaction over time. In other words, people, together, construct their realities as they live them.

Berger and Luckmann distinguish three processes, *typification, institutionalization*, and *legitimation*, which they believe are important in the way that any social group constructs and maintains its knowledge concerning "reality." They use a fourth term, *reification*, to encompass the overall process of which the other three are parts.

Typification is the process through which people sort their perceptions into types or classes. For instance, in my native culture, I (GC) learned to sort people into "Baptists" (us), "other Christians" (almost-but-not-quite us), and "unsaved people" (them). Our realities are constituted through networks of typifications. That is, we tend to accept the typifications that we learn from our families, playmates, teachers, and so forth as real. Yet the typifications that any particular person or culture uses are not the only typifications possible. [5]

For example, Kenneth Gergen (1985, p. 267) describes how

in certain [historical] periods childhood was not considered a specialized phase of development, romantic and maternal love were not components of human makeup, and the self was not viewed as isolated and autonomous.

He goes on to talk about how the emergence of such concepts as "childhood," "romantic love," and "the autonomous self" had to do with "historically contingent factors," not with the sudden appearance of new objects or entities in the universe.

When we talk together about "codependency" or "schizophrenia" or "narrative therapy," it is important to remember that we are actively perpetuating the social construction of these concepts as real elements in the fabric of our daily existence. We all too easily forget that other typifications might lead to the perception of other possibilities. (Would you rather work with "that borderline" or "the woman who is so angry about the way patriarchal, paternalistic staff members are treating her"?)

Institutionalization is the process through which institutions arise around sets of typifications: the institution of motherhood, the institution of law, etc. Institutionalization helps families and societies maintain and disseminate hard-won knowledge. And, like typification, it can blind us to other possibilities. For instance, social class has survived as an institution for thousands of years. For most of that time, most people have accepted it as the right, the proper, indeed the *only* way of distributing certain kinds of rights and responsibilities within a culture. However,

---

[5] George Howard (1991) points out that we all belong to numerous cultures, and as new cultures become more dominant in our lives we tend to leave behind the typifications from less dominant cultures.

the criteria for who belongs to what class, as well as the names for and number of classes, vary greatly from society to society within Western culture. And many people do question the usefulness and certainly the fairness of class distinctions.

Legitimation is the word Berger and Luckmann use to refer to those processes that give legitimacy to the institutions and typifications of a particular society. For instance, writing this book, having a reputable publisher put it forth into the world, and having people such as yourself read it are all acts of legitimation for the institution of narrative therapy. With enough legitimation, "institutions are now experienced as possessing a reality of their own, a reality that confronts the individual as an external and coercive fact" (Berger & Luckmann, 1966, p. 58). We will discuss later in this chapter the important roles of *language* and *narrative* in the legitimation of any particular view of reality.

Reification, according to Berger and Luckmann (1966, p. 89), is

. . . the apprehension of the products of human activity *as if* they were something else than human products — such as facts of nature, results of cosmic laws, or manifestations of divine will. Reification implies that man [*sic*] is capable of forgetting his own authorship of the human world. (emphasis in original)

Reification, the result of the combined processes of typification, institutionalization, and legitimation, seems to be unavoidable. It is *necessary* if we are to think and communicate efficiently. Without it, we could take nothing for granted when we talked together. We would always have to qualify and contextualize even our simplest utterances.

However, necessary as it is, unexamined reification can quickly lead to problems. For instance, in family therapy, "homeostasis" has been a useful concept in describing and attempting to change certain problems that families experience, but when we reify homeostasis as a process that controls the interactions of every family we see, it limits our perceptions and becomes an impediment to progress. The same could be said for "genogram," "boundary," "coevolution," "narrative," and all the other terms and concepts that we use. Each helps us refer efficiently to a certain aspect of experience but can become problematic when we forget that it is a useful social construction and begin to treat it as part of some external, preexistent reality.

The schema of Berger and Luckmann that we have been discussing is only one way of slicing the pie. Lynn Hoffman (1990) and Kenneth

Gergen (1985) have discussed different aspects of the social construction
of reality.

Hoffman describes the difference that she sees between *social constructionism* and *constructivism*. She associates constructivism with the
writings of Maturana and Varela (1980), von Foerster (1981), and von
Glasersfeld (1987). These researchers and theorists, focusing on the biology of perception and cognition, have argued persuasively that since
sensory data go through several transformations as they are received and
processed, it is impossible to know what external reality is "really like."
They say that there is no such thing as "direct perception." Hoffman
(1990, p. 2), writes that constructivists believe that

> constructs are shaped as the organism evolves a fit with its environ-
> ment, and that the construction of ideas about the world takes
> place in a nervous system that operates something like a blind
> person checking out a room. The walker in the dark who doesn't
> bump into a tree cannot say whether he is in a wood or a field, only
> that he has avoided bashing his head.[6]

Hoffman (1990, p. 2) writes that, along with other family therapists
like Paul Watzlawick (1984) and Brad Keeney (1983), she was attracted
to constructivism in the mid-'80s. As many people still seem to do, she
initially assumed that social constructionism was synonymous with constructivism. Then she read Gergen's (1985) paper and realized that the
social constructionists place far more emphasis on social interpretation
and the intersubjective influence of language, family, and culture, and
much less on the operations of the nervous system as it feels its way
along.

Hoffman (1990, p. 3) favors social constructionism because, instead
of seeing individuals as stuck in "biological isolation booths," it

> posits an evolving set of meanings that emerge unendingly from the
> interactions between people. These meanings are not skull-bound
> and may not exist inside what we think of as an individual "mind."
> They are part of a general flow of constantly changing narra-
> tives.

She quotes Gergen (1985, p. 268) as saying, "The move [from constructivism to social constructionism] is from an experiential to a social episte-

---

[6]This constructivist stance is very similar to Paré's second stance regarding human
knowledge of reality, described on p. 20.

mology." That is, there is a shift from focusing on how an individual person constructs a model of reality from his or her individual experience to focusing on how people interact with one another to construct, modify, and maintain what their society holds to be true, real, and meaningful. It is this social epistemology that attracts us to social constructionism. It presents a more satisfying way of conceptualizing the "interactional view" that originally attracted us to systems theory.

Realities Are Constituted through Language

When I (GC) was growing up in eastern Kentucky, both my father and my Uncle T. A. delighted in taking me on long walks in the woods, where they would point out, name, and tell stories about the various plants and flowers we saw. I learned to distinguish a white oak from a black oak. I learned to call the white-blossomed trees that bloomed first each spring "service" trees. My mother once showed me a secret field of blue-eyed Marys that flowered for only a few days each year. My grandmother taught me that mountain laurel was a cousin of bay laurel, and now whenever I put a bay leaf into a pot of soup I think of the mountain laurel's clustered white blooms.

Jill's grandparents often took her brother and her to formal gardens in St. Louis. She has often told me of the delight she took in these outings. But Jill's grandparents would never name the flowers or talk about their properties; their chief interest was in appreciating the beauty that surrounded them.

Consequently, when we walk through the neighborhoods and parks of Chicago each spring, I see daffodils and azaleas and redbuds and bleeding hearts, and note (each and every year as if it were the first) that they bloom all at once rather than in the slow and stately progression they enjoyed in Kentucky.

Jill sees beautiful flowers.

The different linguistic distinctions our families used in our youth continue to constitute different experiences of spring for each of us in our middle age.[7]

Returning to the terminology of Berger and Luckmann, we can say that the linguistic *typifications* and *institutions* of the families into which we were born tend to *legitimate* the *reification* of different worldviews even now. They (Berger & Luckmann, 1966, pp. 37–39) write,

---

[7]We've used this story in an earlier paper (Combs & Freedman, 1994a) to illustrate how knowledge is constituted through language.

Everyday life is, above all, life with and by means of the language
I share with [other people]. An understanding of language is thus
essential for any understanding of the reality of everyday life. . . .
Language is capable of becoming an objective repository of vast
accumulations of meaning and experience, which it can then preserve in time and transmit to following generations. . . . Because
of its capacity to transcend the "here and now," language bridges
different zones within the reality of everyday life and integrates
them into a meaningful whole. . . . Language is capable of "making present" a variety of objects that are spatially, temporally, and
socially absent from the "here and now." . . . Through language
an entire world can be actualized at any moment.

In the modernist worldview, the signs of language[8] correspond in a
one-for-one way to objects and events in "the real world." Within the
modernist belief system, there is a clear distinction between the objective
(real) world and the subjective (mental) world, and language is seen as a
reliable and accurate link between the objective and subjective worlds.
There is a real world "out there," and we can know it through language.
We can use language unambiguously to represent external reality, and
our internal representations are accurate reflections of external reality.

Postmodernists believe differently. We focus on how the language
that we use *constitutes* our world and beliefs. It is in language that
societies construct their views of reality. To postmodernists, the only
worlds that people can know are the worlds we share in language, and
language is an interactive process, not a passive receiving of preexisting
truths. As Richard Rorty (1989, pp. 5–6) puts it,

Truth cannot be out there—cannot exist independently of the human mind—because sentences cannot so exist, or be out there. The
world is out there, but descriptions of the world are not. . . . The
world does not speak. Only we do. The world can, once we have
programmed ourselves with a language, cause us to hold beliefs.
But it cannot propose a language for us to speak. Only other human beings can do that.

In agreeing on the meaning of a word or gesture, we agree on a
description, and that description shapes subsequent descriptions, which
direct our perceptions toward making still other descriptions and away
from making others. Our language tells us how to see the world and

---

[8]When we say "language," we are referring not just to words, but also to vocal inflec-
tions, writing, gestures, pregnant silences—to all the signs we use in communication.

what to see in it. As Harlene Anderson and Harry Goolishian (1988, p. 378) put it, "Language does not mirror nature; language creates the natures we know."

Speaking isn't neutral or passive. Every time we speak, we bring forth a reality. Each time we share words we give legitimacy to the distinctions that those words bring forth. To talk about race is to legitimate race as a concept. Such legitimation tends to reify race or whatever other concepts we discuss, and we can easily forget that other concepts are equally possible and equally valid. The "logic" of language lends an air of logic to our perceptions and descriptions of the social world, and we have been socialized so as to confuse "logical" with "real."

According to Gergen (1985, p. 270), the social constructionist movement "begins in earnest when one challenges the concept of knowledge as mental representation." Knowledge can be viewed as "that which is represented in linguistic propositions," and therefore "not something people possess somewhere in their heads, but rather something people do together. Languages are essentially shared activities." In this view, the study of knowledge becomes the study of "the performative use of language in human affairs."

What is important here for psychotherapists is that change, whether it be change of belief, relationship, feeling, or self-concept, involves a change in language. Fortunately (at least within a postmodernist worldview), language is always changing. Meanings are always somewhat indeterminate, and therefore mutable. Jacques Derrida (1988 and elsewhere) has given numerous examples of this. Meaning is not carried in a word by itself, but by the word in relation to its context, and no two contexts will be exactly the same. Thus the precise meaning of any word is always somewhat indeterminate, and potentially different; it is always something to be negotiated between two or more speakers or between a text and a reader.

We see this inevitable mutability of language as useful. It makes our conversations with the people we work with opportunities for developing new language, thereby negotiating new meanings for problematic beliefs, feelings, and behaviors—new meanings that can give legitimacy to alternative views of reality. Throughout this book, we will describe various ways of inviting people to describe their experience in new language and by so doing bring forth new worlds of possibility.

Realities Are Organized and Maintained
through Stories

If the realities we inhabit are brought forth in the language we use, they are then kept alive and passed along in the stories that we live and tell. The central role of narrative in organizing, maintaining, and circulating knowledge of ourselves and our worlds has been stressed by many postmodern writers. Here is a postmodern sampler of quotes:

> . . . whether you get your literature from deconstructionist critics and university-press novelists, or from the latest item in the airport bookstore, or from the daily news, you are likely to get a similar subtext about the human condition: a message that life is a matter of telling ourselves stories about life, and of savoring stories about life told by others, and of living our lives according to such stories, and of creating ever-new and more complex stories about stories — and that this story making is not just about human life, but *is* human life. (W. Anderson, 1990, p. 102)

> . . . we organize our experience and our memory of human happenings mainly in the form of narrative — stories, excuses, myths, reasons for doing and not doing, and so on. (J. Bruner, 1991, p. 4)

> . . . narrative can provide a particularly rich source of knowledge about the significance people find in their workaday lives. Such narratives often reveal more about what can make life worth living than about how it is routinely lived. (Rosaldo, 1986, p. 98)

> Because postmodern and poststructural ideas were originated by people in semiotics and literary criticism, it is becoming increasingly common, in talking of social fields of study, to use the analogy of a narrative or text. (Hoffman, 1991, p. 4)

> The systems that we, as therapists, work with are the narratives that evolve through therapeutic conversation. (Anderson & Goolishian, 1988, p. 379)

> The conversations that therapists and clients have can be seen as stories, as narratives. Like any story, each case or each session of each case has a beginning, a middle, and an ending, or at least a sense of an ending. Like any story, the conversation is held together by the patterns involved, by the plot. Like many stories, therapy conversations deal with human predicaments, troubles, resolutions, and attempted resolutions. (de Shazer, 1991, p. 92)

> In striving to make sense of life, persons face the task of arranging their experiences of events in sequences across time in such a way as to arrive at a coherent account of themselves and the world around them. . . . This account can be referred to as a story or self-narrative. The success of this storying of experience provides persons with a sense of continuity and meaning in their lives, and

this is relied upon for the ordering of daily lives and for the interpretation of further experiences. (White & Epston, 1990, p. 10)

According to Alan Parry (1991, p. 37), a characteristic of the modernist approach to stories is to explain them through underlying structures or archetypes instead of letting them "tell themselves." In this view, "only a specialist, not so much in stories as in structures or myths, [can] properly understand the story, better even than the story-teller who [is] only the instrument of the structure." Renato Rosaldo (1986, p. 103) illustrates how this search for general patterns or themes that underlie individual stories can rob "lived experience . . . of its vital significance" with the following anecdote:

Imagine . . . the ethnographer returning from the last game of the World Series and reporting these remarkable discoveries: three strikes make an out, three outs retire the entire side, and so on. Eager to learn every move in the game's key plays, the avid fan could only (correctly) say that the ethnographer said nothing untrue, but managed to miss the whole point of the game.

When therapists listen to people's stories with an ear to "making an assessment" or "taking a history of the illness" or "offering an interpretation," they are approaching people's stories from a modernist, "structuralist" worldview. In terms of understanding an individual person's specific plight or joining her in her worldview, this approach risks missing the whole point. Lynn Hoffman (1991, pp. 12, 13) makes a similar observation when, referring to Gergen's (1991a) work, she writes:

. . . traditional therapists believe that there are "essences" in the human experience that must be captured in some kind of narrative and offered to clients in place of their old, illusory narratives. Going in, the therapist already has some idea of what these "essences" are. Postmodern therapists do not believe in "essences." Knowledge, being socially arrived at, changes and renews itself in each moment of interaction. There are no prior meanings hiding in stories or texts. A therapist with this view will expect a new and hopefully more useful narrative to surface during the conversation, but will see this narrative as spontaneous rather than planned. The conversation, not the therapist is its author.

Within a social constructionist worldview, it is important to attend to *cultural* and *contextual* stories as well as to individual people's stories. According to Mair (1988, p. 127),

Stories inform life. They hold us together and keep us apart. We inhabit the great stories of our culture. We live through stories. We are *lived* by the stories of our race and place.

White (1991) writes that cultural stories determine the shapes of our individual life narratives. People make sense of their lives through stories, both the cultural narratives they are born into and the personal narratives they construct in relation to the cultural narratives. In any culture, certain narratives will come to be dominant over other narratives. These dominant narratives will specify the preferred and customary ways of believing and behaving within the particular culture. Some cultures have colonized and oppressed others. The narratives of the dominant culture are then imposed on people of marginalized cultures.

The Just Therapy team (Tamasese & Waldegrave, 1993; Waldegrave, 1990) has reminded us that it is important to respect and try to understand the cultural traditions of all the people we work with, particularly those of people whose cultures have been marginalized. They also assert that when we try to make our work accountable to members of other cultures we can be inspired to reflect usefully on our own. Charles Waldegrave (1990, p. 20) writes,

> . . . the accentuation of cultural meaning and cultural difference . . . inspires reflection on Western meaning systems. . . . It offers a critical contrast to assess major issues like: cooperation as against individualistic competitive, self-determination; subtle indirect and circular processes of interviewing as opposed to direct and linear ones; traditional spiritual and ecological responses as opposed to a dualistic worldview with a separation of physical and spiritual values; and so on.

Whatever culture we belong to, its narratives have influenced us to ascribe certain meanings to particular life events and to treat others as relatively meaningless. Each remembered event constitutes a story, which together with our other stories constitutes a life narrative, and, experientially speaking, our life narrative is our life.

A key to this therapy is that in any life there are always more events that don't get "storied" than there are ones that do—even the the longest and most complex autobiography leaves out more than it includes. This means that when life narratives carry hurtful meanings or seem to offer only unpleasant choices, they can be changed by highlighting different, previously un-storied events or by taking new meaning from already-storied events, thereby constructing new narratives. Or, when dominant cultures carry stories that are oppressive, people can resist their dictates and find support in subcultures that are living different stories.

So, narrative therapy is about the retelling and reliving of stories. As people retell their stories in therapy, they often "notice that they have already experienced participating in an alternative story" (Zimmerman & Dickerson, 1994a, p. 235). Edward Bruner (1986a, p. 17) writes,

> . . . retellings are what culture is all about. The next telling reactivates prior experience, which is then rediscovered and relived as the story is re-related in a new situation. Stories may have endings, but stories are never over.

But it is not enough to recite a new story. In order to make a difference, new stories must be experienced and lived outside the four walls of a therapist's office. Bruner (1986a, pp. 22–25) goes on to say,

> . . . we are not dealing with culture as text but rather with culture as the performance of text — and, I would add, with the reperformance and retellings. . . . Stories become transformative only in their performance.

Therefore, when we use the narrative metaphor to orient our work as therapists, we are intensely curious about the "local knowledge" of each new person we meet. We want to develop an understanding of the influence on particular people of the dominant stories of their culture while cherishing the knowledge that each person's stories are different from anyone else's. We work with people in ways that invite them to celebrate their differences and to develop and perform narratives that they prefer around the particularities of their lives.

There Are No Essential Truths

In the narrative/social constructionist worldview that we have been describing, since we can't objectively know reality, all we can do is interpret experience. There are many possibilities for how any given experience may be interpreted, but no interpretation is "really" true. Where a modernist worldview would invite us to close down options and work methodically to identify a universally applicable interpretation, we invite ourselves to celebrate diversity. We want to think more like novelists and less like technocrats. In this regard, we recommend Madison Smartt Bell's (1987) novel, *The Year of Silence*. Each chapter is told by a different character. As the same "facts" are retold from different points of view they have very different meanings.

Milan Kundera writes about "the unbearable lightness of being." This, the title of his most famous novel, has become a catch phrase among postmodernists, many of whom believe that it is useful to hold our views of reality "lightly." Within the multiple stories and multiple possibilities of the postmodern "multiverse," we believe that there are no "essential" truths.

Consider Clifford Geertz's (1983, p. 62) description of self in Bali:

> . . . there is in Bali a persistent and systematic attempt to stylize all aspects of personal expression to the point where anything idiosyncratic . . . is muted in favor of [one's] assigned place in the continuing and, so it is thought, never-changing pageant that is Balinese life. It is dramatis personae, not actors, that endure; indeed, it is dramatis personae, not actors, that in the proper sense really exist.
> . . . the masks [people] wear, the stage they occupy, the parts they play, and, most important, the spectacle they mount remain, and comprise not the facade but the substance of things, not least the self.

This Balinese conception of self as a character in a timeless, unchanging drama is very different from the individualized, skin-bound "true self" or "deep self" that we hear many Western psychotherapists discussing. The contrast of different experiences of self brings home the notion that ideas of self, like other constructions, are formed through social interaction within particular cultural contexts. We conclude, then, that there is no such thing as an "essential" self.

"Selves" are socially constructed through language and maintained in narrative. We think of a self not as a thing inside an individual, but as a process or activity that occurs in the space between people. Steiner Kvale (1992, p. 15) writes,

> In current understanding of human beings there is a move from the inwardness of an individual psyche to being-in-the-world with other human beings. The focus of interest is moved from the inside of a psychic container to the outside of the human world.

John Neal (in press) notes an implication of this redefinition of self:

> Explanations of behavior based on a psychology of the individual remove the influence of dominant cultural practices from the therapist's lens. A constitutionalist perspective counters this influence with a perspective on persons and problems that locates problems in the operation of power and meaning through the statements,

practices, and institutional structures that share and perpetuate a common world view.

Different selves come forth in different contexts, and no one self is truer than any other. We think that people are continually constituting each other's "selves," and that there are many possible stories about my-self, your-self, and other people's selves.

While no self is "truer" than any other, it *is* true that particular presentations of self are preferred by particular people within particular cultures. But a "preferred self" is different from an essential or "true" self. Instead of looking for an essential self, we work with people to bring forth various experiences of self and to distinguish which of those selves they prefer in which contexts. We then work to assist them in living out narratives that support the growth and development of these "preferred selves."

POSTMODERNISM AND
MORAL RELATIVISM

When we say that there are many possible stories about self (or about other aspects of reality), we do not mean to say that "anything goes." Rather, we are motivated to examine our constructions and stories — how they have come to be and what their effects are on ourselves and others.

As Jerome Bruner (1990, p. 27) has written,

Asking the pragmatist's questions — how does this view affect my view of the world or my commitments to it? — surely does not lead to "anything goes." It may lead to an unpackaging of presuppositions, the better to explore one's commitments.

Richard Rorty (1991b, p. 132) puts it this way:

The repudiation of the traditional logocentric image of the human being as Knower does not seem to us to entail that we face an abyss, but merely that we face a range of choices.

These authors seem to be saying that a postmodern worldview makes it *more* necessary to examine our constructions and to decide carefully how to act on them, not less. The issues of deciding, of choosing, and of examining the effects of our choices are central to the kind of therapy that we practice. Not only do we carefully examine the beliefs and values that we choose, but we invite the people who come to see us to examine their beliefs and values as well.

To this end, we make beliefs and values grist for the therapeutic mill. We try to understand the beliefs that support people's problems. We inquire about where those beliefs come from and what processes of social construction have recruited people into those beliefs. We try to be "transparent" (White, 1991) about our own values, explaining enough about our situation and our life experience that people can understand us as people rather than as "experts" or conduits for professional knowledge.

Even if we wanted to foster a value-neutral, "anything goes" reality, we couldn't. One cannot make up and inhabit a completely new social reality overnight. If you think back to the thought experiment that we described under "Realities Are Socially Constructed" (pp. 22–23), you will remember that it took several generations for the beliefs, practices, and institutions of our fledgling society to take on the weight of reality.

While, as Berger and Luckmann (1966, p. 86) write, "in any developed society there are many subuniverses of meaning," these subuniverses are not infinite in number. The reifying and legitimizing influences of our cultural institutions constrain us very effectively, leading us to see certain possibilities as desirable and completely blinding us to other possibilities. As Joan Laird (1989, p. 430) puts it,

> . . . sociocultural narratives . . . construct the contextual realms of possibility from which individuals and families can select the ingredients and forms for their own narratives.

But some people have readier access to a wider range of sociocultural narratives than others, and some narratives are dominant while others are marginalized. Laird (p. 431) reminds of this when she goes on to write of

> . . . the politics of storymaking or mythmaking. Clearly there are both obvious and subtle differences in the power individuals and particular interest groups possess to ensure that particular narratives will prevail in family, group, and national life. Not all stories are equal.

Social realities may not be "essentially true," but that doesn't stop them from having real effects. The story that "welfare mothers" are engaged in a mini-industry where they get richer and richer as they make more and more babies has had real effects on already underserved women and children. It has provided a rationalization that has allowed those in power to cut funds even further. The story about how women can never be too thin that gets retold every time you turn on the TV or stand in a supermarket checkout line surrounded by magazines has brought forth a real epidemic of self-starvation. The story that inner-city males are only interested in drugs, sex, and killing each other has led to the perverse glorification of certain kinds of misogyny and violence in the media. At the same time, it has served as a rationale for giving up on the establishment of social policies that might offer inner-city males a real chance at a different way of making it in the world.

THE POLITICS OF POWER

One of the most consistently attractive things to us about Michael White's voice has been the way that he addresses the politics of power. He (1991, 1993, 1995; White & Epston, 1990) argues for a "constitution-alist perspective," which proposes that, while we as human beings can know no essential truths, the experiential truths of our daily lives are constituted by the stories we live. He (White, 1993, p. 125) writes

> The constitutionalist perspective that I am arguing for refutes foun-dationalist assumptions of objectivity, essentialism, and represen-tationalism. It proposes . . . that essentialist notions are paradoxi-cal in that they provide descriptions that are specifying of life; that these notions obscure the operations of power. And the constitu-tionalist perspective proposes that the descriptions that we have of life are not representations or reflections of life as lived, but are directly constitutive of life; that these descriptions . . . have real effects in the shaping of life.

In order to understand White's handling of differences in power, it is necessary to understand a little about the work of Michel Foucault (1965, 1975, 1977, 1980, 1985). Foucault was a French intellectual who studied, among other things, the various ways that people in Western society have been categorized as "normal" and "abnormal." He examines madness (Foucault, 1965), illness (1975), criminality (1977), and sexuality (1985) as concepts around which certain people have been labeled as insane, sick, criminal, or perverted, and describes various ways they have been separated, sequestered, and oppressed on the basis of that labeling.

To Foucault, language is an instrument of power, and people have power in a society in direct proportion to their ability to participate in the various discourses[9] that shape that society. The people whose voices dominated the discussion about what constituted madness, for example, could separate the people *they* saw as mad from "polite society," sequestering them in madhouses where their voices were cut off from polite discourse. He argues that there is an inseparable link between knowledge and power: the discourses of a society determine what knowledge is held to be true, right, or proper in that society, so those who control the discourse control knowledge. At the same time, the dominant knowledge of a given milieu determines who will be able to occupy its powerful positions. To Foucault, power is knowledge and knowledge is power.

Within the narrative metaphor, the discourses of power that Foucault studied can be seen as historical, cultural meta-narratives — as stories that have shaped (and been shaped by) the distribution of power in society. As Edward Bruner (1986a, p. 19) writes,

> . . . dominant narratives are units of power as well as of meaning. The ability to tell one's story has a political component; indeed, one measure of the dominance of a narrative is the place allocated to it in the discourse. Alternative, competing stories are generally not allocated space in establishment channels and must seek expression in underground media and dissident groupings.

Three important areas of discourse that Foucault did not discuss (and we do not mean to say that these are the *only* three that he didn't get around to) are those concerning race, social class, and gender. The dominant narratives in our society disempower large numbers of people by excluding them from a significant voice in these particular areas of discourse. For instance, in her monograph *Playing in the Dark*, Toni Morrison (1992, pp. 4, 5) discusses how the "knowledge" of American literary historians and critics

> . . . holds that traditional, canonical American literature is free of, uninformed, and unshaped by the four-hundred-year-old presence of, first, Africans and then African-Americans in the United States. It assumes that this presence — which shaped the body politic, the Constitution, and the entire history of the culture — has had no significant place or consequence in the origin and development of that culture's literature. . . . There seems to be a more or less

---

[9]While *The American Heritage Dictionary, Third Edition* gives simply "verbal expression in speech or writing" as its first definition of "discourse," scholars like Foucault tend to use the word to refer to the ongoing historical conversations within a society that constitute our notions of "madness," "normal sexuality," etc. See Chapter 3, pages 42–44 for a more thorough explication of the importance of this term in postmodernist thought.

tacit agreement among literary scholars that, because American literature has been clearly the preserve of white male views, genius, and power, those views, genius, and power are without relationship to and removed from the overwhelming presence of black people in the United States.

White, following Foucault, writes that we tend to *internalize*[10] the "dominant narratives" of our culture, easily believing that they speak the truth of our identities. Using terminology from Foucault, we can say that people tend to become "docile bodies" under "the [internalized] gaze" of those who control the discourses of power in our culture. Thus, dominant narratives tend to blind us to the possibilities that other narratives might offer us.

White (1991, p. 14) argues that people come to therapy either when dominant narratives are keeping them from living out their preferred narratives or when

> . . . the person is actively participating in the performance of stories that she finds unhelpful, unsatisfying, and dead-ended, and that these stories do not sufficiently encapsulate the person's lived experience or are very significantly contradicted by important aspects of the person's lived experience.

Foucault was especially interested in how the "truth claims" carried in the "grand abstractions" of modernist science constituted a discourse that dehumanized and objectified many people. He was interested in finding and circulating marginalized discourses that might undermine the power of the modernist scientific discourse. He (1980, pp. 80–84) wrote of the "amazing efficacy of discontinuous, particular, and local criticism" in bringing about a "return of knowledge" or "an insurrection of subjugated knowledges." "We are concerned . . . ," he said,

> with the insurrection of knowledges that are opposed . . . to the effects of the centralising powers which are linked to the institution and functioning of an organized scientific discourse within a society such as ours.

Michael White argues that even in the most marginalized and disempowered of lives there is always "lived experience" that lies outside the domain of the dominant stories that have marginalized and disempow-

---

[10]See Adams-Westcott, Dafforn, and Sterne (1993) for an excellent discussion of how dominant stories about abuse and its meaning can be internalized, and the effects of such internalization.

ered those lives. He and David Epston, along with others, have developed ways of thinking and working that are based on bringing forth the "discontinuous, particular, and local" stories of individuals and groups and performing meaning on those stories so that they can be part of an effective "insurrection of subjugated knowledges," an insurrection that lets people inhabit and lay claim to the many possibilities for their lives that lie beyond the pale of the dominant narratives. The rest of this book is an attempt to circulate the story of the work that White and Epston have pioneered.

ELEMENTS OF A NARRATIVE/SOCIAL CONSTRUCTIONIST STANCE

We have evolved a set of questions to help us maintain a narrative/ social constructionist position. We ask ourselves these questions from time to time as we work with people, and we encourage therapists who study with us to ask themselves these questions. The questions keep evolving, so we are reasonably sure that by the time you read this our personal list won't exactly match the one we offer here.

Actually, what is now a list of questions started out as a list of "guidelines" that were phrased as permissive-but-still-rather-prescriptive statements. Phrasing them as questions makes them less prescriptive. Can you see how we would think that being less prescriptive fits with our postmodern worldview?

Here are the questions:

1. Am I asking for descriptions of more than one reality?
2. Am I listening so as to understand how this person's experiential reality has been socially constructed?
3. Whose language is being privileged here? Am I trying to accept and understand this person's linguistic descriptions? If I am offering a distinction or typification in *my* language, why am I doing that? What are the effects of the various linguistic distinctions that are coming forth in the therapeutic conversation?
4. What are the stories that support this person's problems? Are there dominant stories that are oppressing or limiting this person's life? What marginalized stories am I hearing? Are there clues to marginalized stories that have not yet been spoken? How might I invite this person to engage in an "insurrection of knowledges" around those marginalized stories?
5. Am I focusing on meaning instead of on "facts"?
6. Am I evaluating this person, or am I inviting her or him to evaluate a

wide range of things (e.g., how therapy is going, preferred directions in life)?

7. Am I situating my opinions in my personal experience? Am I being transparent about my context, my values, and my intentions so that this person can evaluate the effects of my biases?

8. Am I getting caught up in pathologizing or normative thinking? Are we collaboratively defining problems based on what is problematic in this person's experience? Am I staying away from "expert" hypotheses or theories?

Opening Space
for New Stories

Today, psychologists have a favorite word, and that word is maladjusted. I tell you today that there are some things in our social system to which I am proud to be maladjusted. I shall never be adjusted to lynch mobs, segregation, economic inequalities, "the madness of militarism," and self-defeating phsycial violence. The salvation of the world lies in the maladjusted.

— Martin Luther King, Jr.

. . . I have to give you a warning — if externalization is approached purely as a technique, it will probably not produce profound effects. If you don't believe, to the bottom of your soul, that people are not their problems and that their difficulties are social and personal constructions, then you won't be seeing these transformations. When Epston or White are in action, you can tell they are absolutely convinced that people are not their problems. Their voices, their postures, their whole beings radiate possibility and hope. They are definitely under the influence of Optimism.

— Bill O'Hanlon, 1994, p. 28

People are born into stories; their social and historical contexts constantly invite them to tell and remember the stories of certain events and to leave others unstoried. A number of authors (Foucault, 1980; Hare-Mustin, 1994; Lowe, 1991; Madigan & Law, 1992; Weingarten, 1991) suggest that "discourse" is a useful notion for understanding how this happens. Rachel Hare-Mustin (1994, p. 19) defines a discourse as "a system of statements, practices, and institutional structures that share common values." She (p. 20) suggests that discourses sustain particular worldviews, pointing out, "The ways most people hold, talk about, and act on a common, shared viewpoint are part of and sustain the prevailing discourses." Stephen Madigan and Ian Law (1992, p. 33) add that "discourse can be viewed to reflect a prevailing structure of social and power relationships."

Discourses powerfully shape a person's choices about what life events can be storied and how they should be storied. This is as true for therapists as it is for the people who consult them.

Our stories about therapy have been shaped by a variety of discourses. To name a few, discourses about pathology, about normative standards, and about professionals as experts are quite prevalent. These discourses are propagated by the content of professional education, as well as by the structure of our educational institutions and professional socialization processes. More specifically, most therapists, ourselves included, have been indoctrinated to listen with a diagnostic, pathologizing ear. The medical model, with its emphasis on listening for signs and symptoms of disease, exerts such a pervasive influence that few of us can escape its urgings. Our educational system, with its strong emphasis on knowing the *right* answer, has shaped us to listen for facts of the sort that might appear on a multiple-choice test rather than listening so as to understand a narrator's frustrations, dilemmas, and yearnings.

These discourses also shape and are carried by practices outside of our field: for example, in requirements for third-party payment, such as making diagnoses and keeping certain sorts of records, in self-help books, in depictions of therapists in the media, and in the expectations of the people who consult us. Freudian "archeological" metaphors about the "deep, unconscious truth" have permeated our culture so thoroughly that we often don't notice their influence. These metaphors invite us to listen not for the person's meaning, but for the connoisseur's meaning hidden beneath it.

LISTENING

Given our stories about therapy, which are formed within these prevalent discourses, it is hard for most therapists to learn to listen to people's stories as stories. Our stories about therapy conspire to make us listen with our ears cocked and our mouths set to say "Aha!" when we recognize a "clinically significant item" — something that we know what to do with.

However, as Weingarten (1991) notes, discourses can change and evolve when conversations between people affect culturally available narratives. That is, knowledge at a local level and from subcommunities can influence larger discourses. As simple as it may seem, in the face of prevalent discourses and dominant knowledges, simply listening to the story someone tells us constitutes a revolutionary act.

When we meet people for the first time, we want to understand the meaning of their stories for *them*. This means turning our backs on "expert" filters: not listening for chief complaints; not "gathering" the pertinent-to-us-as-experts bits of diagnostic information interspersed in their stories; not hearing their anecdotes as matrices within which resources are embedded; not listening for surface hints about what the core problem "really" is; and not comparing the selves they portray in their stories to normative standards.

Instead, we try to put ourselves in the shoes of the people we work with and understand, from their perspective, in their language, what has led them to seek our assistance. Only then can we recognize alternative stories. Connecting with people's experience from their perspective orients us to the specific realities that shape, and are shaped by, their personal narratives. This sort of understanding requires that we listen with focused attention, patience, and curiosity while building a relationship of mutual respect and trust.

In spite of all of our education telling us that we do know, we try to listen for what we *don't know*.

Not-Knowing

Anderson and Goolishian (1988, 1990a, 1992; see also Anderson, 1990; Goolishian, 1990; Goolishian & Anderson, 1990; Hoffman, 1991) have written passionately and convincingly about the importance of a "not-knowing" position for therapists. They see therapy as a process in which "we are always moving toward what is *not yet known*" (1990a, p. 159). This implies not asking questions from a position of pre-understanding (Andersen, 1991b; Weingarten, 1992) and not asking questions to which we want *particular* answers.

However, a not-knowing position is not an "I don't know anything" position. Our knowledge is of the process of therapy, not the content and meaning of people's lives. We hope that therapy is a process in which people experience choice rather than "settled certainties" (J. Bruner, 1986) with regard to the realities that they inhabit. As Anderson and Goolishian (1988, p. 381) write,

> The goal of therapy is to participate in a conversation that continually loosens and opens up, rather than constricts and closes down. Through therapeutic conversation, fixed meanings and behaviors . . . are given room, broadened, shifted, and changed.

We are most successful in achieving a not-knowing position when we concentrate on listening and when our talking is guided by and secondary to that listening. As we listen, we notice and question the assumptions we are making. We ask ourselves, "Am I understanding what it feels like to be this person in this situation, or am I beginning to fill in the gaps in her story with unwarranted assumptions? What more do I need to know in order to step into this person's shoes?" If our internal conversation tells us that more information in a specific area would help us step more fully into a person's reality, we ask her to tell us more. Such constant questioning of our own assumptions invites people to question theirs.

Not-knowing fosters an attitude of curiosity (Cecchin, 1987; Rambo, Heath, & Chenail, 1993; White, 1988a). We are curious about people's unique answers and we encourage people to develop them more fully. When an answer takes the conversation in an unexpected direction, we ask even more questions, following that new direction if it seems relevant.

Just listening and asking facilitating and clarifying questions from a position of curiosity can be very therapeutic. Sometimes people get all they want from therapy through this process alone. Therapy of this sort is, as Anderson and Goolishian (1988, p. 380) indicate,

> . . . a process of expanding and saying the "unsaid" — the development, through dialogue, of new themes and narratives and, actually, the creation of new histories.

Interpretation

Postmodernists to the bone, Anderson and Goolishian make it clear that they do not believe that the "unsaid" is something that already exists. It is not lying hidden in the unconscious or waiting, fully formed, to be noticed and described in the cybernetic structures of family interactions. Rather, it emerges and takes shape as we converse with each other. Therefore, it matters what therapists attend to as they listen. In other words, listening is not a passive activity. When we listen, we *interpret*, whether we want to or not.

This may sound like a contradiction to our earlier statement — "We want to understand the meaning of their stories for *them*. This means turning our backs on 'expert' filters." What is important here is the word "expert." While it is impossible to avoid interpretation, we eschew the belief that we know more about a person's lived experience than the person does. The people we work with are the primary interpreters of their own experience.

In our therapeutic conversations, we are "making up" meanings in

interactions with others, not discovering truths. It is inevitable and unavoidable that we will pick out certain things as relevant and meaningful
and that we will ignore others. Our minds are not, and never can be,
blank slates on which other people inscribe their stories. If we think of
ourselves as experts on pathology, we will notice, remember, and inquire
further about things people say that sound pathological to us. If our
listening is guided by a theory that says people must "feel their pain" in
order to be whole, we will bring forth painful stories. If we have a special
interest in disempowerment as an issue, we will invite people to tell us
stories of how they have been deprived of power. We can end up making
the very things that people came to therapy to escape more real, more
vivid, and more oppressive.

Deconstructive Listening

We call the special kind of listening required for accepting and understanding people's stories without reifying or intensifying the powerless,
painful, and pathological aspects of those stories[1] *deconstructive listening*. Through this listening, we seek to open space for aspects of people's
life narratives that haven't yet been storied. Our social constructionist
bias leads us to interact with people in ways that invite them to relate
to their life narratives not as passively received facts, but as actively
constructed stories. We hope they will experience their stories as something that they have a hand in shaping, rather than as something that has
already shaped them. We believe that this attitude helps to deconstruct
the "factity" of people's narratives, and that such deconstruction loosens
the grip of restrictive stories.

In academic circles, the word "deconstruction" immediately brings to
mind the work of Jacques Derrida (e.g., 1988), which explores, among
other things, the slipperiness of meaning. Derrida examines and illustrates how the meaning of any symbol, word, or text is inextricably
bound up in its context. Derrida and other deconstructionists believe that
it is fruitless to search for the one "real" or "true" meaning of any
text, as all narratives are full of gaps and ambiguities. Deconstructionist
scholars focus on these gaps and ambiguities to show that the officially
sanctioned or generally accepted meaning of a given text is but one of a
great number of possible meanings.

So when we listen "deconstructively" to people's stories, our listening

---

[1]This does not mean that we encourage people to ignore or adapt to injustice. It does
mean that we are more alert to events that could be storied as "struggles against injustice,"
than we are to those that could be storied as "person as victim." In so doing, we help
ourselves and the people we work with have roles in deconstructing pathologizing stories.

is guided by the belief that those stories have many possible meanings. The meaning a listener makes is, more often than not, different from the meaning that the speaker has intended. We seek to capitalize on this by looking for gaps in our understanding and asking people to fill in details, or by listening for ambiguities in meaning and then asking people how they are resolving or dealing with those ambiguities.

As people tell us their stories, we interrupt at intervals to summarize our sense of what they are saying. This allows them to tell us if the meaning we are making fits with their intended meaning. Even though our goal is "really" to understand people's realities, those realities inevitably begin to change in the process. In considering our questions and comments, people can't help but examine their stories in new ways. Our very presence makes their world a new and different reality.

As this process continues, new meanings and new constructions emerge. Many of the gaps we notice haven't yet been filled in; people must search their experience to find details that fill the gaps, and as details are added the shape of the narrative changes. Also, when people hear that we are making different meanings from theirs, they can reconsider their own meanings and modify them. Throughout this process we listen with a thoughtfulness about what new constructions are emerging. Are they useful or desirable? If a person doesn't prefer a new construction, we don't pursue it.

Perceiving Problems as Separate from People

White has introduced the idea (1987, 1988/9, 1989; see also Epston, 1993a, and Tomm, 1989) that the person is not the problem, but the problem is the problem. Externalization is a practice supported by the belief that a problem is something operating or impacting on or pervading a person's life, something separate and different from the person.

When listening to people's stories, we ask ourselves questions like "What is problematic here? What is the nature of this problem? How does it show itself? What does it feel like for this person to have this problem in his or her life? What is influencing the person so that he thinks/feels/acts this way? What is keeping this person from having experiences he would prefer?" In asking ourselves these questions, we are taking the first steps in perceiving problems as separate from people.

Externalization is more important as an *attitude* than as a technique (Roth & Epston, in press). We believe, based on our experience in using narrative ideas in therapy and in supervising others who are attempting to apply narrative ideas in their work, that when people approach externalization as a technique or a linguistic trick, it can come off as shallow, forced, and not especially helpful.

Internalizing Discourses

Adams-Westcott, Dafforn, and Sterne (1993) have written compellingly about how people who suffer abuse tend to internalize the traumatizing events to which they have been subjected as inner dialogues, and how these dialogues color the interpretation of subsequent events. They write (p. 262),

> Problems develop when people internalize conversations that restrain them to a narrow description of self. These stories are experienced as oppressive because they limit the perception of available choices.

David Epston (1993a) has pointed out that this process of internalizing happens not just with local and particular experiences of trauma and abuse, but with larger cultural experiences as well. He notes Foucault's description of how death and disease (previously treated as if they were located primarily in a social or spiritual domain) came to be located at specific sites within specific human bodies. Epston (p. 171) writes,

> . . . anatomical space became causal space, the home of both death and disease. This was followed by the body being regarded as the repository of human qualities. Mind, intelligence, madness, and a myriad of human qualities were regarded to be located in living bodies.

In the Middle Ages, if a person was "sick," "crazy," or "criminal," the cause and cure tended to be located in social or spiritual space—his ruler wasn't ruling well enough or he was out of touch with the appropriate spiritual community. In modern times, the emphasis is much more on individual responsibility for properly policing our minds and bodies. If a person has a heart attack, it is because she hasn't properly controlled her diet and exercise. If a person is depressed, it is because of a chemical imbalance in certain circuits of his individual brain and a chemical cure is required. According to Foucault, the most politically powerful discourses in modern society divide us from each other and invite us to treat ourselves and our bodies as problematic objects. Epston has called the kind of dominant discourses that support this process "internalizing discourses."

An externalizing attitude can counter the "objectifying" influences of internalizing discourses, by objectifying and separating what had been internalized. But, in order to adopt an externalizing worldview, we must retrain our perceptions so that we objectify *problems* instead of people.

An Exercise

A turning point for me (JF) in learning to objectify and externalize problems was having an externalizing conversation with myself. I had thought of myself as shy for some time. One day when I was in dread of an upcoming social occasion I decided to talk with myself about the effects of shyness in my life. It was rather remarkable to discover that once I experienced the perceptual shift of shyness taking over in social situations, rather than me being shy, it was much easier to maintain similar kinds of perceptual shifts with others. This discovery inspired us to put together this exercise. You can do it as a "thought experiment."

Pick a character trait, quality, or emotion that you feel you have too much of or that other people sometimes complain about in you. Make sure it is in adjective form, as a description of you, for instance, "angry," "competitive," "guilty," or "nitpicky." In the following set of questions, fill in the trait or emotion where we have "X." As you read these questions, substituting the trait or emotion for X, answer them to yourself.

1. How did you become X?
2. What are you most X about?
3. What kinds of things happen that typically lead to your being X?
4. When you are X, what do you do that you wouldn't do if you weren't X?
5. What are the consequences for your life and relationships of being X?
6. Which of your current difficulties come from being X?
7. How is your self-image different when you are X?
8. If by some miracle you woke up some morning and you were not X anymore, how, specifically, would your life be different?

Note the overall effect of answering these questions. How do you feel? What seems possible in regard to this trait or emotion? What seems impossible? How does the future look in regard to this?

Now, let go of what you have just been doing. Take the same quality or trait that you worked with above and make it into a noun. For example, if "X" was "competitive," it would now become "competition"; "angry" would become "anger." In the following questions, where we've written a "Y," fill in your noun. Answer each of these questions to yourself.

1. What made you vulnerable to the Y so that it was able to dominate your life?
2. In what contexts is the Y most likely to take over?
3. What kinds of things happen that typically lead to the Y taking over?

4. What has the Y gotten you to do that is against your better judgment?
5. What effect does the Y have on your life and relationships?
6. How has the Y led you into the difficulties you are now experiencing?
7. Does the Y blind you from noticing your resources or can you see them through it?
8. Have there been times when you have been able to get the best of the Y? Times when the Y could have taken over but you kept it out of the picture?

Now note the overall effect of these questions. How do you feel? What seems possible in regard to "Y"? What seems impossible? How does the future look in regard to "Y"?

Think back to your experiences with "X." How is your experience with "Y" different from your experience with "X"? By turning the quality or emotion into a noun, did you begin to treat it as an *object*, and in answering the questions did you *externalize* that object? How was this useful in dealing with the quality or emotion?

Stepping into an externalizing worldview requires that we separate our perceptions of problems from our perceptions of people. As we learn to view problems as separate from people, we begin to see people as *subjects*.[2] David Epston (1993a, p. 172) puts it this way:

> If persons fade away or are absorbed into . . . an internalizing discourse, in an externalizing discourse they seem to emerge and come to life as protagonists in their life stories, which can now admit of a life lived forwards rather than one transfixed in various versions of chronicity.

We believe that listening with an externalizing attitude has a powerful deconstructive effect. It biases us to interact differently with people than we would if we saw them as intrinsically problematic. It creates a different "receiving context" for people's stories, one in which we can work to understand their problems without seeing them as problematic or pathological. In this kind of context, the content and meaning of people's stories almost always become less restrictive.

An Example of Deconstructive Listening

The following transcript illustrates deconstructive listening. In it, I (GC) am guided by both a not-knowing position and an attitude of perceiving people as separate from problems.

---

[2]We are using "subject" here in the sense of "subject of a verb, one who acts."

The conversation is with Nan, who moved with her family to Chicago from another city about six months before this conversation. I have been seeing Nan once every three weeks or so since that time. She came to see me so that she could continue the therapy she had started with a therapist in the other town.

Pertinent things that Nan has shared about her story are that she was severely physically, sexually, and verbally abused as a child. The recurring experience of abuse shaped Nan into believing that the way for her to survive was to adopt "hyperconventional" forms of feminine subservience, concentrating on anticipating and satisfying the smallest desires of the people around her. When she was 18 years old, she married Bart — primarily as a means of escaping the household she grew up in. She thought she had chosen well. Bart spoke politely to Nan and provided a house that she had a large say in running. She says that for the first decade or more of the marriage she successfully performed her duties as a hyperconventional wife and mother. However, the "feminine subservience" discourse was still running her life.

While Bart was the master of "his" house, he had recurring difficulties in the world of business. Over time, Bart became increasingly caught up in hierarchical structures in the business world. He didn't like "taking orders" from anybody, but, of course, anytime he started a new job, no matter how high up in an organization, he had a higher-up who "gave him orders." He experienced this as abusive. He would lash out at the perceived abuse and resign or get fired. However, over time he became persuaded that abusive practices were useful and, at times, necessary.

As abuse became more and more a part of Bart's worldview at work, he became verbally abusive toward Nan. He began beating her in their fourteenth year of marriage. During those first 14 years, the family had moved 12 times to cities in three different states as Bart searched for a job where, in his words, he wouldn't be "working for idiots." After Bart started beating Nan, she began to experience panic attacks and extreme depression. "Flashbacks," in which she vividly relived scenes of abuse from her childhood became daily visitors in her life. These problems led to hospitalization; then, while in the hospital, Nan was sexually abused by a therapist who was supposed to be helping her.

At the time of this interview, three and a half years after the traumatic hospitalization, Nan was still struggling with fears and depression. Although Bart had stopped the physical abuse, in Nan's view he was still steeped in the attitudes that supported it. Nan felt neither close to Bart nor safe in his presence. Self-criticism for staying in an abusive marriage fed the depression and fears that were already nearly overwhelming her.

Given Nan's experiences, and the real effects of those experiences, I keep a number of things in mind while we're talking. I'm aware that, as a man who lives in this patriarchal culture, I am not immune to patriarchal attitudes and beliefs that make it easy for me to treat women in abusive ways. I particularly want to guard against unwittingly duplicating the traumatizing experiences Nan has had with the dominant culture. For example, imposing my ideas instead of listening to hers would duplicate certain undesirable aspects of her childhood and her marriage. I try to guard against this in a number of ways. I have talked with Nan about my dilemma, wondering if she would prefer to work with a woman. When she decided to continue to see me, I arranged, with her permission, to consult with Jill in an ongoing way so that I would be accountable to women in this work. In order not to duplicate her abusive experiences of being coerced, I am particularly careful about following Nan's lead. Deconstructive listening is perhaps the most important practice in this regard.

As we begin to listen in on this particular conversation, Nan is talking about fear and how it immobilizes her at times.

NAN   I was never a fearful person. I took risks. But now it really, really gets bad, I guess, during traumatic times, like when Bart threatens me. Like that. . . . And it gets to the point where it almost immobilizes you. To have something control you like that is . . .

GENE   Are you saying that the fear immobilizes you?

NAN   It's like if you move away from this one spot, it will take over. It doesn't give you answers. It just gives you feelings, that's all. Physical feelings. Physically fearful feelings.

GENE   So, is it here right now?

NAN   Not to a great degree, no.

GENE   How do you understand that? I mean, what's . . .

NAN   Well, it works on its own. It controls when it wants to control. It's like, as I said, a separate thing. That's what causes the anxiety. And it's, you know, and it's just stupid things you try to talk yourself out of, and it's like, you wake up in the middle of the night and look out the window and it just feels really fearful. And you feel, "This is so stupid." But it's like, it has its own place in you that you can't control. You can't talk yourself out of it or do anything to make it go away. It just will be there.

GENE   So it feels like you don't have any direct power over it, like it kind of comes and goes as it pleases?

NAN   Um-hum . . . but I can act through it, too, sometimes when it's not so bad. I can pick up Mary Pat at school. You can still function some of the time.

GENE   And when you go ahead and function in the face of it, What's that like?

(Up to this point, I have been "just listening." I have been conceptualizing fear as an externalized entity, and she has been talking about it that way. I have only asked facilitating, clarifying questions phrased in externalized language, to fill in gaps. With this question I make a somewhat bolder choice. Rather than inviting her to keep telling the story of the fear, I ask what it is like when she functions in the face of the fear. Still, my role is primarily one of listening to and understanding her story as she tells it.)

NAN   I like to feel like I'm controlling it by functioning while I have it. (Pause) But I know I'm not. It's like it's just letting me.

GENE   It's toying with you?

NAN   It's just . . . "Okay, go ahead, you do what you've got to do, but I'm going to still be around." You know? "I'm going to get you. I'll get you later." You know? Is this like psychosis or something? Am I getting unbelievable? I don't know.

GENE   Well, I'm more interested in this notion that there is a sense that you've got some times that you can have some influence over it. That you can diminish its grip on you. That even though it's there, you can function in the face of it.

(Here, I am acknowledging that my interest is in a specific part of her story. I am interested to know how she can diminish fear's grip on her, but I am not attempting to teach her anything or convince her of anything, just to learn what she knows about diminishing the grip of fear. I also hope she might construct something new in puzzling about how she diminishes fear's grip.)

NAN   Not all the time.

GENE   I hear that.

(I take "not all the time" to mean that the story about the times fear does have a grip on her is more relevant to her at this time. I follow her lead and listen.)

NAN   Like I had an appointment last Friday with an orthopedist to get my cast off.

GENE   Um-hum.

NAN   I couldn't leave the house. There was no way.

GENE   And what was it about that particular situation? What was the
fear doing that was so effective?

*(I maintain the use of externalized language, but otherwise just invite
her to tell me more about the fear and how effective it is.)*

NAN   It was like . . . it was my whole body, inside, like I had to be
in a real tight ball and not move.

GENE   What was the fear doing to keep you in that tight ball?

NAN   The feelings. Making me feel the feelings.

GENE   And what are those feelings? What were those feelings then?

NAN   That I was just going to break apart into many pieces if I didn't
just stay curled up in one little area. I had some of this when I
was having flashbacks real bad. Flashbacks.

GENE   Um-hum. Um-hum.

NAN   It . . . at that time it seemed more controllable. Because I
guess I knew what it was about. You know, I could . . . I
could say okay, this is what happened, this is why you're feeling that way. It was more okay to feel that way. But these are
just coming from nowhere.

GENE   Well, if you look back at that situation now, now that you're
not in the middle of it, can you see something different about
the feelings?

*(Here, I offer a gentle invitation toward a different viewpoint, but I
don't suggest what she should see from that viewpoint. I just listen to her
description in her words.)*

NAN   Well, I think it's fear of losing complete control. It's the only
thing . . . . I mean, I'm not really convinced that's it. You know
what I mean? But, it's just a thought.

GENE   How long, total, did it have that . . . was it able to keep you
curled up in a ball?

NAN   A few hours. Two or three hours. The phone would ring and I
couldn't answer it, you know? Oh, there are days when I can't
talk on the phone. Or answer the door or . . . (pause) maybe,
maybe it's because I just . . . at that time, just don't want to
exist. (Pause) And I know I have to exist, so it's like mid-

existence, you know what I'm saying? It's like I have to be there, but I'm not really there.

GENE I think that makes a certain sense to me. It's like you'd like to just disappear for a while. But you know that Mary Pat's going to be coming home from school or that . . . I don't know what other reasons. What are some of the reasons that you have to exist?

(I realize that I don't know why she "has to exist," so I ask her to fill me in.)

NAN I have a responsibility to myself to exist.

GENE Well, say more about that. I mean, I'm interested in that, that responsibility to yourself to exist. What do you believe or understand about that?

NAN Well, I have tried the inappropriate methods. I realized they don't work and I really don't want them to work. I know I need to live. And, ah, I don't know. It's just . . . as I said, it's like I really don't want to be here, but you know you have to be here. And that it's not always . . . it's not always . . .

GENE It's not always going to be like that?

(This is the meaning I'm inferring. I say it out loud with a rising inflection so she can correct me if I'm not understanding her meaning.)

NAN Well, it's *not* always like that.

GENE It *already* isn't always like that?

NAN Right.

GENE Well, you said, "I know I need to live." You also said, "I know I don't want those inappropriate methods, I know I don't really want them to work." Both of those statements are interesting to me. I mean, why not? Maybe that sounds like a stupid question on my part, but why do you really need to live? Why don't you really want these methods to work?

*(I **don't** know why she "needs to live," and I really am interested to know why.)*

NAN Because I know sometimes I want to. It's just that I feel like my whole life has been so damned hard. And I don't like not being able to shut off my feelings any more like I used to. I

mean, I'm still feeling my brother's suicide and my mother's
death and that was four years ago, you know? Why should it
feel as painful, physically painful, now? . . . But I don't want
to die.

In the remainder of this session, Nan and I talk about her mother's
funeral. She tells me about the family tradition of not showing feelings
and how it kept her from crying or talking about her grief. Earlier in her
life, she had been able to completely shut down her feelings, and that
had helped her get through some harrowing experiences. Now she is
becoming a feeling person; although she thinks this is in general a good
thing, it leaves her more vulnerable to the attacks of panic and depression. As the session closes, she reflects on her growing determination to
live and to feel — to face the fear and depression and build a meaningful
life for herself in the face of them.

At the time of this writing, Nan is still living in the same house as
Bart, but they are divorcing and will soon be living separately. They will
continue to raise their daughter jointly. Nan has a growing circle of
supportive friends and she has gone back to school to finish a master's
degree in education. Panic and depression have not vanished from her
life, but she is facing them more confidently, and it is only rarely and
briefly that they immobilize her.

DECONSTRUCTIVE QUESTIONING

So far, we have discussed deconstruction as something that is a natural and inevitable byproduct of our efforts to understand people's life
stories through a narrative/externalizing filter. Our primary intentions
have been to listen to people's narratives and to *understand* them, not
change them in any major ways. As we listen in a way that brings forth
an awareness of either assumptions that narratives are built on or gaps
and ambiguities in people's narratives, space opens for stories to shift as
they are being told.

That said, we often feel that it is important to take a more active role.
We agree with Karl Tomm (1993, p. 66), who writes:

Hermeneutic listening, circular questioning, empathic reflection,
and systemic understanding are not enough, especially when problematic patterns of injustice are entrenched.

At some point, usually when it seems that a certain degree of trust and
mutual understanding has been achieved, we begin to ask questions of a
more purposefully interventive nature. That is, we shift from deconstructive *listening* to deconstructive *questioning*.

Deconstructive questioning invites people to see their stories from different perspectives, to notice how they are constructed (or *that* they are constructed), to note their limits, and to discover that there are other possible narratives (Combs & Freedman, 1994b). Another name for this process is "unpacking." As people begin to have ideas about how the narratives they are living out have been constructed, they see that those narratives are not inevitable, that they do not represent essential truth. Instead, they are constructions that could be constructed differently. The intent of this kind of deconstruction is not to challenge a narrative (Griffith & Griffith, 1994), but to unpack it or to offer the possibility of considering it from a different perspective. Once this occurs, people can commit themselves to protesting it.

The Politics of Deconstructive Questioning

Michael White defines deconstruction more actively and politically. He (1991, p. 27) says,

> According to my rather loose definition, deconstruction has to do with procedures that subvert taken-for-granted realities and practices: those so-called "truths" that are split off from the conditions and the context of their production; those disembodied ways of speaking that hide their biases and prejudices; and those familiar practices of self and of relationship that are subjugating of person's lives.

Following White (and Foucault), we believe that dominant stories can be "subjugating of person's lives." We have already discussed, in Chapter 2, how the medical model can lead people to a sense of themselves as "docile bodies," subject to knowledge and procedures in which they have no active voice. There are also subjugating stories of gender, race, class, age, sexual orientation, and religion (to name a few) that are so prevalent and entrenched in our culture that we can get caught up in them without realizing it.

Deconstruction in White's sense can help us unmask the "so-called 'truths'" that "hide their biases and prejudices" behind the "disembodied ways of speaking" that give an air of legitimacy to restrictive and subjugating dominant stories. In adopting and advocating this type of deconstruction we are taking a political stand against certain practices of power in our society.

When we say taking a stand we do not mean lecturing the people we work with. In the context of therapy, like it or not and even though we take steps to minimize it, the therapist's words are privileged. Inflicting our beliefs on the people we work with would replicate the effect of the dominant culture's privileged knowledges and practices on those in subjugated positions.

However, not taking a stand supports the status quo. In that sense, one cannot *not* take a political stand. In a racist society, for example, to ignore racism (to "take no stand on it") is to support its continued existence. We believe it is our responsibility as therapists to cultivate a growing awareness of the dominant (and potentially dominating) stories in our society and to develop ways of collaboratively examining the effects of those stories when we sense them at work in the lives and relationships of the people who consult with us.

Rachel Hare-Mustin (1994, p. 22) has used the metaphor of a "mirrored room" to talk about how the only ideas that can come up in therapy are the ideas that the people involved bring into the therapy room:

> The therapy room is like a room lined with mirrors. It reflects back only what is voiced within it. . . . If the therapist and family are unaware of marginalized discourses, such as those associated with members of subordinate gender, race, and class groups, those discourses remain outside the mirrored room.

This notion implies that therapists must continually reflect on the discourses that shape our perceptions of what is possible, both for ourselves and for the people we work with. Although we can never obtain a detached or objective view, we can open up, rather than close down, the number and variety of possibilities available in the mirrored room of therapy. We can reflect on the power relationships implicit in each possible discourse. We can seek new possibilities through self-education and through ongoing, regular deconstruction of our beliefs and practices. We pursue such deconstruction by reflecting with our colleagues and with the people who consult with us on the effects of the stories and discourses that guide our beliefs and practices.

Externalization and Deconstructive Questioning

We believe that people can most easily examine the effects of problem-saturated stories on their lives when they do it in the context of an externalizing conversation. We have already acquainted you with how we listen with an externalizing attitude; now we want to discuss how we ask questions that invite not just therapists, but also the people they work with, to experience problems in an externalized way. The first step in this process is simply taking the language the person uses to describe the problem, modifying it so that the problem is objectified, and asking the person questions about it.

For example, in North American culture, people involved in a whole range of experiences are being labeled as "co-dependent." There are institutions, such as 12-step groups, that reify the label. "Co-dependency" becomes an internalized discourse, so that people begin to make "co-dependent" a part of their identities. When the co-dependency discourse takes over, they lose touch with a multitude of lived experiences that lie outside its confines. People are objectified as co-dependents, and other, once vibrant, aspects of their experience cease to count. To engage in an externalizing conversation with a person who has been subjected to this process, we might begin by asking how co-dependency has influenced her life. If she joins us in this conversation, we, together, will be turning the tables on the internalizing discourse, placing co-dependency outside of the person. Since she is no longer being defined as a "co-dependent," she is free to reclaim other aspects of herself and her experience. She is now in a position to decide what to do with co-dependency. She may decide to kick it out of her life or she may rename it — perhaps as "a caring attitude."

The following transcripts, excerpted from two consecutive meetings, illustrate the impact this kind of conversation had on one person I (JF) worked with.

LAVERNE So, this is big, this is like a really big problem to me . . . because it never used to be like that. And it's getting, it's getting progressively worse. It's not getting better.

JILL How do you know it's getting worse?

LAVERNE Well, I feel like it's getting worse because I'm more scared. You know what I mean? I've never felt like this before. I mean, I felt like this before when they'd be like, LaVerne Skolnik, please step to the front and read like your twenty-page whatever.

JILL Mm-hmm.

LAVERNE You know. It's not as, it's not as intense as that. But somethin' starts stirring. You know? And I just got like . . .

JILL So, I just want to really, really slow this down.

LAVERNE Okay.

JILL And hear what it is.

LAVERNE Okay.

JILL So, when you say, something starts stirring. What do you mean?

LAVERNE Okay. I get this overwhelming feeling of nausea. Not the throw-up nausea.

JILL Mm-hmm.

LAVERNE My heart starts to beat fast. I almost feel like I have to go to the bathroom? Um. I mean, I start to sweat.

JILL Mm-hmm.

LAVERNE And then I start doing the whole like, oh, we're going to be sitting there. They're all going to be looking at me. Not so much, I don't go through the like, I'm going to say something stupid thing. It's just, I'm not going to have anything to say. Which in turn is going to make me have absolutely nothing to say, because I'm going to start analyzing the whole thing.

JILL Okay. Um. How does the fear know when to, when it can get you? When it can come in and start creating this overwhelming nausea? And . . .

LAVERNE Well, that's an interesting way to pose the question. How does the fear know when it can come and get you? Huh, that's pretty interesting.

JILL Why? Why's that interesting?

LAVERNE I don't know. I just like the way you said that. As if like the fear wasn't, like the fear wasn't part of, you know what I mean? The fear was something like over there, as opposed to being inside of me.

JILL That's how I think of it.

LAVERNE That's how you think of it? Yeah, I think I knew that. That's a pretty interesting way to ask that. I like that. You've given me a different way to look at it now. It's pretty interesting.

JILL Hmm.

LAVERNE I have to tell you something that's going to sound pretty strange?

JILL What's that?

LAVERNE But I feel strange anyways. Um. I mean, when you just said that and I said, I thought, oh, that's an interesting way to say it. And then I was like, oh, it's over there. I almost felt like that. I got that, you know what I mean? Like I felt like some of that shit was kind of lifted out.

JILL That's great.

LAVERNE For some reason. Yeah, it's good. It bothers me that I feel like that.

JILL Well, I can understand how you would feel that way. Because of the way people talk about problems. So, I can see how that would feel like, you know, sort of a relief.

LAVERNE Yeah. I mean, literally though.

JILL Yeah. Yeah. And let me just ask you for, do you think that with that off of you in some way, that you're, that you can be more aware of some of your own strengths?

LAVERNE Yeah. I don't know if that, if, if I'm going to be able to control the feeling, cause I just got like a hint of it. As soon as I said I was relieved?

JILL Mm-hmm.

LAVERNE I said that. And it was like right here. Kind of like a, like, ooo hoo. I mean not like a soothing feeling.

JILL Mm-hmm.

LAVERNE Like a tossing kind of, but, in here. I think that I can, I mean when I start to feel I can be like, you know, like I can say, "Get out of there, man." You know what I mean? Like to myself, of course.

JILL Yeah. Well, let me just ask you, back to that question I was asking. How do you think the fear knows when it could, when to sort of get in there? And try to take over?

LAVERNE Um. I mean. If you think about that literally, it, it doesn't. I almost like I invite it to come in. Cause how could it, you know, realistically thinking. If we did think it was over there. I'd have to let it come in. It couldn't just come in.

JILL Well, I guess what I was thinking is that it might be, there might be certain things it pairs up with that would make you vulnerable to it.

LAVERNE Oh.

JILL Like self-doubt. And I wondered if there were particular, you know, if we could begin to identify. Like for example . . .

LAVERNE Right, I see what you mean. I see what you mean.

JILL Would that be helpful to know about?

LAVERNE Right.

(This next excerpt is from our next meeting two weeks later)

LAVERNE   I've thought about the fear being outside me. I've thought about that all week. Or, all two weeks.

JILL   You did?

LAVERNE   Yeah, totally.

JILL   What'd you think?

LAVERNE   I just, it was on my mind and then I had to. . . . Like that guy, Craig wanted me to meet him at his friend's house. And that was the guy that I like took this trip with for the weekend. So, we had a bond.

JILL   Mm-hmm.

LAVERNE   But, I started to get myself like, I started freaking out a little bit? So, I was on the way there and I like had, this fear was there. I shut the radio off. And started, I mean, I was talking out loud to it. Just being like, no. I was being like, I have complete control over it and if I don't wanta, you know. I was being, you know. As I was doing it I was like tapping my finger on the steering wheel, cause there were a lot of people out. You know. So, I was pretending maybe I was singing.

JILL   (Laughing) You did that?

LAVERNE   You know, like.

JILL   So, you were sort of talking back to the fear? Is that what you were doing?

LAVERNE   I was just basically like telling it that I wasn't going to allow it to come into my body kind of thing. As if it were sitting next to me.

JILL   Wow.

LAVERNE   But I just like, I just like, that just seems like a good way to think about a lot of things, not just that, you know.

JILL   Mm-hmm. Why do you think it's a good way to think about a lot of things?

LAVERNE   Well, cause it's very, I just think it's very, like it could really give you like a good reality check.

JILL   Mm-hmm.

LAVERNE   You know what I mean? Puts things like in perspective, kind of?

JILL Mm-hmm.

LAVERNE Yeah, I like that.

One criticism that we hear of externalizing conversations is that they might encourage people to abdicate responsibility for their behavior. We've found just the opposite. Externalizing conversations make it possible for many people to experience themselves as choosing responsibility for the first time. When a problem defines someone, there is little she can do about it. It is her. When a problem is external to a person, she can take responsibility for how she interacts with it. Laverne began putting the fear in its place almost immediately.

In Chapter 5 we will give examples of specific questions that can be used in deconstructive questioning. Here let us describe several concepts that we find helpful in the practice of deconstructive questioning.

Naming of the Plot

Naming of the plot (or problematic story) is a useful adjunct to externalizing the problem. Often the same name works for both the problem and its associated narrative. ("Lying" can be both a problem and a plot.) But sometimes different names work better for the two. (The problem might be named "Anger" and the plot named "getting tricked into flying off the handle.")

In regard to naming the plot, Tomm (1993, p. 69) writes:

Such naming, as a labeling process, pathologizes the pathologizing pattern itself, rather than the persons enacting it. Any exclusion practices that might be mobilized by this kind of negative labeling are then harnessed as resources in the protest because they are automatically directed towards the problematic pattern rather than the persons involved.

In the following transcript, Hector talks with me (GC) about the benefits he is discovering of naming various aspects of the plot and the problem. He has been talking about his struggles with depression, and just before we join the conversation, he has mentioned that he is no longer "scraping the bottom of the barrel."

HECTOR Something's making it easier for me to, um, (long pause) to keep things in perspective. So that it's . . . it's much easier now for me, than it has been in the past, for me to step outside of the depressive feelings, and try to see them for what they are. Rather that just taking them to heart and wallowing in them.

GENE   Something . . . Can you characterize what the "something" is that's making it easier?

HECTOR   Um. I think some of it might be awareness. (Long pause)

GENE   Awareness of?

HECTOR   Well, aware with the symptoms, for one thing. So that . . . in the past it's been, I wake up one day and suddenly realize, "Hey, I'm being stupid." You know. Depression. Whereas now I can see the things as they happen, or I can, you know, as the feelings start to come I can recognize them.

GENE   Mm-hmm.

HECTOR   Which doesn't make them any easier to handle. Um. Except for the fact that once I've named it, it's, it's easier to . . . I wouldn't say categorize it, but, well . . . maybe . . . maybe it *is* easier to handle. (Gene and Hector both laugh.)

HECTOR   Yeah.

GENE   Yeah. Well, what is it about that? I mean, other people say that, too. That, once they put a name on something . . . um, once it's not just this formless kind of experience that happens and they wake up in the middle of one day and it's already very intense . . .

HECTOR   Mm-hmm.

GENE   . . . uh, there's something about naming it that makes it more . . . more possible to deal with, to struggle with it. To do something. But, I mean, can you say anything more about how that works for you? About what it is about calling it by name that makes it . . .

HECTOR   Well, I think in general human beings have a need to categorize.

GENE   Mm-hmm.

HECTOR   And I know I'm that way. And the unknown is much more fear-generating than the known. So that, if there's a nebulous cloud of emotion that I can't put my finger on, I'm . . . I allow myself to be much more open. To being hurt by that.

GENE   Hm.

HECTOR   Whereas if I can get a hook into it. Sort of like . . . What's a good analogy? The difference between . . . can you imagine this sphere of water and this sphere of ice? Okay? (Laugh)

GENE   Okay.

HECTOR   The water, the water is, when you have no hold on it you can't, it's formless pretty much.

GENE   Mm-hmm.

HECTOR   But, but the ice, you can at least feel and do something about. You can get a hook into it. You know?

GENE   So, ah, I'm not sure what level you're talking at here. So, if you say, "Oh, this. This is lethargy. Oh, this is that trouble getting out of bed in the morning."

HECTOR   Mm-hmm.

GENE   Um, is that the kind of naming you're talking about? Or are you just talking about calling depression, depression? Is it one of those?

HECTOR   No, it's much more specific. Yeah. First of all, recognizing the overall thing . . .

GENE   Mm-hmm.

HECTOR   . . . is helpful.

GENE   Mm-hmm.

HECTOR   Ah, because then that allows me to go in and pick out the individual things. And then, if I have enough stamina for it, I can actually try to do something about it. But, you know, if I'm just moping around, you know, and I'm not interested in doing anything, can't seem to draw up interest in anything, and I suddenly realize, "Hey, this is the same thing that I've noticed in the past me doing!" A lot of times then I can force myself to go outside, or go do something. Anything. Go play piano, or something, you know? Just to break the mood.

GENE   So, I just want to be sure I'm following this and I'm not reading meanings in you wouldn't want me to. Um . . . so, naming it "lethargy," or, um, or "the kind of difficulty doing accounting that I have," identifying it as the first steps toward that kind of mood motivates you to do something about it. Is that what you're meaning to say?

HECTOR   Well, the mood is the depression itself.

GENE   Okay.

HECTOR   And then the naming of this other stuff lets me break that.

GENE   Right.

HECTOR   Yeah.

As you can see, naming the plot or problem facilitates finding out about tactics and means of operating that the problem employs. This knowledge helps people know how to respond. As therapy progresses, naming and renaming the plot can continue as people's stories develop.

Relative Influence Questioning

Michael White (1986a, 1986b, 1988a, 1988/9) introduced "relative influence questioning" as a way to structure externalizing conversations. In relative influence questioning people are asked first to map the influence of the problem in their lives and relationships and then to map their influence on the life of the problem.

In these two sets of questions it becomes established that, rather than *being* the problem, the person has a relationship with the problem. Everyone participating in the conversation has the opportunity to describe this relationship in a variety of ways. One of the consequences of these questions is that it becomes clear that everyone — not just the "problem bearer" — has a relationship with the problem.

For example, this afternoon Lashawn called our office because her seven-year-old daughter, Lynette, has had a series of problems at school. From our telephone conversation, I (GC) got the impression that unhappiness has made an appearance in Lynette's life and that it has recruited her into a lying and stealing lifestyle. As I talked to Lashawn I discovered that the problem has affected her as well as Lynette. Lashawn had always been close to her daughter before, but now this unhappiness seems to have sealed Lynette off. The unhappiness is coming between Lashawn and Lynette. Lashawn said that in an attempt to "get to the bottom of it," she has talked to people at the school a number of times. So many times, she said, that no one there wants to talk to her any longer.

"So this unhappiness has ended up getting you a reputation at Lynette's school?" I asked. Lashawn agreed that it had, adding that it might end up being a problem for her other two kids as well, since no one at the school wants to hear from her anymore. She used to be active on the P.T.A., but now this unhappiness is taking so much of her time and affecting her energy so much that she doesn't want to go around to the school anymore.

Further questioning will undoubtedly establish that the problem has had other effects on the lives and relationships of family members.

There are several advantages to bringing forth the problem's effects on a number of people. First, it helps keep the identity of the problem separate from any person. Second, it creates a broader landscape about which we can ask the second set of questions (the influence that the people have had on the problem). Third, it mobilizes people to join together in working to oppose the effects of the problem. This is particularly helpful in situations where the problem has kept them apart.

For example, while unhappiness has come between Lashawn and Lynette, pushing Lashawn out of the picture, we wonder if in the course of relative influence questioning they might decide to team up, working together to keep unhappiness out of the picture.

Once we have constructed some understanding of the influence of the problem on the lives and relationships of family members, we ask what effect family members have had in the life of the problem. In Chapter 5, we will give examples of questions that we use for this purpose. We call them "opening space questions" and use them to bring forth "unique outcomes" (White, 1988a). Unique outcomes are experiences that would not be predicted by the plot of the problem-saturated narrative. Once the landscape of the problem has been broadened by mapping its effects on the lives and relationships of the people involved, there can be many openings in which unique outcomes might appear. These include experiences that are exceptions to the problem, such as times when Lynette has been happy, but are not limited to those exceptions (White, 1995).

For example, our training team is currently working with a family who requested therapy because the oldest son, who is a senior in high school, is skipping school. The school has indicated that if this pattern continues Juan will not graduate with his class. As Dina Shulman, the therapist working with the family, asked questions, Juan and the family named the problems as "skipping school" and the "not caring attitude" that made way for skipping school. As Dina asked deconstruction questions, the family members spoke of the problem's effects on them as a family — including unpleasant involvement with the school, distrust, anger, and frustration — all of which had begun to color different aspects of family life.

Dina's questions also brought forth the unique outcome that the oldest child, Rosa, had escaped the grip of anger and frustration enough to stop lecturing Juan about what he should do. She had begun to spend more of her time on her own interests and less of it on anger and frustration. Even though Rosa's new actions are not an exception to the problem of skipping school, they certainly would not have been predicted by the plot of the problematic story. Her actions constitute a unique outcome or opening that might be expanded to develop a less problem-dominated strand in the family's narrative.[3]

So, as we ask questions about people's effects on the life of the prob-

---

[3]See Chapter 8 for a letter that the training team wrote to the family including a discussion of this unique outcome.

lem, we begin to see that people's lives are more multi-storied than the problem would have us believe. Unique outcomes or openings are doorways to alternative stories.

Exposing the Role of Subjugating Dominant Discourses

We can expose subjugating dominant discourses by asking about contextual influences on the problem. What "feeds" the problem? What "starves" it? Who benefits from it? In what settings might the problematic attitude be useful? What sort of people would proudly advocate for the problem? What groups of people would definitely be opposed to it and its intentions? Questions such as these invite people to consider how the entire context of their lives affects the problem and vice versa.

Deconstruction of this sort often unmasks dominant stories that are politically oppressive. As David Reiss (1985, p. 257) indicates, a family's construction of reality requires some support from outside the family. "Indeed, the family is sustained by, and contributes to, the constructions of the community in which it lives." Many power imbalances in families are coached and supported by power imbalances in the larger culture, imbalances that are supported by the dominant stories about class, sexual orientation, race, gender, and so on. When people, through the "unmasking" process of relating problems to societal discourses, see their local problems as particular instances of political problems in the larger society, they can become motivated to deal with them differently. When people stop living by the dictates of a political problem at a local level, they help deconstruct the problem at a societal level.

In working with Ruth Ann, I (JF) didn't have to ask many questions about contextual influences in order to unmask the discourse that was coaching depression in her life. A year after she had consulted with me, Ruth Ann called to tell me that she had gone forward with a racial discrimination suit that she had been considering filing. For the purposes of that suit, she asked me if I would write a summary of our work together. This is the summary I wrote:

> *I saw Ruth Ann Wilson for three sessions of therapy in April of 1993 and for a follow-up appointment in January of 1994.*
> *Ms. Wilson sought therapy because of depression and anger. She was without a job and having difficulty mobilizing herself for a job search because of depression and self-doubt. This difficulty in facing a job search led to extreme stress because of Ms. Wilson's responsibilities as a parent. Anger, particularly brought on by unwanted and intrusive memories of specific incidents in which she*

was mistreated as an employee of _____, and accompanying feelings of frustration and hopelessness seemed to be dominating her life.

During this time the only relief and sense of peace that Ms. Wilson got was through the support of her church and from friends.

It became apparent during the course of therapy that the depression and feelings of anger, frustration, and hopelessness were caused by mistreatment by her former employer during the entire course of events leading up to and including her being fired. The very real consequences of this job loss included financial jeopardy, loss of a home, and disruption in schooling and security for Ms. Wilson's children. Additionally, the experiences that Ms. Wilson suffered resulted in loss of trust and feelings of security for her, making job interviews and social connections intensely difficult.

Racism and racial discrimination brought Ruth Ann Wilson's life to near ruin. However, through her personal strength and resources and community connections, particularly through her church, she has been able to persevere in getting her life back on track.

The therapy served to support this process of getting her life back on track against considerable odds.

After she received the report Ruth Ann sent me a note. These reflections on our work together were very important to me.

Dear Jill,

Your report reminded me of what the therapy was like. I don't know if I ever told you that I didn't want to come. That old misery had taken hold, I knew that, but I hated the idea of seeing a professional for help when I knew (I hoped) that there was nothing wrong with me. It was a great dilemma, knowing I was depressed and knowing I needed help, and I kept thinking it was so unfair that I needed help. I thought that getting it would divert from what I thought was really wrong — how they treated me at _____. But the misery got so bad that I came along to see you anyway.

I never dreamed that in that kind of setting we would call the problem racism. If I wasn't relying on the EAP I would never have seen a white therapist and, to tell the truth, I didn't expect a white therapist to understand. You said you probably wouldn't understand and then went ahead and really understood (most of it, anyway!). I hadn't imagined that I could know it was racism and still attend to my depression. In fact, calling it racism helped a lot. The depression was real and it did have to do with racism.

I don't know if I would have filed the racial discrimination suit without the therapy. I'm very glad to be filing it and hope that that organization won't be able to do this to anyone again!

The therapy really helped.

Thank you,
Ruth Ann

We can also expose dominant discourses by asking people about the history of their relationship with the problem. Especially useful in this regard is to ask how people were recruited into acting or believing according to the dictates of the problem: "Where did you learn this way of thinking about relationships?" "What models were there for these kinds of attitudes?" "How did fear so easily coach you to believe that?" This type of inquiry often encourages people to consider the discourses of power that shape ideas and actions.

These questions do not have to do with teaching or imposing. As people begin to consider the effects of politics in their own lives, they almost invariably want to pursue the conversation. [4]

For example, Ryan came to see me (JF) alone several years after I had worked with him and Darlene in couples therapy. He told me that in the last couple of years there had been periods of time in which he was not attracted to Darlene. They could last days or weeks or even months. His explanation for the lack of attraction was that Darlene had gained a considerable amount of weight. His dilemma was how to approach Darlene on this topic. His attempts so far had resulted in Darlene making it clear that he was "not allowed to talk about it." Although their relationship was very satisfying in other respects, this problem bothered Ryan more and more.

After Ryan and I had mapped out some of the effects of the lack of attraction on him, on Darlene, and on their relationship, I asked about the tactics that the lack of attraction used to get between Darlene and Ryan. After some thought he said that "perfect images of women" enter his mind from time to time.

I then began to ask questions about how these kinds of images had gotten such a strong grip on Ryan's mind — "Where did they come from? Who put them into circulation?"

"Wow," he said. "I had no idea it had to do with this." He went on to tell me that he had a job helping out in a drugstore when he was a kid.

---

[4]See Freedman and Combs (in press) for an account of this work with patriarchal stories.

The store carried a number of pornographic magazines, which he pored over whenever he had the chance. As he got older he began to buy these kinds of magazines. "So this is about pornography?" he asked me.

"Well, what do you think the effects of pornography have been in your life?" I asked.

Ryan began by saying that he had pretty much put pornography aside, so he thought that it didn't affect him at all.

I wondered, then, about the images. When he considered the images again, he concluded, "I think that the influence of pornography has clouded my mind. These perfect images cloud my mind for sure."

As we talked more, Ryan said that pornography had a different way of seeing women. He characterized this different way as "not as people." When he realized that the influence of pornography and associated ideas that define women as nonpeople had taken hold in his relationship with Darlene, he was very clear in stating that he was opposed to this state of affairs. When I asked about how such ideas might affect his daughters, he became even more committed to opposing pornography and its effects.

He said that he realized two things. One was that he had been able to keep the idea of women as "nonpeople or as lesser people" out of his life in other contexts. He now saw, though, that pornography had confused him in the sexual realm. His second conclusion was that he had let physical appearance dictate his feelings. This did not fit with how he wanted to do things. In the course of talking about this, Ryan decided he could guard against pornography's specifications for physical appearance by saying to himself, "This isn't about sex. It's about love. I want sex to be about love and I love Darlene."

"You know what?" Ryan asked. "I think that pornography was a major factor in the demise of my first marriage, and I won't let it happen again."

In further conversation, it became clear that Ryan had walked away from actually looking at pornography, in the process of putting his life back together after a divorce. He was appalled to discover how some of the associated ideas had stuck around.

I knew from the couples therapy with Ryan and Darlene that religion was very important to him. Inspired by Melissa and James Griffith's work (Griffith, J. L., 1986; Griffith, M. E., 1995) I asked Ryan if he would be interested in having a conversation with God about this. He said that he would do so on his own. In our conversation, he said that he felt that he already had God's direction in putting these images and ideas about women out of his life. He believed that he could gain strength through prayer to fight any vestiges of these ideas. But he also said that he was quite confident that the images and ideas would not be a problem anymore. He didn't really believe in them. He just hadn't known that they were there. Now that he was alert to them, he thought he could keep them from having an influence.

We agreed to meet again with Darlene to make sure the ideas about women as nonpeople hadn't snuck into the relationship in any other ways.

A THERAPY CONVERSATION

We end the chapter with a therapy conversation that illustrates many of the ideas we've been writing about.

The conversation is with Fran, who came to see me (JF) because of struggles with what she calls depression. In our work together we have found it useful to a name a number of problems that make up depression. This excerpt is about "the voice of insecurity." My questions are not the only ones that could have been asked; you may think of others.

FRAN   I've been really bummed out, just really moody in the month since I've seen you. . . . I don't know if it's because of Nathan. I don't even know if I told you but I found out that Nathan is seriously dating someone and has been for the last six months. I don't know if it's an engagement or what. Loretta told me last week. She said it has possibilities.

JILL   Yeah.

FRAN   But you know I've been seeing this guy Chris and I'm just really aggravated with him. He doesn't seem to want to spend any time alone. Like, to me that's what a relationship is about. I want to get to know the other person. But he's really hard to get to know. Saturday night he said to me, "Let's sleep in on Sunday and go to brunch." I never do that. I like to get up, go to the gym and work out, and get my day started, but I did. We got up around noon. He took a shower and then kind of nonchalantly told me that he was meeting his buddies to play pool and drink beer. I was really bummed out. He could tell, too. So he said, "Well, we could stop and grab something to eat and I'll just be a little late." I told him, "No. You said you'd be there. You should keep your word." Then he said we could get dinner that night, but I just said, "No." Then, he said, "You're a tough chickie." I could tell he probably won't put up with that. Now I've just been in this bad mood ever since. I don't know if I'm just not ready to date . . .

JILL   And what part is the mood playing?

FRAN   I don't know. Maybe I should be more laid back, not care. I mean, I've only been dating him a month and already I've told him that I don't want to just be with big groups of people. I want to get to know him. I mean, I don't want to just have fun.

JILL   Hmm. I'm a little confused. How is caring a problem?

FRAN   Well. After I left Sunday, I was thinking, "What's wrong with me? Why doesn't he want to spend time with me? And Nathan wouldn't make a commitment to me. And now it looks like he is with someone else."

JILL   So this voice has a lot to do with . . .

FRAN   I'm just really insecure.

JILL   I guess I'm wondering if the voice of insecurity sort of makes room for moods to take over?

FRAN   I just wish I wasn't so insecure.

JILL   You know, I just don't know how to put this together. You told Chris what you wanted in a relationship. I would think you'd really have to feel secure in yourself to do that. Am I missing something?

FRAN   . . . I didn't look at it that way. . . . I guess it's true. I've changed. A year ago I would have said, "Oh, you go ahead. It's all right. I'll see you tonight." But I didn't do that.

JILL   What did you do instead?

FRAN   I stood up for myself, but then I started asking myself, "What's wrong with you? Why doesn't anyone want to be with you?"

JILL   So even though security really comes through in your behavior, the voice of insecurity speaks to you?

FRAN   Yeah.

JILL   It almost sounds like when it speaks to you, it keeps you from noticing how you've been able to stand up for yourself. Is that right?

FRAN   Yeah.

JILL   How else does it affect you?

FRAN   How else . . . ?

JILL   Well, let me ask you something else first. What ideas do you think make room for the voice of insecurity?

FRAN   I don't know what you mean.

JILL   Well, I guess I was thinking that you were talking about this dilemma about whether to accommodate yourself to a man and I was thinking that I've heard a lot of women talk about that and not many men.

FRAN   It's true. I always ended up scheduling myself around Nathan but he didn't schedule around me. Even when I cooked dinner for him, he'd call and say, "Can we do it at 7:30 so I could go to the gym first?"

JILL   Where do you think that comes from?

FRAN   Umm. My mother always did everything around my father's work schedule and it seemed like that's the way it was for everyone.

JILL   Yeah. What do you think pushed your parents into that pattern?

FRAN   Umm. It's just all around you — television, your neighbors, the church.

JILL   Yeah, so you grew up with these ideas kind of directing your future?

FRAN   Yeah, and I don't think it's really changed. Now women are working but they're still supposed to make the dinner, clean the house, and work around the man's schedule.

JILL   So do you think that's fair?

FRAN   No.

JILL   What do you think is fair?

FRAN   I think both people have to pay attention to the other's schedule and what they want.

JILL   Okay. So it seems like you've been taking some steps to change a pattern that's been around for a long, long time.

FRAN   Yeah, but last night he wanted to get together and I said no because I have an important meeting at work today but I ended up seeing him. But I wanted to see him. Oh, I don't know what's wrong with me.

JILL   Is that you speaking or the voice of insecurity?

FRAN   I guess it's the voice of insecurity.

JILL   Yeah, it seems like it keeps you from noticing that you're standing up for yourself and it seems like it paves the way for moods to taint your life. Do you agree?

FRAN   Yeah. It makes me lose track of how much I've changed.

JILL   What else does it do?

FRAN   I think it makes me want to stay isolated, not get involved with anyone to keep from getting hurt.

JILL   What kind of effect does it have on your friends and family?

FRAN   I guess it keeps me away from them a lot.

JILL   And would you say that that cultural pattern we were talking about sort of sets the stage for the voice of insecurity?

FRAN   Yeah, because the whole world practically is going in a different direction. Well, maybe not some young people but it's just all around you.

JILL   Even though it's all around you, have there been times that you've been able to not listen to that voice?

FRAN   Yes! On Sunday, after Chris dropped me off, I called up some friends because I wanted to be with somebody. Usually I would just stay home alone and cry, but Sunday I called up some friends and Patty came over and we were going to go to the movies but we ended up getting a video and staying home and I told her what happened and I told another friend, too. And both of them said, "Fran. We're so proud of you. He's lucky to be with you. You don't have to take that."

JILL   If I could have talked to your friends about what you did, how do you think they would have described you? I mean, what characteristics would they have said you have?

FRAN   They would have said I'm getting better, but they know I was thinking all this negative stuff about myself.

JILL   The voice of insecurity we were talking about?

FRAN   Yeah.

JILL   Can I just ask you a question about that? If the voice matched what you were doing on the outside, what would it be saying to you?

FRAN   It would say, "You are ready for a real relationship with someone who wants to get to know you. You deserve that. It's fine for you to see if that's what's happening and if it's not say, 'You know, this doesn't seem like it's going to work out.' That doesn't mean anything bad about you."

JILL   Wow.

FRAN   Yeah, now it says, "What's wrong with you? He has a right to be with his friends. He's getting all this hassle from you. He's probably not going to put up with it, because I could sort of tell he's getting sick . . . "

JILL   So the difference would be that the voice would talk about
        what *you* want instead of what he wants?

FRAN   Yeah.

JILL   Has that ever happened?

FRAN   Yes! On Sunday. That's why I ended up calling my friends
        instead of just being isolated.

JILL   So you were able to talk to yourself instead of letting insecurity
        take over?

FRAN   Yes.

JILL   What kind of preparation went into being able to do that?

FRAN   (Laughing) Years of therapy! No, but it does have to do with
        therapy.

JILL   But therapy wasn't happening when you did it. How did you
        do it?

FRAN   I did it by reminding myself that I'm important. What I've
        learned in therapy is to speak my mind because others don't
        know if I don't tell them and not speaking feels horrible.

JILL   What does this experience mean to you?

FRAN   That I can get to security if I work at it.

JILL   So would you name the project you're working on "security"
        or would it be another name?

FRAN   Security.

Story Development

4

. . . the narrative metaphor proposes that persons live their
lives by stories—that these stories are shaping of life, and that
they have real, not imagined, effects—and that these stories
provide the structure of life.

—Michael White, 1991, p. 28

Our prevailing narratives provide the vocabulary that sets our
realities. Our destinies are opened or closed in terms of the
stories that we construct to understand our experiences.

—Harry Goolishian

There are always "sparkling events" (White, 1991) that contradict problem-saturated narratives. In this chapter, we look at how we can invite
people to take such events and transform them into stories that they can
live—and in the living know themselves in preferred, satisfying ways.

We want to emphasize that the narratives we are talking about are the
stories that people *live*. They are not "about" life; they *are* life as we
know it, life as we experience it. Since, as far as meaning, hope, fear,
understanding, motivations, plans, and the like are concerned, our life
narratives are our lives, it makes all the difference in the world what sort
of narrative is available to a person. To illustrate this point, let us tell
you a story.

JESSICA'S STORY

This is Jessica's story,[1] and we think you will agree that the changes
that occurred in her life were spectacular. While our experience with

_____

[1]We have told this story before (Combs & Freedman, 1994b), but we think it deserves
telling again.

people is often less dramatic, we chose this story because, as well as being dramatic, it is very clear, straightforward, and easy to follow. Remember, however, that what you are reading is a much simplified and "cleaned up" report. It is edited to emphasize how using narrative as a guiding metaphor contributed to a satisfying outcome for Jessica.

At the time I (JF)[2] met Jessica, she had just completed several years of therapy. She felt that her therapist[3] had been helpful and supportive, but Jessica had not perceived any progress for a number of months before stopping therapy, and she had come to believe that "it had gone as far as it could go." At a conference she attended in Chicago, Jessica heard me give a talk on sexual abuse which gave her hope that maybe she could go farther. She called me to set up an appointment, explaining that she hoped I would see her even though she lived three hours away and didn't know how often she could come to see me.[4]

The First Meeting

Jessica worked as a nurse in the emergency room of the only hospital in a farming community in southern Illinois. She lived alone in a farmhouse on the edge of town, had a sizable circle of female friends, and enjoyed participating in sports.

In the first meeting she told me that she was 35 years old and had never had a romantic relationship. She described growing up in a family where women were treated as the property of men. Her father and uncle touched her, her mother, and her sister in any way they liked at any time they liked. The touching was often rough and often sexual, including having her breast or crotch grabbed while she was helping with kitchen chores and being forced into sexual contact with one man while the other looked on.

I asked Jessica what the effects of this abuse were on her, both in the past, as a child, and now, as an adult. She said that when she was a child the abuse brought forth feelings of fear, insecurity, confusion, helplessness, and isolation. She elaborated on incidents that illustrated these themes in some detail. The effects of the abuse on Jessica as an adult were different. She experienced an inability to engage in a romantic

---

[2]We will refer back to this story throughout the chapter, using it to illustrate our ideas in practice. For the sake of ease in reading, when we refer to Jessica's story, it is written as though I (JF), who worked with Jessica in therapy, am commenting. I would like to acknowledge that Gene's ideas play at least as great a part in this commentary as mine.

[3]In many ways I felt that this therapy was really co-therapy. Jessica saw another therapist both before and after our work together. Much of the work we did was built on and later supported by work she did with the other therapist.

[4]One of the ways we accommodated the distance was by incorporating the possibility of phone calls between meetings.

relationship, difficulty in friendship, and feelings of worthlessness. Again she gave examples of how these problems played out in her life.

I wondered, and asked aloud, how she had moved from a childhood in which she struggled with nearly incapacitating problems to the different emotional place that she now inhabited. Jessica wasn't sure how, but she did help me to understand that, while the present effects were the remnants of the earlier difficulties, the feelings of worthlessness were now limited to social situations. In fact, it turned out that all the effects of abuse had become contextualized and no longer took over her life as they had when she was a child.

Jessica had a master's degree and she described her nursing job as a good one that she had held for a number of years. I asked her how it would have affected the fear, insecurity, confusion, helplessness, and isolation of her childhood if she had been able back then to see these things in her future. She said that she would have realized that the fear and related feelings were not inherent truths about her. If they were, she would not have been able to accomplish as much as she had professionally. I was very interested in how she had been able to stand up to the effects of the abuse over the years and to determine her own career. I hoped we would be able to talk more about this.

Jessica commented that, now that she thought about it, her accomplishments really were remarkable, especially because no one else in her family had ever gone to college or become a professional.

The Second Meeting

At the second meeting, six weeks later, Jessica said she now realized that she was no longer the child that she once had been, and that life was very different for her as an autonomous adult than it had been for her as a dependent child. Now she felt ready to get married and raise a family. She wanted to use our meeting to work on smiling, because people kept telling her to smile.

I was caught off guard by how she was leaping forward and asked if it would be all right to slow things down a little so that I could keep up with her. When she said that would be all right, I asked her how she had come to this realization that she was no longer the child she once had been. She answered by going over some of the same ground as she had in the first meeting, this time going into more detail about the differences between her past and present experience. This time she had more ideas about things she had done to create an identity for herself instead of letting the effects of the abuse create her identity. Experiences at school—a place where she excelled, got positive comments, and was treated with fairness—turned out to be very important sources of self-knowledge that she had used in creating her identity. She told me that these experiences of mastery and of being treated as a person rather than as property nurtured a secret part of her. Over time she was able to develop that part, and it enabled her to stand up to the effects of the abuse and limit their area of influence.

I asked her what it meant to her that she had accomplished so much in spite of the abuse. With some hesitation, averting her eyes from me, she said it meant that she was smart and tough. I said I understood that her home situation was a secret, but I wondered, if other people had known about it, who might have predicted that she would be able to stand up as successfully as she had to the effects of the abuse. She said that teachers and kids at school knew she was smart and tough. Had they known about her situation at home, they would probably have predicted that she would find a way to oppose the abuse and take her life back for herself. Her previous therapist also recognized how tough and smart she was.

I then wondered aloud, "If we look back over the years at how you have used your strength and intelligence to take charge of your life — you got an education, became a nurse who handles life-and-death situations, and found ways to limit the effects of the abuse — is this readiness to get married that you are talking about the next step? She thought maybe it was. As we began to talk about what that meant, Jessica acknowledged that it was different to think of herself as someone who could have an intimate life with another person. Not only was she smart and tough, but now she could begin to imagine herself having warm and tender feelings and connecting with someone special. In fact, in her previous therapy she had felt connected to her therapist and had a variety of pleasant feelings towards her. She could now see that relationship as preparation for other relationships. In friendships with women she had also experienced some positive feelings and connection, even though these relationships were often rocky.

As we talked more about the possibility of moving into the realm of romantic relationship, we discovered that simply thinking about herself as someone who could live in that realm was an important step in taking her life back from the effects of the abuse. Because the effects of the abuse had held her social life hostage for so long, there were probably a number of important social experiences that the effects had robbed her of until now. For example, Jessica did not really think of men as people,[5]

---

[5]A number of men who have engaged in abusive behavior have told us that one thing that makes this behavior possible is an attitude that women are not really people. One of the ways Jessica had storied the abuse was the inverse, that is, that men are not really people. Her plan to make friends with a man demonstrated that she had begun to deconstruct this story.

so making friends with a man might be an important step, and now she knew that her intelligence could help her pick a safe man for the project.

The Third Meeting

In the third meeting, one month later, Jessica was taken over by distress about events in one of her friendships. In her estimation, a close woman friend often treated her badly — criticizing her, refusing to talk to her — but Jessica had chosen so far to continue the friendship. It was after a recent bout of these incidents that the distress had taken over. The belief that other people they knew sided with her friend made the distress even stronger.

I asked if Jessica's implied desire to do something different with this friendship was a part of her project of rescuing her social life from the effects of the abuse. When she considered it in this light, she thought that, although the effects of the abuse had influenced her up to now in the relationship, she was at a turning point. I reminded her of the personal qualities she was beginning to own more closely — strength, intelligence, the ability to have warm and tender feelings, the ability to connect — and wondered how these might be useful in this problematic relationship.

She decided to put her professional self — the part of her who had done well at school and work, and whose intelligence and strength she trusted — in charge of setting limits and deciding what she should do to take care of herself in this relationship. I asked if she thought this would move her toward being more secure in other relationships. She thought it would.

The Fourth Meeting

Jessica came to the fourth meeting (again, one month later) taken over by distress and also by confusion about the friendship we had discussed in our last meeting. She had consistently used her intelligence and strength in setting limits and making decisions regarding the relationship. Her friend had countered with criticism and name calling, which brought forth self-doubt for Jessica. She particularly began to experience doubt about whether it was possible for her to be healthy, normal, or playful.

I wondered if there were times when she had been sure of her ability to be "healthy," "normal," and "playful," even for a moment. With some encouragement, Jessica remembered learning a song at school. Her grandmother, who lived out of town, was visiting, and when Jessica came home from school that day her grandmother was there alone.

Jessica remembered sitting on her grandmother's lap and teaching her grandmother the song, singing with her grandmother, who looked into her eyes, smiled, and sang with Jessica, clearly enjoying her company.

I asked what her grandmother recognized in her and most appreciated about her. She said "that I am lovable" and explained that being lovable meant many things. She listed the many things: she was a good person; she was warm; she was fun; she was normal; she was healthy; she was playful; she was receptive; she recognized good things in others.

Then we spent a long time talking about how her life might have been different if she had lived with her grandmother. We developed the story of those differences through time, starting with when she was very little and coming all the way up to how things might be different for her now if she had grown up living with her grandmother.

I asked her to list again what her grandmother knew about her, and I wondered what life would be like if she owned the qualities on that list as truths about herself. She was more thoughtful than verbal in response to this last question.

The First Phone Call

Jessica called me five days after the fourth meeting. She began the conversation by asking, "Do you know what it would be like to wear new shoes, new clothes, new makeup, and new breast implants all at the same time?" I had to admit that this particular combination of events was completely outside my experience, so I asked her to explain. She told me that on the morning after our meeting she drove through McDonald's on her way to work, as she had every morning, to pick up a cup of coffee. She was handed the coffee through her car window, as she had been every morning, and was asked if she would like sugar and cream, as she had been every morning, and automatically said "No, thank you" (not just "No" as she had every other morning)! She found this quite startling and absolutely normal at the same time.

She said now that she realized who she was, she knew that she was the kind of person who would say "thank you," and so she did. Hearing herself actually say "thank you" out loud was a startling and clear confirmation of her new identity. She didn't remember ever having felt this strong for this many days in a row. She noticed that she was both more concerned about other people and more tuned into herself. This was scary, too, because of how different it was. She was feeling strong all the time, but was afraid she must be denying other feelings because she couldn't believe she was so strong. She was afraid the changes weren't real, and said that may have been why she used the unreal example of breast implants. But then she said, "The neatest thing about this is I have something to guide me—my new image."

Since the last appointment she had also stopped smoking; this was because she now knew she was the kind of person who wouldn't smoke. She said two things about stopping smoking that were particularly interesting to me. One was, "Cigarettes are taking my energy and I need it for other things." The other was that in the past, when she was around people she liked, if they smoked, she smoked. She said that now it was important to be able to stay on her own path and have them go on their own.

She ended the phone call saying, "Having a new image of myself has affected me in ways I could never imagine. My car broke down, and I didn't meet the man of my dreams, but it's all right."

The Second Phone Call

Jessica called again eight days later. She had ended the relationship with her friend because she couldn't tolerate all the blaming. With everyone else, she reported, she was being her new self and liking it. When she was her new self with her friend, it had begun to seem like their relationship would end, so at first she had gone back to her old self in that context. She then decided that she couldn't do that anymore, so she had ended the friendship. She felt strong but very sad. She believed that she was mourning the loss not only of her friend but of her old self.

I wondered if the new self had been there all along, hidden under the effects of the abuse. That made sense to Jessica, but she said she was still sad. I said that I was not trying to take the sadness away. I was sad, too, that she had been through all that abuse and had been forced into hiding.

I asked about ways other than the sadness that her experience was different. She answered that she felt safer, more open, and more understanding. She said that this process had worked to give permission to parts of her that had already changed and to those ready and waiting to change, as well as giving her something she could use to live by every day, a new image of herself.

The Fifth Meeting

The fifth meeting was one month after the fourth. Jessica's very positive experience of getting to know herself in new ways had been interrupted and then overcome by a flood of graphic memories of the abuse that she had suffered. The central memory was of her uncle repeatedly thrusting his penis into her mouth while her father looked on. Her voice became very small and shaky as she described this memory. She reported that after it happened she went into the bathroom and washed out her mouth and then rode off on her bicycle.

I was very distressed to hear of this event. I looked directly at Jessica and said, "I'm sorry that happened to you."

Then, with her permission, I read her the notes from our two phone calls after the last meeting. She seemed to relax and began nodding as I read the notes. I said, "You were telling me in that first phone call that you know the kind of person that you are. If you really owned that new self-image, and looked back through time with the knowledge and feelings that are part of the new self-image, what would that you appreciate about the you that went through the abuse?"

"Appreciate?" she asked.

"Yeah, what can you appreciate or learn about the you that survived this abuse?"

As she reviewed the memories, Jessica identified that she was strong and resilient, and after some thought she even realized that she was creative. She silently began to weep. She said that in the past when she had these kinds of memories she had felt helplessness, terror, worthlessness, and shame, but she believed that this was the first time she had ever felt grief about everything she had endured. She said that the grief felt like a good, pure feeling. It signified to her that she was worthy of sadness over something that had happened to her. We agreed that it was a joyful grief.

The Third Phone Call

Three weeks later Jessica called and said that she was thinking about canceling her next appointment. Her life was not perfect, but she was feeling free. Her new image was guiding her and the power had gone from the memories. Also, her car had broken down on the way home from the last meeting and she had had to spend the night in a hotel. When things had been really bad, the three-hour drive each way had seemed worth it, but now that things were going more smoothly for her, six hours seemed a long time to drive. She canceled the appointment, arranging to talk again a month later.

The Fourth Phone Call

Jessica called again in a month. She said that before she had seen me she felt stuck, but now she was "over the hump." She liked herself. She was thinking about going back to her previous therapist to get some support for the new way she was thinking about herself and about life.

I asked her what had been most important in getting over the hump. She said it was the memory of singing with her grandmother and learning what her grandmother must have felt about her. It completely changed how she knew herself. I congratulated her on knowing herself and said I was curious to hear where her new knowledge might lead her. She thanked me and we ended therapy.

The Sixth Meeting

Four years (to the day) after our last meeting, Jessica came to see me again. The first thing she told me was that she was buying a new house. I asked her what meaning this had for her. She said that it meant that she is going for what she wants and breaking family traditions.

She came to consult with me because she was involved for the first time in a romantic relationship. Gary, she told me, was different from her family. He was fun-loving, a traveler. He didn't have traditional values about relationships between men and women. He was sexual and playful and didn't use sex as power. "If this works," Jessica said, "I will be different from the women in my family." I wondered, wasn't there already lots of evidence that she was? She agreed that she was, but said that what worried her was that she reacted to Gary like her sister and mother would when it came to sex. In her family she had learned that women are not supposed to like sex and now she was finding intercourse to be painful. She reported that she was businesslike and efficient, wanting "to get in, have an orgasm, and get out."

When I asked how she was *different* from people in her family, she said that she was the most playful person in her family. She had always had fun at school and work, but in recent years she has also played in other situations. She had taken up a number of team sports and thought that she had more fun in general than she used to. She also had more friends.

These changes had led her to see herself as being more active, involved, and free. She listed friends who had noticed the changes and told me that some of her friends had predicted that she would become involved with a man.

Our conversation brought forth the knowledge that she had prepared for these changes by coming to therapy and by taking chances. For instance, she had begun frequenting a riding stable where she initially knew no one, and she had joined a dart club as its only female member. She had discovered that a lot of what is involved in play is being open to whatever pops into your mind. As she said this, she realized that there were precursors in her youth to these events. As a kid she was good at making something out of nothing and enjoying daydreams. As a teenager she got into telling jokes.

I summarized these events chronologically and asked what might come next. Jessica thought becoming more playful sexually and playing without structure would be next, but fear stood in the way of taking the next step and had also kept her from getting very close to Gary.

I wondered if going to a stable where she knew no one was an example of overcoming fear. She agreed it was, and added that she had become close friends with a man she met there. Other examples that she offered of overcoming fear included being the only woman to join her dart club and telling Gary about the abuse in her past and the difficulties it had caused her.

I asked Jessica how she had been able to overcome fear in these instances. She said that in the case of telling Gary about the abuse she knew that because of the trouble she had with intimacy she would lose him if she didn't. So she took the risk and stood up to the internal voice that argued for silence. In a larger sense, Jessica said that she knows that a lot of what we fear in this world doesn't matter that much. She trusts her Higher Power. This knowledge and trust help her overcome fear.

I asked what these examples of taking risks and overcoming fear said about her. Jessica responded, "that I can do it, that there is some part inside of me that is compelled to do it. I guess also that I have perseverance and a belief in my own growth and development."

When I asked what difference it would make if she took these descriptions of herself to heart in the context of her relationship with Gary, she said that owning them in that way could make a difference sexually. She grinned and said, "It makes me want to practice more." She added that she had been trying to please Gary but this conversation was making her interested in practicing for her own pleasure, like she had at horseback riding and darts, for fun and so that she could relax. She also said that thinking about it as practicing made her feel like she could be more in charge. She intended to talk to Gary about these ideas.

As the conversation drew to an end, I asked Jessica if it had been helpful. She said, "Yes. It hadn't occurred to me how much I have changed and accomplished until now."

The Fifth Phone Call

Jessica called one month later. After our meeting she had talked with Gary about wanting to practice and be more in charge. They went through some "misunderstandings about this but then things got comfortable." Sex stopped hurting and Jessica had been enjoying it more and more. She said that it got more playful and sensual. She and Gary had been having other problems, and she didn't know if the two of them would end up together, but she felt very pleased with the possibilities she had begun to realize for herself as a sexual and playful person. She hoped the two of them would work things out, but if they didn't she understood that it wasn't because there was something wrong with her. It was because they didn't fit. She now believed that it was possible for her to have a satisfying intimate relationship.

IMPORTANT CONSIDERATIONS IN STORY DEVELOPMENT

We will return to Jessica's story throughout this chapter, using episodes from it to illustrate elements of the process through which we invite people to develop sparkling events into robust, richly experienced narratives. But before we get back to Jessica, let us share a couple of other stories.

Transformative Stories Are Performed Stories

One day in therapy, Crystal told me (GC) a story. Her extended family was gathered for a weekend at her mother's house. She and her sister, Carmen, were in the kitchen leaning against the kitchen counter, talking, with a bag of potato chips open on the counter between them. As they talked they ate potato chips. At regular intervals Crystal thought to herself, "I'm going to stop eating these," but as the conversation continued she and Carmen kept on eating potato chips. Finally, at one point in the conversation, Crystal said out loud, "I'm going to stop eating these." Carmen nodded. Crystal closed up the bag and put it in a cabinet, and the two continued their conversation.

Crystal told me this story because it reminded her of what happens in therapy. "It becomes more real when you say it out loud," she told me. "Maybe we're talking about something I haven't thought about in years, but we're having this whole conversation, and you keep asking me more and more about it. By the time I leave it's like it just happened. You ask me what I'm going to do next, and I say it out loud, and then I do it. Just like the potato chips. You were thinking some of these kinds of things before but they didn't get into what you were doing. Once you say it out loud it's more real. Then you do it."

Milton Erickson used to tell a story about being on a road trip with a friend. As he was driving, Erickson told his friend about another trip he had taken years ago on the same road. As he was telling the story he began trying to manually shift the car. His car was an automatic shift car, and he had been driving an automatic shift car for years, but the story he was living happened twenty years before—when he drove a manual car—so he automatically moved his feet and reached out to shift as he was telling the story.

This "performance" of stories does not happen automatically or every time someone tells a story. It does happen when a person is immersed in the story and when he experiences the story as meaningful.

We sometimes view therapy as a ritual or ceremony that centers around the "performance of meaning" (E. Bruner, 1986a; Myerhoff, 1986; White, 1991; White & Epston, 1990) on people's "preferred" stories (White, 1991) about themselves, their relationships, and their experiential realities. Along with Edward Bruner (1986a, p. 25), we believe that "stories become transformative only in their performance."

Our intention, then, is not to co-construct stories that represent or describe experience, but to co-construct stories through which people can live in preferred ways (Anderson & Goolishian, 1992; White, 1991). Returning to Jessica's story, an event in her life on which she performed meaning was the childhood experience of sitting on her grandmother's lap and teaching her grandmother a song. Jessica immersed herself in that memory and saw herself through her grandmother's eyes. Then she developed the story through time, authoring and experiencing a speculative history of what her life would have been like if she had lived with her grandmother. After this conversation, Jessica found herself doing a whole range of things that were unusual, from saying "thank you" to quitting smoking. She said that she had gained an understanding through our work of the kind of person she was and that she was being the person she now knew she was. She began living a new story, not simply telling it. The story was both shaped by life events and shaping of life events and self-image.

The People We Work with Are the Privileged Authors

Stories are authored through conversation, and in therapy the stuff of stories is the experience of the people we work with. The story that is constructed is clearly the person's or family's own, and it is deeply personal.

We can't know where people's stories will go. We can only co-author a story a piece at a time. Each detail stands on the one before and can only be constructed as the one before begins to find form and definition (Tomm, 1993; White, 1991). This is very different from developing a goal and then finding experiences to support it (Chang & Phillips, 1993). It calls for curiosity and involvement in each bit of the story as it emerges. Each bit of construction can be responded to with an infinite number of questions, each of which would lead in a different direction. An important part of our job as co-constructors is to be very alert to the nonverbal and verbal communication of the people we work with so that we can recognize and ask questions about the experiences that seem most meaningful to them (Andersen, 1991a, 1993).

I (JF) didn't know about Jessica's experience teaching her grandmother a song until she brought it up. However, since it was very obviously meaningful for her, I asked her many questions about it.

Because we don't know where a story will go and because we are not its principal authors, we often use the subjunctive mood. David Epston (1991), following Jerome Bruner, refers to this as "subjunctivizing," a term Bruner (1986, p. 26) uses in reference to "trafficking in human possibilities rather than in settled certainties." Along this line, we use "would" or "could" instead of "will" as a way of introducing possibilities, but not prescribing them.

Lynn Hoffman makes a similar point about the work of Tom Andersen and his colleagues. She (Hoffman, 1992, p. 18) writes, "They tend to begin their sentences with 'Could it be that?' or 'What if?' . . . and the effect on clients is to encourage both participation and invention."

OPENINGS TO NEW STORIES

Listening for Openings

As we discussed in Chapter 3, we generally focus on deconstructing people's problem-saturated narratives before attempting to bring forth new stories. However, although we are presenting the processes separately for sake of clarity, the construction of preferred stories almost always goes hand-in-hand with the process of deconstruction.

Our entryway for inviting people to author and live new stories is through "unique outcomes," that is, anything that wouldn't have been predicted in light of a problem-saturated story. Unique outcomes constitute openings that, through questions and reflective discussion, can be developed into new stories.

The way unique outcomes or "sparkling events" become apparent can vary tremendously. A delightful example is Jessica's phone call beginning with, "Do you know what it would be like to wear new shoes, new clothes, new makeup, and new breast implants all at the same time?" and continuing through her description of saying, "thank you," at McDonald's.

I (JF) am currently working with a family whose members are struggling with worries about Alexis, the 17-year-old daughter. They came to see me the day Alexis had been sent to the principal's office at school following a challenging confrontation with a teacher. We had an externalizing conversation about the effects of anger in her life and in the life of other family members. I wasn't sure whether this conversation was meaningful to Alexis. When I asked questions searching for unique outcomes such as, "Have there been times when you've been able to keep the anger from determining your behavior?" she responded with shrugs and "I don't know."

At our next meeting, two weeks later, just after the family entered my office, before she even sat down, Alexis announced, "I did great! I was great! Have you ever read *The Fall*, by Albert Camus? Well, we had this test on it and first we had a matching section and then there were quotes, not where you identify quotes but where they give you quotes and you have to say who said it and what was happening right before and after it, which is absurd for *The Fall*, I mean it's this existential novel where they go to this cafe in Amsterdam and talk about their opinions about everything in the world all night long. So how could you know when a particular thing was said? But anyway, then there were short answers like about stuff about symbolism and then an essay. And we had forty minutes to do this whole thing. And I could just feel the anger creeping up on me more and more. So I just said to myself, 'If you were in a college class with like a thousand students where the teacher would never know you or anything and you let this anger get you to blow up, you would just never get through college.' So I just said, 'Nope!' to the anger. And at home a couple of days ago my mom shrunk this shirt that I really like," Alexis said dramatically, glancing at her mother, "and she's always doing that and I told her not to put it in the dryer. But I just went, 'Anger? Nope!'" Alexis made a brushing away gesture with her arm as she said, "Nope!"

Sometimes people offer unique outcomes quite directly, but with less drama than Alexis did. For example, someone may be describing a problem and then say, "It's not always like that," and go on to describe a unique outcome.

It is not unusual as people become involved in re-authoring their lives to save up new unique outcomes to tell a therapist about. At other times, it is important to listen very carefully if we are not to miss the mention of unique outcomes buried in people's descriptions of their problematic stories (Lipchik, 1988). For example, if a father says, "Once in a while I get through to him, but usually . . . " and then proceeds to describe the dominant story, we can be curious about the "once in a while" part, just as we would be curious about the answers to unique outcome questions.

Sometimes we can observe something happening that, given the problematic story, we wouldn't have predicted — people who believe they have communication problems eloquently describing the problem, kids behaving well in a session although they are being described as always misbehaving, or a teenager showing up on time to meet other family members for therapy although the problematic story is one of irresponsibility.

In the first meeting with Jessica, when Jessica compared the past with the present effects of the abuse it seemed to me that the present effects were milder and were limited to a smaller range of contexts. This difference struck me as a candidate unique outcome, because somehow Jessica had shrunk the effects of the abuse. Therefore, I asked questions about how she did it, inviting her to story her achievement.

Asking for Openings

Most often, openings develop "spontaneously" in the process of listening deconstructively and asking people about the effects of problems on their lives and relationships. If openings don't develop spontaneously, we can inquire more directly about their existence. As we mentioned in the discussion of relative influence questioning in Chapter 3, when we are working with an externalized problem, the most straightforward way of looking for openings is to ask about the influence of the person on the life of the problem. That is, we ask questions like, "Has there ever been a time when the problem tried to get the upper hand, but you were able to resist its influence?" or "Have you ever been able to escape the problem for even a few minutes?" or "Is the problem *always* with you?" When questions of this sort follow a detailed inquiry into the effects of the problem on the person, people can usually find instances in which they were able to elude the problem's influence. Each such instance is a potential opening onto an alternative life narrative.

In the fourth meeting with Jessica, we were working with the externalized problem of "self-doubt." Through questioning, we found that one of the effects of self-doubt on Jessica was that it led her to ask herself whether she would ever be "healthy," "normal," or "playful." Then I asked whether there had ever been times when Jessica had been sure of her ability to be healthy, normal, or playful, even for a moment. This inquiry led to an experience that proved to be a pivotal opening for Jessica, the one of teaching the song to her grandmother.

There are other kinds of questions that can also bring forth unique outcomes.[6] Here we'll limit ourselves to a few examples of some of these questions in relation to Jessica's story.

If Jessica hadn't told me about learning the song, I might have said,

---

[6]See Chapter 5 for discussion of hypothetical outcome questions, questions from others' points of view, and questions about different contexts and different time frames.

"I understand that you don't see yourself as healthy, normal, or playful, but if I were to interview other people who know you, who might say that you are? What have they noticed about you that would make them say that?" Or I could have posed a hypothetical outcome question, such as, "If you grew up in a different household and no abuse had occurred, do you think self-doubt would have been able to get such a hold on your life? Do you think you might be more playful now? What do you think there is about you that would have developed in this way in better circumstances?"

Making Sure the Opening Represents a Preferred Experience

Once we perceive a candidate "sparkling moment," we ask a question such as: "Does this interest you?" "Did that surprise you?" "Is this something that you want more of in your life?" or "Do you think this is a good thing or a bad thing?" Questions like these invite people to consider whether something that we see as a possible opening is really new for them and whether it opens in a direction that they prefer over the direction of the problem-saturated story.

In addition to asking questions, we pay attention to nonverbal communication. When I (JF) wonder aloud how Jessica has moved from one set of effects to the other (p. 79), Jessica readily begins to fill in details of the differences between the past and the present. We see this kind of easy and willing response as evidence that a person thinks an opening is relevant and meaningful, so we feel comfortable in continuing to ask for more details. If someone does not responded so readily, we would drop our inquiry into the particular events in question and go back to listening and questioning deconstructively.

Remember that, especially in the beginning, as we are becoming acculturated to people's experiential worlds, we listen to their existing narratives. As we listen, we orient ourselves to their values, customs, and preferred ways of relating. The intimate and graphic details that Jessica volunteered were evidence that a relationship of trust and mutual respect was developing. Only as such evidence is perceived do we feel comfortable about moving our focus to the construction of a new story. Especially for people with stories of abuse like Jessica's, attempting to move too quickly can be yet one more violation and disqualification by a powerful other. At the same time, it is important to be careful not to reify or replicate the abuse by becoming voyeuristically involved and pushing for more detail about the problem story than the person freely and comfortably gives (Durrant & Kowalski, 1990).

DEVELOPING AN OPENING INTO A STORY

Once we have agreed upon a preferred opening that seems relevant and interesting to the people we are working with, we invite them to develop it into an alternative story. For Jessica, teaching her grandmother a song was a sparkling moment that opened onto a vivid and compelling story. Not only did Jessica "re-collect" the story of that event itself, but she storied a speculative history and a future based on it. As we have seen, although the future was speculative, Jessica began living it.

We don't have a formula to follow in this process, but we do keep in mind that stories involve events that happen through time in particular contexts and that they usually include more than one person. Remember that a big part of what lets new stories make a difference in people's lives is that, in telling them to other people, a performance of meaning occurs. In order to make the therapy conversation a "ritual space" in which the performance of meaning can occur, we strive to maintain the kind of focused attention and mutual respect that will make it easy and natural for people to become experientially involved in the stories they are telling. Ideally, people should be reliving the events as they tell them.

Think Like a Novelist or Screenwriter

If you talk to me (GC) while I'm reading, I probably won't answer. It's not that I'd be ignoring you. It's just that I wouldn't be there. I'd be in a different city or country, in a different time. I'd even be a different person.

Good novels, plays, and poetry create worlds that the reader enters into. We've found it helpful to think about what makes stories compelling and how our experience and imagination are recruited by particular stories (White, 1988/9).

One way that novelists, playwrights, and other accomplished storytellers make their stories experientially vivid is by including detail. Consider this excerpt from *Franny and Zooey* (Salinger, 1955/61, p. 12 in the 1986 Penguin paperback). In this scene Lane is meeting Franny's train:

Franny was among the first of the girls [*sic*] to get off the train, from a car at the far, northern end of the platform. Lane spotted her immediately, and despite whatever it was he was trying to do with his face, his arm that shot up into the air was the whole truth. Franny saw it, and him, and waved extravagantly back. She was wearing a sheared raccoon coat, and Lane, walking toward her quickly but with a slow face, reasoned to himself, with suppressed excitement, that he was the only one on the platform who really *knew* Franny's coat. He remembered once, in a borrowed car, after kissing Franny for a half hour or so, he had kissed her coat lapel, as though it were a perfectly desirable, organic extension of the person herself.

'Lane!' Franny greeted him pleasurably — and she was not one for emptying her face of expression. She threw her arms around him and kissed him. It was a station-platform kiss — spontaneous enough to begin with, but rather inhibited in the follow-through, and with somewhat of a forehead-bumping aspect.

In other hands, the same ground might have been covered by writing, "Lane picked Franny up at the train station." As you can see, detail creates this scene, pulling us into it.

Similarly, when people search for specifics of detail in memories, they tend to become experientially involved. (Notice what happens if you find a memory from a few years ago, then begin to flesh out its details: what you and other people were wearing, who spoke to whom when, what time of day it was, how bright or dim the light was, etc.)

We think that in countering the effects of a problem-saturated story, it is important to develop as rich, detailed, and meaningful a counterstory as possible. In our second meeting, Jessica and I (JF) talked about how Jessica had managed to attenuate and compartmentalize the effects of the abuse in her life. Although it was quite abbreviated in our retelling here, a wonderful and richly detailed story came forth.[7] The story was always a possible part of Jessica's life narrative, but until the previous six weeks the events from which it was constructed had been lying around disconnected and gathering dust in seldom-visited memories.

One way of being sure to invite people to include detail in their stories is to inquire about multiple modalities of experience. In the excerpt from *Franny and Zooey*, J. D. Salinger describes what Lane was thinking as well as what he was doing, and what he was feeling as well as what he was thinking.

We've found that people become more experientially involved in an emerging story if they include more than one modality of experience. We were particularly impressed with how different modalities drew us into a story when watching a videotape of David Epston's work. In the conversation we were watching, a teenage boy was telling David about a conver-

---

[7]See the transcript at the end of this chapter for more examples of detail in authoring stories.

sation he had had with his grandfather. "What was the look on his face when you told him?" David asked. "What did he call you? When he was saying that, did he refer to you by a special name?" And later, "Had you planned what you were going to say?"

It can be helpful to ask what people are thinking as well as what they are doing, what they are feeling as well as what they are thinking. And we have also found it helpful to ask about seeing, hearing, and feeling.

I (GC) don't know all the details that Jessica experienced in re-collecting the memory of teaching the song to her grandmother, but every time I hear her story it takes me back to an experience of sitting in *my* grandmother's lap. I must have been about four, and we were in the porch swing that hung to the left of her front door. It was late on a summer afternoon, and the tiger lilies in her fence row were casting long and very distinct shadows across her clover-strewn lawn. She had on a blue print housedress. Her big, soft, warm, pale arms were gently, loosely, cradling me and we were swinging slowly and almost-but-not-quite imperceptibly back and forth. She had bet me that I couldn't count out loud to a hundred, and when I reached a hundred she bet that I couldn't make it to 200. I could feel her breath lightly moving the hair on the crown of my head. . . .

Characters and Multiple Viewpoints

Most stories have a number of characters. Since we think about reali-ties as being socially constructed, including others in re-authoring makes sense. A major way that we do this is through asking about other peo-ple's points of view.

> The novelist's substitute for the appearance-reality distinction is a display of diversity of viewpoints, a plurality of descriptions of the same events. What the novelist finds especially comic is the attempt to privilege one of these descriptions, to take it as an excuse for ignoring all the others. What he [*sic*] finds heroic is not the ability sternly to reject all descriptions save one, but rather the ability to move back and forth between them.
> (Rorty, 1991b, p. 74)

Changing point of view almost always brings out different details, different emotions, or different meanings. There are many different points of view that we can propose: looking through the eyes of other people (a relative, a co-worker, a best friend, a tormenter), looking through one's own eyes at a different age, "stepping back" and looking at the story from a reflecting position, looking back from the future, looking forward from the past, and so on.

I (JF) asked Jessica who might have predicted that she would be able to stand up to the effects of the abuse, had they known about it. Jessica said that certain teachers and classmates would have predicted it. They knew she was tough and smart. Through the eyes of these teachers and classmates, with the knowledge that she was tough and smart, Jessica re-saw her plight in a different way—with the belief in her ability to oppose the abuse.

Later, when I asked Jessica what her grandmother recognized in her and most appreciated about her, I was asking Jessica to tell a portion of her story from her grandmother's point of view. From that point of view, she recognized that she was lovable (something she did not recognize from her usual point of view). This recognition pointed the way for Jessica to reexperience many "lost episodes" from her life that had to do with being a good person, being healthy, being warm, being fun, being receptive, and being able to recognize good things in others. As she tells these stories and I listen, thoroughly eliciting details, we are engaged in a ceremony; we are performing meaning on the stories, allowing the emotions, actions, and beliefs associated with them to become part of the official record of Jessica's life.

Attention to the scene or setting of a story is another aspect of making it experientally compelling. It can be important, then, to ask questions that bring forth knowledge about the various contexts of a person's life. For Jessica, the problem-dominated story took place mostly in the realms of her childhood home with particular family members and in social situations. It also took place in the context of patriarchy, where women are seen as the property of men. The alternative story that she authored included the contexts of school, her professional settings, and being home with her grandmother. These were all less patriarchal contexts than the one supporting the problem-saturated story.

In other situations, drawing out descriptions of context grounds stories in actual places. This can be important in making sure that these stories are lived stories. Situating their experience in these places draws people into performance of stories.

Dual Landscapes

Michael White (White & Epston, 1990), following Jerome Bruner (1986), speaks of the "dual landscapes" of *action* and *consciousness*. He believes that since the stories that constitute people's lives unfold in both those landscapes, therapists should inquire about both. Let's look first at the landscape of action. Bruner (J. Bruner, 1986, p. 14) writes that its "constituents are the arguments of action: agent, intention or goal, situation, instrument, something corresponding to a 'story grammar.'" This is similar to the "who, what, when, where, and how" of journalism. In the landscape of action, we plot sequences of events through time.

You can see that much of what we have already discussed under "developing an opening into a story" relates to the landscape of action: *detail in multiple modalities* involving the viewpoints of *multiple characters* in a particular *scene or setting*. What we need to add now is the action itself. What happened, in what sequence, involving which characters?

There were many times when Jessica and I worked together to expand Jessica's preferred stories in the landscape of action. She told the story of her achievements at school. We explored events from her professional life, where the effects of the abuse had less power than in her social life. She told me in detail, and from two vantage points, the story of teaching her grandmother the song, describing the actions involved and fleshing them out more in each telling. When Jessica returned after four years, she told me the story of her forays into horseback riding and playing darts, and I invited her to expand on these events.

In the landscape of action, we are interested in constructing an "agent-ive self" with people. That is, we ask questions with an eye to enhancing those aspects of the emerging story that support "personal agency" (Adams-Westcott, Dafforn, & Sterne, 1993). The very act of re-authoring requires and demonstrates personal agency, and most people experience that in this work. We go a step farther in making personal agency apparent by asking in a variety of ways how people have accomplished what they have. With Jessica, one example is the question about what she had done to create an identity for herself, instead of letting the effects of the abuse create her identity.

Asking "how," or some question that implies "how," is especially useful for inviting stories of personal agency. The answers to "how" questions can also make stories experientially vivid and develop sequences of events through time. Questions like, "How did you do that?" "What did you do that led you to feel this new feeling?" and "How did you notice this different way of perceiving the situation?" are examples. Answers to such questions almost always come in the form of stories.[8]

We think about the *shape* of a story as it comes forth: What happened

---

[8]You might want to try this yourself. Identify a behavior, perception, or emotion from your recent life experience. Ask yourself how that behavior, experience, or emotion came about. Isn't your answer a story of sorts?

before the unique outcome? How smoothly did things unfold? Were there false starts involved? What did this particular episode lead to? In this regard, we are especially interested to know if there is a *turning point*, a place where the story changes for the good. Although "turning point" is not a fitting metaphor for everyone in every situation, when it is, it becomes a significant event that we can plot in time, so that it becomes a story. If there is such a point, it creates a focus for when a problematic story becomes a preferred one. As such, we believe it is useful to focus special attention on it, bringing forth even more shape and detail, perhaps even treating it as a story-within-a-story.

No matter how vivid a story is in the landscape of action, if it is to have *meaning*, it must also be developed in the landscape of consciousness. By "the landscape of consciousness" we refer to that imaginary territory where people plot the meanings, desires, intentions, beliefs, commitments, motivations, values, and the like that relate to their experience in the landscape of action. In other words, in the landscape of consciousness, people reflect on the implications of experiences storied in the landscape of action. Thus, when Jessica named the new account of herself "my new image," she was in the landscape of consciousness.

Jerome Bruner (1986) has discussed how the interplay between these dual landscapes invites empathic and experiential involvement in the lives and minds of the characters in a story. As we read a novel, watch a movie, or listen to a friend recount an amusing anecdote, we only become really involved as we reflect on what people's actions *mean* — why they do what they do, what they hope will or won't happen next, what their actions say about their character, and so on. Earlier, we described asking people how they do things as a way of storying agentive selves. The sequences of events they tell us about in response to "how" questions only come to embody personal agency when people enter the landscape of consciousness and make meaning of them.

In order to explore the landscape of consciousness, we ask what we (Freedman & Combs, 1993) call *meaning questions*. These are questions that invite people to step back from the landscape of action and reflect on the wishes, motivations, values, beliefs, learning, implications, and so forth that lead to and flow from the actions they have recounted.

In the second meeting with Jessica, I asked what it meant that she had accomplished so much already in her life in spite of the abuse. Jessica replied, after some thought, that it meant that she was smart and tough. We believe that Jessica had not previously linked the personal attributes of smartness and toughness so directly to the actions of getting a nursing degree, doing well at a difficult job, and establishing a nice home for herself in spite of the abuse. Even if she had, both the landscape of action and the landscape of consciousness became more real, more vivid, and more memorable as she reflected on the story she constructed.

Again, when I asked Jessica what her grandmother recognized in her and most appreciated about her, we were trafficking in the landscape of consciousness. The meaning question I asked this time was from the grandmother's point of view. Jessica replied that her grandmother recognized and appreciated that she was lovable. She went on to explain that being lovable meant many things: it meant she was a good person; it meant she was warm; it meant she was fun; it meant she was normal, healthy, playful, and receptive; it meant she recognized good things in others. In the therapy conversation, even if they had never been linked before in her experience, this rich and wonderful complex of meanings became linked for Jessica to the memory of sitting in her grandmother's lap and teaching her a song. And together, the meanings and the actions made a narrative that was detailed, vivid, and experientially involving.

In co-authoring stories, we move between the landscape of action and the landscape of consciousness, weaving the two back and forth again and again.

Hypothetical or Speculative Experiences

Fiction has taught us that truth can be found in descriptions of events that never occurred. After all, as Edward Bruner (1986a, p. 18) reminds us,

> . . . stories serve as meaning-generating interpretive devices which frame the present within a hypothetical past and an anticipated future.

Consider the speculative history that Jessica developed of how her life might have been "starting with when she was very little and coming all the way up to how things might be different for her now if she had grown up living with her grandmother." To us, it seems more appropriate for that history to speak of Jessica's identity. It speaks of the identity she prefers and has been working hard for years to construct. The one that had to do with being fearful to enter public spaces in her own house because of years of abusive treatment was never her preferred identity, it was a "ruse" perpetrated by the abuse.

Isolated sparkling moments can easily be lost. Once they emerge, using them as a basis to speculate about how things might have been or could be is one more way to keep them alive and storied. A hypothetical story can become the basis for actual present and future events.

DEVELOPING A "HISTORY
OF THE PRESENT"

Michael White (White & Epston, 1990, p. 9) writes:

Social scientists became interested in the text analogy following
observations that, although a piece of behavior occurs in time in
such a way that it no longer exists in the present by the time it is
attended to, the meaning that is inscribed into the behavior survives
across time. . . . In striving to make sense of life, persons face the
task of arranging their experiences of events in sequences across
time in such a way as to arrive at a coherent account of themselves
and the world around them.

In rendering such accounts, once a preferred event has been identified, we want to link that event to other preferred events across time, so
that their meanings survive, and so that the events and their meanings
can thicken a person's narrative in preferred ways. Therefore, once a
preferred event is identified and storied we ask questions that might link
it to other events in the past and the future.

Before we adopted a narrative map, we worked to help people identify
"resources" from nonproblematic life contexts and to use those resources
in problematic contexts. It was quite common for us to search through
past experiences for these resources. However, we thought of the resources as states of consciousness and used past experiences only as a
way to help people access resourceful states. We made little effort to
connect experiences and states into a narrative that could persist through
time. Now, we think of such experiences as important life events that,
through performance of meaning and connection with other such events,
can alter problematic narratives in satisfying ways. This leads us to de-
vote much of our time and energy to re-viewing, reexperiencing, and
linking together the antecedents of present unique outcomes. Michael
White (1993) calls the kind of story that results from this process a
"history of the present."

In working with Jessica, her accomplishments in spite of the abuse
stood out as unique outcomes. In asking who would have predicted that
she would stand up to the effects of the abuse (as shown through her
accomplishments), I was inviting Jessica to co-construct a history of the
present with me. This history included more details than we have recorded in the written narrative. It included a number of people who
would have predicted that Jessica could stand up to the abuse and the
stories of a number of events they witnessed at different times in her life.

We storied each of these events as a precursor to standing up to the abuse. Together they constituted a history of her present accomplishments.

EXTENDING THE STORY
INTO THE FUTURE

We can also ask how the emerging new story influences a person's ideas about the future. As people free more and more of their pasts from the grip of problem-dominated stories, they are able to envision, expect, and plan toward less problematic futures.

In our second meeting, when I asked Jessica, "If we look back over the years at how you have used your strength and intelligence to take charge of your life—you got an education, became a nurse, and found ways to limit the effects of the abuse—is this readiness to get married you are talking about the next step?," I was recounting a history of the present and asking her to extend the story into the future. In responding to my question, Jessica began to imagine herself having warm and tender feelings and connecting with another person. She could now really believe that it was possible for her to move into the realm of romantic relationships, something that had seemed only a fantasy before.

When Jessica returned four years later, we could see her beginning to realize the future she had begun to author in our work together.

A PRACTICE FORMAT
FOR STORY DEVELOPMENT

We offer you this practice format as a tool for learning, not a prescription or a recipe. It outlines an idealized shape for a therapy conversation that puts together many of the ideas we have talked about in this chapter. In our actual work, things rarely follow the shape we describe here. As with any interesting conversation, there are digressions, recapitulations, and changes of order.

1. **Begin with a unique outcome.** Even when people are describing problem-saturated stories, they often mention or imply experiences that do not fit with these stories. Ask about such events.

   You've said that, even though moods of hopelessness often lead you to suicidal thoughts, you know that you don't really want to die. When was the last time this knowledge helped you turn suicidal thoughts away?

You've said that your son woke you up four nights last week. What happened on the other three nights?

If such events are not alluded to, ask about times or places they might have occurred.

Has there been a time when the arguing could have taken over, but it didn't?

When was the last time your son got himself to school?

2. **Make sure the unique outcome represents a preferred experience.** Ask people to evaluate the unique outcome.

Was that a good experience or a bad one?

Do you want more of this kind of interaction in your relationship?

3. **Plot the story in the landscape of action.**

How did you prepare yourself to take this step?

What do you think was the turning point in your relationship that led to this being possible?

What exactly did you do?

Were you guided by an image or something you said to yourself? Did you have a plan?

Was it a decision you made on your own or did other people play a part?

What exactly did your partner say when you told him? What was the look on his face?

4. **Plot the story in the landscape of consciousness.**

What does it say about you as a person that you would do this? What personal characteristics does it show?

What do you see in your relationship when you look at this event?

Is there something you learned in that conversation with your aunt that might be important in other areas of your life?

What went into doing this at this point in your life?

What does this show about your goals for your life?

Note that questions from points 3 and 4 can be woven back and forth:

How did you prepare yourself to take this step? What does it say about you as a person that you would do this? What personal characteristics does it show? Knowing that about yourself, did that have something to do with how you did it? Were you guided by an image or something you said to yourself? Did you have a plan? What went into your doing it at this point in your life? What do you think the turning point in your relationship was that led to this being possible? What do you see in your relationship when you look at this event?

5.[9] Ask about a past time that has something in common with the unique outcome or the meaning of the unique outcome.

Were there times when you've done this kind of thing before? What example are you thinking of?

Who would have predicted this event? What have they seen you do before that would have led them to believe you would have done this?

Now that you recognize this quality in your partner do memories come to mind of times where you have experienced this quality in him before?

What time in your life best illustrates your perseverance? What incident stands out for you from that time?

6. Plot the story of the past event in the landscape of action. (as in 3)
7. Plot the story of the past event in the landscape of consciousness. (as in 4)
8. Ask questions to link the past episode with the present.

Now that I understand its foundation in your past, do you see how this recent development in your relationship makes even more sense to me?

If I could ask the you back then what she thinks of these recent developments, what would she say?

When you think about that past time, does it put the experience that you had last week in a different light?

9. Ask questions to extend the story into the future.

If we look at these events that we've been talking about as a trend in your life, what do you expect the next step will be?

Does looking at these events today have an impact on what you see in your future?

---

[9]Steps 5 through 8 serve to facilitate developing a history of the present. They can be repeated with a number of events.

Given these experiences we've been talking about, what do you
predict for the coming school year?

A TRANSCRIPT

We offer the following transcript so that you can get a feel for how
we put the ideas we have explicated in this chapter into action moment-
by-moment in a single therapy conversation.

I (GC) am talking with Emma, who first came to see me when she was
nearly immobilized by depression. She had lost her job as production
manager in a large plant when the company "downsized." When she was
unable to find another job like her old one, she went to work for her
younger brother, who was a real "wheeler-dealer." He soon had her
working two jobs: managing a diner he had won in a poker game and
keeping the books for his real estate company. For this, he was paying
her half the salary she had earned as a production manager.

As you will read, Emma had grown up with many responsibilities and
little support. At the point I met her, fear that standing up to her brother
would alienate her other siblings and cause a family uproar had immobilized her. This led her to characterize herself as having no voice and no
spine.

Just before the meeting prior to this one, Emma had "told her brother
off." He had given her a "ton of paperwork" to do late on a Friday
afternoon, expecting her to do it before she left for the day, and she
rebelled, yelling at him and storming out. We spent most of the meeting
before this one developing the story of that incident.

At the start of the meeting from which the transcript is taken, Emma
told me she had been job hunting for the first time in a long time, and
that she had found a job! She thought she had handled the interview for
this job superbly. We developed the story of the interview. Then I
learned that she had had another confrontation with her brother, Ray.
This time she had handled herself calmly and with strength, saying that
she would be resigning soon and that she expected him to give her two
weeks of paid vacation when she left!

GENE   So you said that your big fear was talking to Ray.

EMMA   Uh-huh.

GENE   And, if I understood you correctly, that didn't stop you at all
       from talking to him. You went ahead and talked to him. Then
       you did some stuff that you kind of . . . you kind of hoped

you wouldn't have to say some stuff, but you felt like you had to.

EMMA Uh-huh.

GENE And you said the stuff you had to say calmly, and from strength. . . .

EMMA Uh-huh.

(In these first few questions, I have identified a unique outcome which was quite clearly a preferred one for Emma, and reviewed some of the developments she had already described in the landscape of action.)

GENE Well, what does that say to you about yourself? What kind of a person does that say to you that you are, that you've been able to do that now?

(I now inquire about the landscape of consciousness, and Emma becomes involved in a very substantial answer.)

EMMA Hmm . . . well . . . (under her breath, to herself) what kind of person am I? (addressing Gene again) Well, it made me realize that I had been taken advantage of and that angered me. But, I don't know. I guess it goes back to that, what I said before, that I'm a lot stronger than I thought I was.

My self-worth is a lot more than I thought it was. A lot more. I'm finding out that I'm a pretty good person. I'm starting to lose that insecurity and that self . . . self . . . I don't know. Is "deprivation" the right word?

I don't put myself down as much verbally — I never thought out loud to myself "You're stupid! You're bad!" — I just had this feeling. I was "adequate," and not really good. Ray reinforced that feeling in me over the past year, I've come to realize, that I was adequate, or I'm expendable, or I was one that could just be walked all over, and he pushed me aside. And that's one thing I said to him on Wednesday when we were having this heated discussion.

I said to him, "Ray, I was always your safety net. I was always there for you. You could treat me however you wanted." And I said, "You can't do that anymore." And "It's rotten that you're doing it." And "I'm wondering if you even realize you're doing it to me, but you are doing it to me, and it will not be tolerated."

I mean, I feel bad for him, he's so caught up in himself. And he said to me, "We sat in Jack's office," that's his partner, "and we never discussed this first month's salary."

I said, "No, we sat in your living room and discussed it. You, me, and your wife."

And he said, "Well, that's another thing. Reba doesn't remember that conversation either."

And I said, "Really? If I call her up and ask her, is she going to remember? She doesn't even know that you owe me this money, does she? She doesn't even know about it."

And he goes, "No she doesn't." He hasn't even been truthful with her.

GENE If you think of people that knew you when you were a kid . . .

EMMA Uh-huh.

GENE . . . friends, family, teachers — who from back then would be least surprised to see you taking the stand that you've taken with Ray, or to see you being the way you were in that job interview?

(Here I ask Emma to begin thinking about past events that have something in common with the present unique outcome.)

EMMA Who would be least surprised?

GENE Yeah. Who would say, "I knew she had it in her."

EMMA Well, my Uncle Patrick. Hmm . . .

GENE Yeah?

EMMA Yeah. I have an uncle. . . . Now he would read it — he's the one person in my life who would read it — as, "I knew she had it in her. Good for her." The others in my life wouldn't have been surprised that I did what I did, but they would have read it as, "She's just a pushy bitch! Always has been, always will be."

GENE But what was it that your Uncle Patrick saw as different about you?

(Emma has identified a person from the past who would appreciate the sparkling event in her present life. I invite her to explore the meaning of her life from Uncle Patrick's viewpoint. When she takes up my invitation, she experiences a flood of memories. She tells several stories about past experiences. These stories are rich in detail and she spontaneously develops them in both the landscape of consciousness and the landscape of action. On her own, she introduces another key character, Aunt Joan.)

EMMA He's like my kindred soul. He was always able to understand the inner me for some reason. I don't know if it's because he's a kind, gentle, individual who always took the time to listen to me or to talk. . . .

He's only 13 years older than I am and to this day I still tease him about the time. . . . He was in the seminary; he was studying to be a Jesuit for nine years before he left – and came out and got married and had kids. . . . But I remember him coming home for a weekend visit and we went up to the local malt shop, and he was 20 years old and I was seven. And I was on a date with my uncle who I absolutely adored. And there are all these teenagers around. Just like something out of "Happy Days," you know?

And he goes, "Sit down kid. Take a load off." And I wasn't a heavy kid.

And I went, "He thinks I'm fat." And to this day, to this day, every time I see him, I tell him. I say, "Do you remember the time?"

He goes, "Will you ever forget it?"

And I say, "No. I never, never, will." (Emma laughs) "I'll never let you forget it either!"

Umm . . . but he always talked *to* me. Not down to me. He always talked *to* me. There was always something special about him that I connected with.

I also have an Aunt Joan who's the same way, which is really strange. This woman is my dad's youngest. . . . Now, my Uncle Patrick is my mom's youngest brother, and my Aunt Joan is my dad's youngest sister. That woman has been a force in my life since I re-met her 15 years ago. And by "re-met," I mean she and her family lived not far from us on the South Side, and then my uncle was stationed – he was in the army – he was stationed over in London for a couple years, and when they came back from London they lived in Chicago for maybe a month, or a year, or whatever. And then they moved out to the West Coast. And then we didn't see them for 10 years, 15 years.

And then we had a tragedy in our family. One of my cousins was shot and killed, and she came in for the funeral. And she happened to stay at my house, instead of at my mom and dad's. I had a two-bedroom apartment at the time. And she and I sat up – literally sat up all night long – talking.

And about dawn I looked at her and I said, "I have just been talking to my father in a skirt. But a sober 'my father.'" Because he was an alcoholic.

And she just started laughing. And it was shortly after that, my parents lost their house to foreclosure. And I had all this responsibility on me.

She always called me once every other week. Just to see how I was. I didn't have anybody else. And to this day, we talk at least once a month. And when they come to town, they stay with me. It's just a given.

I had talked to her a couple weeks ago, and told her about the awful fight I had with Ray, and how awful it was.

And she's going, "Get out of there. You just get out of there. Get another job."

So Sunday, I came back from church. What I usually do on Sunday morning, I read the newspaper. I turn on the stereo. You know, I just have some quiet time. I was thinking to myself, "You know, I should call Aunt Joan with some good news for once. I'm not going to wait for her to call me. I'm going to call her." I literally got up from my chair and went to get my phone book. My phone rang. It was her. And I screamed.

I went, "I can't believe this."

And she's going, "What? Did I interrupt something? What? What?"

And I went, "Aunt Joan, I was just picking the phone up to call you. Literally, just picking the phone up."

And she starts to giggle. She goes, "I've been thinking about you all morning."

I said, "All morning? If it's 9 o'clock here it can only be 7 o'clock there." (You know, because they're in Vegas.)

And she said, "I was up really early." And she said, "Something good?"

And I went, "Well, maybe."

She goes, "Do you have a smile on your face?"

I went, "Yeah. It's about as wide as the Mississippi. I think I got the job!"

She goes, "Good."

You know? But it was so strange. It was so strange . . . yeah.

We had a long time. . . . They came and stayed with me right after my mother passed away. My uncle was in the other room. He's an alcoholic, and he was just drinking. And I told her about my mom and dad always making me feel or telling me that I was adequate, "But that was fine because it was the best you can do. But, you're not as good as so and so."

And I can remember seeing the fire in her eyes. She was so furious. And it was the first time. . . .

GENE Now when was that?

EMMA This was four years ago.

GENE Uh-huh.

EMMA My mom will be dead four years this May. It was the first time that I can vividly remember thinking to myself, "Geez, maybe it's not true. Maybe those feelings aren't true. Maybe I am pretty good at what I do."

GENE Now, what was it about that interaction that made it possible for you to think that?

EMMA Because of her instant reaction to the statement that I made. That, you know, they made me feel like . . . they told me I was adequate at best. And you know how you can see in somebody's look on their face like they were shocked? That that was the last thing they expected to hear?

GENE Yeah.

EMMA When I saw her initial reaction. . . . Of course after her initial reaction, then came the typical aunt accolades and, "No. No. You're wonderful. You've done a lot for your family." And . . .

GENE But it was more the reaction than the words?

EMMA It was more the reaction that got through to me.

GENE Yeah.

EMMA People's reactions get through to me faster than words I've come to. . . . They do, because words mean nothing. Most of the time.

GENE Now . . . so she knew something about you for a long, long, time. . . .

EMMA Uh-huh.

GENE . . . that that adequate stuff just didn't fit with at all. It just made her blood boil.

EMMA Yeah. It did! Instantly.

GENE So, what do you think you would see if you were able to look at you when you were a kid through your Aunt Joan's eyes, and see that kid the way Aunt Joan saw that kid? What do you think she saw back then? What do you think you would see?

EMMA Well, through my young adolescent years, she wasn't around. She was out on the West Coast.

GENE   But if we go back to when she did. . . .

EMMA   Before that?

GENE   Yeah . . . what do you think she saw that maybe nobody else except maybe your Uncle Patrick saw? What did she notice in you?

EMMA   I don't know. I think that. . . .

GENE   Well, what would be your guess? Best as you can imagine, kind of crawling inside her body. . . .

EMMA   That here is a kid that has overcome what for some people would be insurmountable odds. I think.

GENE   So if I were able to go back and interview her, back then, at that time, and I'd say, "What insurmountable odds? What are you talking about? What is it that she's overcome?" What do you think she would say?

EMMA   "Taking care of her family during really rough times. Keeping them together." Because that's what I did. I did do that. At a very young age. I did do that. She would have seen a girl that had a lot of potential but wasn't able to develop then because she wasn't given the opportunity.

GENE   And if I said to her, back then, if I somehow could do that, "You say potential. Potential for what? What kind of potential do you see in this girl?"

EMMA   Hmm . . . Aunt Joan's response would be, "She should get a better education to reach whatever she would want to be. Be it a doctor or lawyer or an artist or an author, whatever it would be."

GENE   So she saw somebody that had a lot of . . .

EMMA   Yeah . . . yeah.

GENE   lot of stuff.

EMMA   Yeah. Aunt Joan's kids are all real educated except for her oldest son. They all went on to . . . you know, it's her daughter that's the Ph.D. in physics. She has another daughter that's a dancer. And she has another son that's. . . . She has a daughter that's a social worker and another son that's a very successful businessman. And then she's got two that are a little goofy, but you know, out of seven kids she did pretty well.

       She always told me later. . . . That week that they stayed with me, after my mom died, she and I did a lot of talking.

And she said, "It used to always anger me that you kids weren't given the opportunities that you should have been given."

GENE   What difference did it make for you to hear that from her?

EMMA   Back then it made me feel real sad and real forlorn, like, "Gosh, I was cheated. I was cheated."

Now I feel that it's time to stop blaming other people and just go on with it, and stop dwelling on the past. Which I don't think I was doing consciously, but subconsciously I think I was. I had a lot of years of garbage to get out of myself. You know?

GENE   Yeah.

EMMA   After my mother passed away, when it came up to my dad's birthday time, and I couldn't stop crying, which made me go in to see a therapist back then, he very kindly said to me, "Oh, and you miss your mom and dad, don't you?"

And I looked around and went, "No. I'm sorry but I don't. They weren't nice people to me."

They *weren't* nice people. I mean, if you sat down and met them, you would have enjoyed their company. They weren't nice people to *me*. I don't think. So no.

I was mourning. I don't know what I was mourning but it wasn't their passing. I was mourning probably their living, instead of their passing. I think that's what I was mourning all those years. All these past four years.

And now it's like, "Okay, so you did the best you could do." You know, they danced as fast as they could, and God bless them. And so you just . . .

GENE   And now you're in a position where you can realize some of that potential that Aunt Joan always saw in you?

EMMA   Yeah. That's what I'm seeing this job. . . .

GENE   Yeah. So, if you sit there for a second, and you think back over everything you've said here today . . .

EMMA   Uh-huh?

GENE   What stands out for you? What pieces of that are. . . . If you kind of think of yourself as somebody that's been sitting here off to the side (gesturing to an area in a corner of the room) listening to Emma over there, (gesturing towards Emma) what stands out?

EMMA   What stands out . . . well, I think I was a lot better person. Much better than I realized. At a much younger age. . . . But I'm just coming to realize it now, I think.

GENE What difference does it make to be . . . not just realize that
you're a good person now, but to realize that you've been a
good person all along? That you were a much better person
than you realized at a much younger age? What difference
does it make to come to that realization now?

*(Here I am inviting Emma to connect the meaning of the past experiences
she has been relating to the context of her present life. She goes me one
better by extending the past and present meaning into the future.)*

EMMA My feelings won't get hurt as easily as they have in the past. So
I will be a lot stronger. I will feel a lot stronger within so people
won't walk all over me. It's been almost like a vicious circle.
You know? My feelings get hurt because somebody walks all
over me, and somebody walks all over me because I let them
hurt my feelings. And it's like, suddenly I feel like this circle is
going to be ending. You know?

GENE Yeah. Cause the possibility for . . .

EMMA Expansion.

GENE Yeah, who knows what . . .

EMMA Yeah, I know. I know. I remember last week we said something
about . . . I said, "God, you know, if I just didn't have all that
stuff happen to me when I was a kid, what could I have been?"
      And I remember you saying, "What? Is it too late now?"
      And I thought, "Yeah." But now I think, "No, it's not.
Who knows what I'm going to be?" I mean who knows? Who
knows?

Questions

5

Every time we ask a question, we're generating a possible version of a life.

— *David Epston in Cowley and Springen, 1995, p. 74*

There are some questions that linger in the minds of clients for weeks, months, and occasionally years, and continue to have an effect.

— *Karl Tomm, 1988, p. 14*

We've all been asking questions for almost as long as we've been talking. However, as narrative therapists we think about questions, compose them, and use them differently than we did before. The biggest difference is that we ask questions to *generate experience* rather than to gather information. When they generate experience of preferred realities, questions can be therapeutic in and of themselves. While many people (e.g., Campbell, Draper, & Huffington, 1988; de Shazer, 1994; Fleuridas, Nelson, & Rosenthal, 1986; Freedman & Combs, 1993; Lipchik & de Shazer, 1986; O'Hanlon & Weiner-Davis, 1989; Penn, 1985; Tomm, 1987a, 1987b, 1988; White, 1988a) have written about this idea, it may have been expressed first by the Milan team (Selvini Palazzoli et al., 1980) when they wondered whether change could occur solely through their interviewing process (which consisted largely of circular questions) without any final intervention.

We first began thinking about how questions can generate experience a number of years ago, when we were using ideas primarily from strategic therapy.[1] At that time we saw a family who came to therapy because

[1]We have described this experience elsewhere (Freedman & Combs, 1993). Because it was a turning point in our own stories of ourselves as therapists, we describe it again here.

Kathy, the 12-year-old daughter, wouldn't go to school. She didn't like it that some of her classmates at the girls school she attended were showing increasing interest in boys, alcohol, and drugs. She had the idea that if she started thinking about any of these particular classmates when she was involved in an activity, she would somehow become like them. The fear led to some problematic behaviors. For example, if a thought about one of the classmates came into her mind while she was putting on a shoe, she took it off and put it on again. She would repeat this behavior until she was positive that she had completed it with none of her classmates in mind. She approached opening and closing doors, turning on and off lights, and an ever-increasing number of other activities in the same way. Because her classmates surrounded her when she was in the classroom, Kathy had to contend not only with her thoughts but also with the possibility of actually hearing their voices or seeing one of them while she was opening her desk or changing into gym shoes. Because of this, she found it intolerable to be in the classroom, and refused to go to school.

By the time we had met with Kathy and her parents five times, the situation had not changed. When they let us know that the two older children were coming home from school for a winter break, we arranged for the whole family to come in. We split the group for the first part of the meeting, with one of us (JF) seeing the siblings and one of us (GC) seeing the parents.

In conversation with the siblings I (JF) learned that the parents both smoked heavily and that all the children, especially Kathy, were very worried about the effects of the smoking on their parents' health. Kathy was terrified that they would die.

Kathy seemed more actively involved in the discussion about her parents' smoking than she had been at any other point in therapy, so I wanted to utilize this interest if I could. I asked her, "Who would be in greater danger — your parents if they continue smoking or you if you go to school?"

When she answered "Mom and Dad," I began to wonder if Kathy would be willing to make a bargain, going to school in return for her parents' quitting smoking.

To test my idea, I inquired further: "Are you the kind of person who will take a risk for the welfare of someone you care about?"

She said that she was, and her brother and sister agreed, citing an incident in which she had rescued a neighbor's toddler from a locked bathroom through a small second-floor window.

"Would it help you to do something that seemed dangerous if you knew that it was really benefiting someone important to you?" She said that it would.

I asked, "How would it help?" and she answered that the benefit to another person would put things in perspective. She would have a compelling reason for facing the danger.

I asked, "Could you go to school if you knew it might save your parents' lives?"

She unhesitatingly answered, "Yes."

I asked, "What would you do if you looked at someone and thought you might become like them?"

She answered, "Just concentrate on the work and on being there."

I asked, "Even if it is really difficult, if you agree to do something are you a person of your word?"

She said she was.

During a break we (GC and JF) conferred and agreed that, since the parents had repeatedly committed themselves to doing whatever it would take to get Kathy back in school, they would certainly be willing to give up smoking. When we met together with the whole family, we stated that everyone knew how important the parents thought it was that Kathy go to school. They had already put a lot of time and energy into this, first trying to handle the situation on their own, then meeting with school officials, and finally coming to therapy. We said that we had just discovered how important it was to Kathy that her parents quit smoking, and that she was willing to put time and energy into making that happen. We then proposed the trade, asking Kathy if she would go to school if her parents would quit smoking. Beaming, she said she would. We asked the parents if they would quit smoking if Kathy went to school. They, too, agreed.

When we met again two weeks later, we were shocked to learn what had happened. Both parents were still smoking, but Kathy had gone to school every day since our meeting! From that point on, Kathy continued going to school and her parents continued smoking. Although she still wanted them to quit smoking, Kathy never even threatened to stop going to school. The repetitive behavior seemed to just disappear. We found this extremely puzzling.

It wasn't until about six months later that we found a way of thinking about what had happened that made sense to us. We began wondering if in the mental search involved in answering my (JF) questions, Kathy had experienced a different way of being. That is, when I asked, "What would you do if you looked at someone and thought you might become like them?" might Kathy have vividly imagined herself in the context of school, concentrating on the work without fear taking over her experience? Her answer, "Just concentrate on the work and being there," implied just such an experience. She must have experienced herself as someone who could take risks and handle being in dangerous situations by focusing on the task at hand rather than letting the danger terrify her. In answering the questions, she must have entered a different reality than the one she usually inhabited. She must have experienced herself as someone who could go to school. So she did.

We wondered what would have happened if we hadn't been so certain of the parents' willingness to do whatever it took to help Kathy go back to school. If we had asked them questions similar to the ones we asked Kathy, might they have entered into a different experience of themselves, one in which they were already nonsmokers?

This incident was a turning point in our way of thinking about and practicing therapy. Our background in Ericksonian approaches had grounded us in the importance of associational searches, experiential learning, and alternative realities (Dolan, 1985; Erickson & Rossi, 1979, 1981; Erickson, Rossi, & Rossi, 1976; Gilligan, 1987; Rossi, 1980a, 1980b; Zeig, 1980, 1985). However, we thought of lived experience as being stored "inside" of people.[2] We knew that by asking questions we could help people access and relive "resourceful" experiences. For example, we might ask someone, "What time in your life did you feel most comfortable?" with the hope that he would access and relive an actual experience of comfort (or a representative sample of such an experience) and feel comfortable in the present.

The experience we had with Kathy did not fit that way of thinking. For one thing, it was clear from previous conversations that Kathy had not thought of herself as a risk-taker. The example her brother and sister provided of her rescuing a toddler from a locked bathroom may have originally meant to her that she was obedient (if someone had suggested that she do it), or small and agile (since she could fit through the window), or perhaps caring. But it was only in relation to my question that the past event began to take on the new meaning of taking a risk. "Taking a risk" was not stored inside Kathy. She constituted herself, perhaps for the first time ever, as a risk-taking person when she stepped into the new reality that my questions brought forth.

Up to this time, we had thought of experience as simply what happens, and we thought all experiences were stored as they happened and were retrievable through memory. We now think that experience is colored and shaped by the meaning people make of it and that it is attended to or not as it seems relevant to the stories people are living. Therefore, when we ask questions, rather than believing that people can retrieve particular experiences with particular predetermined meanings, we are very aware of how our questions *co-author* experience (Anderson &

---

[2]Remember our conversations about "resources" with David Epston and Michael White in Chapter 1?

Goolishian, 1990b; Penn, 1982; Tomm, 1988). They put a spin on the experiences that they call up; they suggest beginnings and endings for those experiences; they highlight portions of experience while dimming or excluding others.

Our questions don't access experience. They generate it (Campbell, Draper, & Huffington, 1988; Freedman & Combs, 1993; Penn & Sheinberg, 1991). We are reminded of this each time one of our questions is met by a long pause, after which a person says, "I never thought of this before . . . " or "I didn't know this until you asked that question." We think it is not just that the person did not know it; we think it had never been so until the question and person came together to constitute it that way.

A therapist's values shape the questions that she asks. So do her stories about people and therapy. With this understanding we find it interesting to look back on our work with Kathy. At the time, we didn't pay very much attention to Kathy's experience of being with girls who were interested in boys, alcohol, and drugs. Now we would be very interested in finding out the impact of that experience on her. We would wonder if social pressures and expectations were creating an atmosphere that was intolerable to her and was threatening her sense of herself as a person. If we had asked questions along that line, we wonder if the way Kathy's family thought about her and the problem and the way that she thought about herself might have been different. We now believe that, in effect, we conspired with social pressures to get her to go to school, not recognizing that she found the social pressures there intolerable. If we could travel back through time, we wonder if our questions might have enlisted the family's help in fighting against social pressures. By avoiding school, Kathy found a way of not letting social pressures take her over. We wonder if we might have been more helpful if we had asked questions about ways she had been able to do that (or ways she might be able to do that) while she attended school.[3]

In this work, we hope to privilege the knowledge of the people we work with over ours. For this reason, we think it is very important to be aware of the influence our questions have in setting the direction of the conversation. One of the ways we try to balance the influence of our questions is by periodically asking questions that invite the people we work with to evaluate the process. For example, we ask, "Is this what you want to be talking about?" and "Is this conversation helpful to you?

---

[3]Part of what we are trying to express in this critique of our own work is that we are part of the dominant power/knowledge domain. We cannot be completely outside of dominant practices, but we can take responsibility for working to see through dominant cultural stories. This requires that we deconstruct our practices and situate our ideas in our experience.

How is it helpful?" We modify our questions in response to the answers. We also ask questions about our questions, such as, "Were there particular questions that seemed more helpful and others that you didn't find helpful? Why?" and again, we pay attention to the answers.

Even though we recognize the influence of questions in specifying the domain of "appropriate" answers, we think that interacting mainly through questions helps us privilege the knowledge of the people we work with. As Karl Tomm (1988, p. 2) writes,

> In general, statements *set forth* issues, positions, or views, whereas questions *call forth* issues, positions, or views. In other words, questions tend to call for answers and statements tend to provide them.

In another place, Karl Tomm (1987a, pp. 4–5) reminds us that, although we may have a particular idea in mind when we ask a question, the person who answers it determines the direction it will take. He writes,

> . . . the *actual* effect of any particular intervention with a client is *always* determined by the client, not the therapist. The intentions and consequent actions of the therapist only trigger a response; they never determine it.

As we have described in Chapter 3, we strive to work from what Harry Goolishian and Harlene Anderson call a "not-knowing" position. We endeavor not to ask questions that we think we know "the" answers to, or ones that we want *particular* answers to. That is, we are not asking questions from a position of pre-understanding (Andersen, 1991a; Weingarten, 1992).

Even though we value a position of curiosity and not-knowing, we do have intentions or purposes. We think that all therapists follow some sort of intentionality, even if the purpose is a very general one, such as "opening space." Our intentions are more specific. We hope to engage people in deconstructing problematic stories, identifying preferred directions, and developing alternative stories that support these preferred directions. The narrative metaphor shapes our curiosity, but doesn't stifle it.

Even though we have dedicated this chapter to offering examples of and a structure for thinking about "types" of questions, we can think of several reasons not to give these examples or that structure. First, the examples will be out of context. Each question we ask in therapy comes from what has just been said in the conversation. When, as here, we focus on particular types of questions, rather than on a living conversation, we tend to forget that any single question might be useful only in particular contexts. You can see by looking at any of the transcripts in this book that we do not ask the exact questions that we give as examples here, that our questions are in response to moment-by-moment shifts in the conversation, and that we don't follow the idealized structures that we offer here.

Second, the examples illustrate only words, not voice tone, gesture, or relationship. People respond to much more than words. As Karl Tomm (1988) and James and Melissa Griffith (1992a, 1994) suggest, the emotional postures from which questions are asked are of primary importance. We strive to ask questions from a position of respect, curiosity, and openness, but we doubt that these positions can be adequately represented through written words. We hope that as you read the examples here you will supply an appropriate tone.

Third, we know that some people follow examples as though they are "the" way to do something. Our examples are certainly not meant to be that, and we sincerely hope that they do not restrain your creativity.

In the face of all our hesitation, we offer the following examples. The shift from gathering information to generating experience is a monumental one—and it's not an easy one for every interested person to make. For our own learning, we have found studying examples of other people's experience-generating questions extremely useful.[4] In this way we stop time and focus on single questions, one at a time.

Using narrative as a guiding metaphor is another large conceptual and practical shift, requiring particular kinds of questions. Coordinating both curiosity and the narrative metaphor while at the same time attending to the relationship feels like a lot of juggling at first. Although in practice they all work together, it is helpful to look at the components separately.

The main reason that we offer these examples is because people in our training programs tell us that having examples, to which they can add their own, is useful and that having categories helps them to organize their thoughts. In other words, for many people examples and categories are on the side of practice and learning.

We have found it helpful to divide the questions we use in this process into five major categories: *deconstruction questions, opening space questions, preference questions, story development questions,* and *meaning questions.* These categories are fluid, in that a particular question could,

---

[4]Our dog-eared copies of the following articles, each of which offers categories and examples of questions, have been particularly helpful in our own learning: White, 1988a, 1988b (both of these articles are reprinted in White, 1989); Tomm, 1987a, 1987b, 1988. Also invaluable are the transcripts that appear in many of David Epston's articles—see Epston, 1989a, and Epston and White, 1992.

for example, both open space and lead to the construction of new meaning. Also, a therapist could intend for a question to invite someone to state a preference and that person could nevertheless respond with an answer that began to develop an alternative story. The categories we give refer to the therapist's intentions in asking questions. They are meant to help therapists think clearly about the process of narrative therapy. While the order in which we list these examples does follow a certain linear logic, we do not follow a strict order when we ask questions in actual conversations. We will offer some thoughts about what to ask when toward the end of the chapter.

DECONSTRUCTION QUESTIONS

Deconstruction questions help people unpack their stories or see them from different perspectives, so that how they have been constructed becomes apparent. Many deconstruction questions encourage people to situate their narratives in larger systems and through time. In bringing forth the history, context, and effects of people's narratives, we are broadening their scope, depicting entire landscapes that support problems. Within these broader landscapes, more (and more varied) "sparkling events" can be brought forth.

Bringing Forth Problematic Beliefs, Practices, Feelings, and Attitudes

Almost all of the deconstructive questioning we do takes place within externalizing conversations. Although our intention is to deconstruct problematic narratives, no particular question is aimed at an entire narrative. Instead, each question addresses something that is part of a problem-saturated story or that maintains a problematic narrative. Generally, as we listen to problematic narratives we hear about beliefs, practices, feelings, and attitudes, and these are what a particular deconstruction question addresses. If, in a person's telling of his story, we do not learn about beliefs, practices, feelings, and attitudes, we can ask questions to constitute them or bring them forth. Such questions might include:

- What conclusions about your relationship have you drawn because of this problem?
- What behaviors have you found yourself resorting to in relationship to the situation that you have described?
- Does this situation that you describe encourage particular feelings in your life?

- What attitudes do you think must be there to justify the behaviors that you have described?[5]
- What gets in the way of developing the kinds of relationships you would like to have?

As these questions help people to distinguish particular beliefs, practices, feelings, and attitudes, we ask about:

1. the *history of a person's relationship* with the belief, practice, feeling, or attitude,
2. *contextual influences* on the belief, practice, feeling, or attitude,
3. the *effects or results* of the belief, practice, feeling, or attitude,
4. the *interrelationship* with other beliefs, practices, feelings, or attitudes, and
5. the *tactics or strategies* of the belief, practice, feeling, or attitude.

We ask all these questions within the context of an externalizing conversation. Can you see how each of these types of questions presupposes that the belief, practice, feeling, or attitude is separate from the person, and would thus serve to externalize it further? As you know, we generally use externalizing language whenever our intention is to deconstruct problem-saturated narratives. It is such an important part of deconstruction that we often compose questions with the sole intention of engaging in an externalizing conversation. Most of the questions that we compose with a "pure" externalizing intent inadvertently ask about at least one of the other areas we've identified as well. Conversely, all the questions in the other areas serve the purpose of externalization, whether a therapist consciously intends it or not.

The above five categories of deconstruction questions are not the only kinds of questions that could be used to deconstruct narratives. Rather, they represent types of questions we use often in our work. We ask numerous questions of this sort, not a single question, in inviting the deconstruction of a narrative. A question about one belief, feeling, practice, or attitude leads to another belief, feeling, practice, or attitude. So we then ask about that one, as this short excerpt from a therapy conversation illustrates.

I (JF) was working with Louise, who had landed a new job and was preparing for the change. "Several people at work came up to me and

---

[5]As we look at some of these questions in black-and-white, we see that they may sound like we engage in heavy duty confrontation. This is not the case. Our use of externalizing language makes it possible to engage with people in mutual puzzling about the answers to these questions.

told me not to tell the people at my new job that I'm half African-American," she told me.

"What do you think about that idea?" I asked.

"I think they're right," she declared. "It won't do me any good. People will consider me black and be biased against me, and since I don't look black, the blacks won't accept me anyway."

"I'm at a disadvantage here. . . . I can't know what your experience is like. Can I ask you a little bit more about this?"

"Sure."

"Well, what beliefs or attitudes do you think a person must have in order to suggest that you shouldn't let people know that you are biracial?"

"The people who said this to me were black, and I agree with them. Black people are more rude and mean."

"I haven't found that myself, but can I ask you about another part of this? What do you think the effect on your life will be of keeping your heritage secret?"

"I'm not ashamed of who I am. I mean, I didn't have to tell people at my last job."

"Yeah, and I'm not telling you what to do at all. I don't really know. I'm just wondering, if you do keep it secret, what will that do to you?"

"Probably keep me from being close to people. Maybe make me feel worse about being black. I used to like to be black."

Keeping in mind that we use a number of these questions together, as the excerpt begins to demonstrate, let's look at each of our five categories of deconstruction questions one at a time.

History of Relationship. In addition to enlarging the landscape within which the problem exists, asking about the history of a person's relationship with a belief, practice, feeling, or attitude may expose the role of dominant cultural practices or knowledges in supporting the problem. As Lynn Hoffman (1992, p. 14), writing about Foucault, notes,

Once people subscribe to a given discourse — a religious discourse, a psychological discourse, or a discourse around gender — they promote certain definitions about which persons or what topics are most important or have legitimacy. However, they themselves are not always aware of these embedded definitions.

"History of relationship questions" can reveal taken-for-granted or embedded practices or knowledges.

- How were you recruited into this way of thinking?
- Where did you witness these ways of responding to problems?
- What experiences did you have in the past that encouraged these feelings of guilt?
- Has solitude *always* been your best friend?
- When in history did these sorts of ideas gain prominence? How were they used? How did you learn of them?

Contextual Influences. These questions are aimed at depicting the ongoing contexts that serve as support systems for problematic stories. "Contextual influence questions" may also expose the role of cultural practices or knowledges.

- In what situations would you most expect these kinds of ideas to be advocated?
- Are there places where it is more likely you'll be pulled into drinking?
- Who in your life supports anger taking over?
- Who benefits from this way of doing things?

Effects or Results. These questions broaden the domain of the problematic story by showing the impact of the problem in people's lives and relationships. Seeing the real effects of a belief, practice, feeling, or attitude can put it in a different light.

- What are the effects on your life of this belief that you are not a good person?
- What has self-doubt talked you into doing in your relationships with people at work?
- How has this pattern influenced other family members?
- How has pessimism affected your relationship with yourself?
- If you were to step futher into this way of being, how would that affect your future?
- What has the idea of self-reliance promoted in relationships?

Interrelationship. "Interrelationship questions" can help deconstruct the web of beliefs, practices, feelings, and attitudes that constitute the life of a problem.[6]

---

[6]See Rick Maisel's paper (1994) on "Engaging men in a re-evaluation of practices and definitions of masculinity" for an excellent discussion on helping men attend to contradictions between intentions and effects and between ideas (and their effects) and relationship preferences.

- Are there other problems that anorexia teams up with? Some people have told me that they think self-blame and isolation are partners with anorexia. What do you think?
- Does the belief that things should be this way encourage anger taking over or leave more room for other feelings?
- What does this idea have you doing?
- What conclusions have you drawn about your relationship because of all this fighting?
- What ideas, habits, and feelings feed the problem?
- If we look at the effects of this attitude, does it match your hopes for your relationship?

Tactics or Strategies. Since we treat problematic beliefs, practices, feelings, and attitudes as externalized entities, we can think about them as having plans and preferred ways of working. Unmasking these tactics and strategies can have a powerful deconstructive effect.

- How does the anger worm its way between the two of you?
- If I were going to be the fear in your life, what would I do to make my presence known? How would I make things worse? What times would I pick?
- What does the voice of depression whisper in you ear? How does it manage to be so convincing?
- Which does the bulimia do first, flash the pictures of whole sheet cakes in front of your eyes or give you that certain taste in your mouth?
- What ways of life does racism ride piggy-back on?

OPENING SPACE QUESTIONS

Once the landscape of the problem has been broadened through deconstruction questions, there are numerous vantage points from which unique outcomes or sparkling events—those experiences that lie outside of the problem-saturated narrative and would not be predicted by it—might be brought forth. We use opening space questions to construct unique outcomes.

Because this is a chapter on questions, we are emphasizing the questions we use in constituting unique outcomes with people. In practice, though, people are likely to mention unique outcomes or demonstrate them spontaneously. In such situations, rather than asking any opening space questions we can simply respond to what a person has mentioned, most likely with a preference question or a construction question.

If we don't observe openings to alternative stories or if the people we work with don't tell us about them, we can co-construct them by asking:

1. questions about *unique outcomes* that have occurred.
2. Or, we can ask about unique outcomes in the realm of imagination through *hypothetical experience questions*,
3. questions that ask about different *points of view*, and
4. *future oriented questions*.

We group these different types of unique outcome questions together under the name "opening space" because each inquires about the possible presence of an opening that, if taken, may lead to an alternative story.

Unique Outcomes

Inviting a search for exceptions to the problematic story is the most straightforward way to contribute to constructing an opening:

- Has there ever been a time when the arguing could have taken control of your relationship, but it didn't?
- Have the two of you ever stood up to some of these cultural prescriptions and decided to do something your own way instead?
- In what situations do you make decisions easily?

A unique outcome does not have to be a triumph over the problem. A thought at odds with the problematic story, doing something differently in response to the problematic story (even if the problem eventually dominates), or making preparations to have a different relationship with the problem can all be unique outcomes. When asking questions along these lines it's often useful to acknowledge the hold of the problem so that people know that its presence and influence are understood. Often this frees them to describe the instances in which it doesn't have a hold:

- Even though the bulimia convinced you it was too dangerous to go out to eat with other people, did you hold out against its arguments longer than you had at other times?
- I understand that the fears are still keeping your life very narrow and confined, but do you have a sense that you are working up to changing that? Can you tell me what's giving you that sense?
- So in the last two weeks the conflict continued, but were there any points at which, even for a moment, you felt hopeful?

When direct inquiry about unique outcomes fails to open space, we try other types of questions.

Hypothetical Experience Questions

If people have difficulty locating exceptions to dominant stories in their lived experience, "hypothetical experience questions" may help them imagine those experiences (Penn, 1985; Penn & Sheinberg, 1991). In the first story we told in this chapter, Kathy's answers to hypothetical experience questions created an opening for an alternative story. Once Kathy imagined herself doing something that was at odds with the dominant story—going to school—she and other family members could see her past in light of that imagined experience. She entered an alternative story that supported the imagined-but-experientially-real experience.

Here are some hypothetical experience questions:

- If one of your children had been born with a serious illness, do you think you would have pulled together to face the crisis? . . . And how do you think you would have functioned as a team?
- What would happen if you didn't take all the responsibility for child care? For example, if you didn't get up when your son couldn't sleep, what would happen?
- If you were to discover with certainty that your mother works overtime not to avoid your Little League games, but to provide the things you want for your future, how would that knowledge change things for you?

Point of View

We have a colleague who has more referrals than she can see. She sometimes asks us if we have time to see a person or family who has been referred to her. We have discovered that, if we are very interested in working with the people she describes, although she originally set out to refer them, by the end of the conversation she decides to see them herself. The way we make sense of this experience is that she has entered our point of view. If we are interested or excited about working with the particular family or person, she begins to see the individuals involved as we do, to notice what is interesting or exciting to us about them. Even though she is short on time, she does not want to lose the opportunity.

Similarly, when a person is living a problem-saturated story, the problems sometimes blind her to unique outcomes, as time constraints blind our colleague to what might be interesting. Since she is living a particular story, she tends to see all of her experience in line with that story. People outside of the story are more free to make different meaning of the events she experiences. As the person considers the meaning from someone else's perspective, she can adopt the meaning as her own (or at least try it on). It may provide an opening to an alternative storyline.

Questions such as these ask about other points of view:

- What would your grandmother say about how you're coping with this dilemma?[7]
- Can you understand how from my point of view you are ready to take on this responsibility? What do you think I've noticed that makes me think so?
- What do you think your daughter is learning as she sees your husband making almost all of the decisions for the family? Is that what you want for her? What would you prefer her to see? Have there been times she has seen what you describe?
- Are there certain friends who influence you more when it comes to taking drugs? Do you have other friends and associates who are more of an influence to do otherwise? What is the difference in how those two groups experience you? What characteristics does one group see that the other doesn't?
- What are you aware of about yourself that the fighting has blinded your family to?

Different Contexts

If someone is living a story dominated by helplessness he probably thinks of himself as a helpless person. Even though there have been countless events in his life that don't fit with his story, these events may not be part of what he thinks of as his life. Since people are living stories, not simply reporting them, problematic stories often blind them to the significance of contexts other than the problem-saturated one. In other words, problems often stand between people and their knowledge of themselves in such a way that they lose preferred aspects of their identities. Since problems are constructed in and supported by particular contexts, unique outcomes can often be constituted by asking about other contexts.

- I understand that anger has really come between the two of you as you work on building a business together and has caused you to say things that are not representative of how you most want to be. But I'm

---

[7]Linda Bailey-Martiniere (personal communication, 1995) has suggested asking questions from a grandmother's point of view.

wondering if there are other situations where you are able to keep anger in its place?

- Has laziness affected all the areas of your life or only school?
- I think I understand something about how self-doubt is robbing you of confidence at school. When we were just getting to know each other a little bit at the beginning, I got a different picture of you when you talked about playing basketball. Do you see how I got a different picture? (This question is also a point of view question.)

Different Time Frames

From my (JF) point of view, my grandfather had a glorious life. At the age of 16 he escaped the pogroms of Eastern Europe to arrive in this country with little money but close family connections. He was successful in his business endeavors, he had a wonderful 63-year marriage, he traveled extensively, he was self-educated and politically active, he had close relationships with family and friends and lived to see his children and grandchildren realize dreams that he helped them build. However, he spent the final years of his life in a nursing home, after losing his health and being afflicted by painful confusion about what was real, surrounded by strangers, bereft of almost all personal possessions. When I visited him in those last years, images of his earlier life would bombard me, torturing me with the comparison. I remember trying to explain to one of his attendants that the man in the nursing home wasn't really him. To her, though, the man I described wasn't really him. I don't know what was real for my grandfather at that time, but I hope that when he made meaning of his life, he drew on all the wonderful years of satisfaction, relationships, and accomplishments. Those are certainly the times that speak to *me* of who he was.

In asking questions to develop unique outcomes, we hold close the knowledge that the problematic stories that drive people to consult with us do not represent the entirety of their lives, even if they seem to fill the present. The following questions are examples of unique outcome questions about different times in people's lives:

- I hear that you experience this as a lifelong problem, but if you compare different times in your life, was there a time when desperation played a lesser role?
- At what time in your life did you feel most secure?
- During which period in your life were you least susceptible to panic? Was there a particular incident from that time that you thought of when I asked the question? Could you tell me about that incident?

In Chapter 6 we include a transcript of a therapy meeting that illustrates deconstruction and opening space questions. You may want to read it before moving on to other kinds of questions.

PREFERENCE QUESTIONS[8]

Since we co-construct alternative stories a bit at a time from experiences that do not fit with dominant, problematic stories, it is important that therapists check frequently to be sure that the direction or meaning of these experiences is preferred to that of problematic stories. This point may seem academic but we, at least, are not always right about what different people actually prefer.

For example, I (JF) recently saw a family that was referred to me by a colleague who had seen them for some time but was getting ready to move away from Chicago. As I caught up on the work they had done with my colleague, I discovered that 45-year-old Glenn was engaged in what he described as a lifelong struggle with severe depression. Family members told me about the effects of the depression on their lives and on the life of the family. They shared with me the knowledge they had gained about the depression—signs that it was beginning, what its boundaries were, and so on.

What stood out to me from this description was that, if the depression began at times, then it must also end. If it had boundaries, there were places outside of it. I began to ask about those aspects of their experience. I was quite interested in hearing about these depression-free times.

Family members, though, and particularly Glenn, seemed somewhat reluctant to enter wholeheartedly into this conversation. I asked, "Is this what you want to be talking about or is there something else?"

Glenn answered, "There are times when the depression isn't present in my life, and I think all of us agree that there are very good things about those times. But focusing on them has not been especially helpful."

"I think it's scary," added 13-year-old Karin.

I thought this was a curious comment, so I asked more about it and discovered that the ideas that Glen instead of the depression could be in charge of his life and that family members could have a part in making that happen were not ideas that family members preferred and in fact were ideas they considered to be dangerous. When they had tried these

---

[8]We are indebted to David Epston and Sallyann Roth (1994) for the name "preference questions." Previously, we were calling these questions "suitability questions" as they invite people to evaluate suitability, but we much prefer "preference."

ideas out in the past, the depression had taken Glenn and the family by surprise. No matter how strongly they believed it was a thing of the past, it would always rear up again.

Their experience told them that what worked best was to have a different relationship with depression. They didn't think that they could kick it out of their lives, but they did believe that they could coexist with it. They learned the early signs of its return and a number of things they could do to keep it at a "low level." It no longer took over completely but it had a place in their lives that required watchfulness and quick responses. "Sort of like a roach problem," explained Margaret, Glenn's partner. "It doesn't go away, but if you do something when you notice more of it, it doesn't get very bad."

Experiences such as these have taught us the importance of asking people what they prefer instead of assuming that we know. We ask preference questions throughout our interviews to make sure we are moving in people's preferred directions.

However, this is not just a simple matter of providing an occasion for people to make their preferences known. To choose a preference out loud is to commit oneself to a direction in life. Many of our questions such as, "Do you think dishonesty suits you best as a way of life or would you prefer a life of honesty?" ask that people pick between two possibilities.[9] When we pose these questions we are constructing particular dilemmas. People do occasionally tell us that neither possibility is preferred, but we suspect that much of the time people approach the two possibilities offered as though they really are the only two available choices and stretch to align themselves with one or the other.

As Karl Tomm (1993, p. 67) notes, "These kinds of questions, which juxtapose two contrasting options . . . and invite the client to state a preference, are obviously 'loaded.'" Tomm calls these "bifurcation questions" and believes that they are helpful in mobilizing and aligning a person's emotional responses. He writes that they create a bifurcation or branching of alternative meanings and alternative directions. When a person chooses one, different sets of emotion become oriented to each branch. Presumably, if a person stated that honesty suited her, not dishonesty, her negative emotions would become oriented to dishonesty, which could help her fight against it, and her positive emotions would become oriented toward honesty, helping her align with it.

At times, one of the branches is only implied. When we ask, "Do you

---

[9]When Michael White and David Epson have raised these questions around participation with problem lifestyles, they (Epston, 1989a; White 1986a, 1986b) have called them "dilemma questions" or "raising dilemmas."

consider this type of thinking to be helpful?" we are implying, "Or not helpful?"

Earlier, we did a lot of work with hypnosis and saw a great many people who wanted to stop smoking. When we asked them what was most helpful in stopping smoking, many people told us that making the commitment to stop was by far the most important element. In asking preference questions, we create a context for the making of commitments.

We often ask "Why?" after people have stated a preference. This invites people to justify their choices and describe their motivation, and in the course of their explanations, people have the opportunity to clarify and elaborate on their preferred directions in life, identities, and values.

The following are some examples of preference questions:

- Do you think this reputation should speak for you or do you think it would be better for you to speak for yourself?
- Is that a useful practice? How? Why?
- Does this idea suit you? Why?
- Do you think it's best for anger to run your life or for you to run your life? Why?
- Is this a good thing or a bad thing for you?

STORY DEVELOPMENT QUESTIONS

Once space has opened enough to reveal a unique outcome or preferred development, we can ask questions to develop the story of it. All of the questions we talk about in this chapter are used to invite the reauthoring of stories. By referring to "story development questions" in this section we are referring to that part of reauthoring that makes events into a story in the usual sense. That is, story development questions invite people to relate the process and details of an experience and to connect it to a timeframe, to a particular context, and to other people. In this way an event is expanded in space and time, it is peopled, and it is reexperienced in a detailed way. It becomes a story! Such stories can be constructed either from actual events or from hypothetical ones.

Our hope when we ask story development questions is that people will come to experience their lives and themselves in new ways as they focus on previously neglected and unstoried aspects of their experience, aspects that lie outside the realm of the problematic stories they find themselves caught up in when they seek therapy. To that end, it seems to be important that these stories be developed in ways that are compelling and experientially vivid (Freedman & Combs, 1993).

Process

In asking questions about process, we invite people to slow an event down and notice what went into it. As a person works to retrieve the sequence of important elements involved in a unique outcome, he relives it. In this process, he has the opportunity to create a map that will then be available to follow during future challenges. Since they ask people to review their own actions, these questions almost always contribute to stories of personal agency.

- What were the steps you took in doing this? What did you do first? Then what?
- How did you prepare yourself to see things in this new way?
- As you look back at this accomplishment, what do you think were the turning points that made this possible?
- Were there particular things that you said to yourself that supported this new resolve?
- How did you do it?

Details

Details help make an event vivid. Questions about detail offer people the opportunity to remember aspects of events that may have been neglected or forgotten. Full, detailed descriptions foster an intensity of experiential involvement that generalized accounts do not. This is true even for hypothetical events. Also, some of the different details brought forth may play a more significant role in the reauthoring than those details that are most readily remembered.

- What was the look on his face when you told him you won the award?
- What particular things would I have noticed if I were there when you two experienced this breakthrough?
- What was it like to grasp that award in your hands? Did you hear the sound of the crowd or make out any particular faces?
- What was happening in the rest of the room while you were coming to that realization?
- What exactly did she say when you told her the news?

Time

Finding the *historical antecedents* of unique outcomes and preferred developments can lend particular significance and credence to the preferred self-identity stories that result from this work. Often, unique outcomes have historical roots to which problems have blinded people. "History questions" can help people identify and reclaim them.

- Who would have predicted that you would have made this shift in your understanding? What would have led them to make this prediction? Would they recall a particular memory or event?
- When in the past has your daughter shown this kind of courage before?
- Was this a new development or do you have a history of speaking out in difficult situations? What situation comes to mind?

Asking *future-oriented* questions can extend alternative stories into the future, changing people's expectations about what is ahead for them and, as Peggy Penn (1985, p. 301) notes, they can " . . . cut into ideas of predetermination."

- What do you think your next step might be?
- Now that you've discovered these things about your relationship do you have a different vision of the future?
- Do these new developments inspire any predictions you might make about your son's future school career?
- Three months from now, who do you think will be most pleased by the consequences of this new understanding? What are the consequences that will please them so? (This question could also be listed under "people" on pp. 134–135.)

Questions that *contrast* the past and either the present or future emphasize the changes a story has taken over time.[10] In answering these questions, people can notice many changes and differences that they had been tending to take for granted.

- How is this different from what you would have done before?
- Okay, so this time you didn't let bulimia trick you into staying away from a social situation. How is that different from when bulimia controlled your life?
- You seem pretty pleased about the reports you're getting from John's teachers. What did it used to be like when you went to parent-teacher conferences? And now . . . ?

---

[10]David Epston uses these kinds of questions quite extensively. As people contrast what is happening in the present or what they plan for the future with the past, they seem to become more committed to the new direction.

Questions that *link the past, present, and future* dramatize the time-span and directionality of a narrative and add relevance to the events in different time frames.

- If we link the self-confidence from your past with your current ideas, where do you think you might go along these lines in the future?
- You said that in high school you stood up for yourself on a number of occasions and that just recently you've been back in touch with that ability and told your best friend what was on your mind. If we think of these events as a kind of trend in your life, what do you expect might happen next?
- Who from your past would have predicted this new development in your life? Knowing what he does about your past, if he were in on this current development, what would he predict about your future?

Context

Stories develop within particular contexts. Problematic stories may be coached or supported by different sociocultural contexts than preferred stories. As people construct alternative stories, new contexts may become important. Some narratives are more highly dependent on context than others, but every story has a setting. Asking questions about context can anchor a story to a particular place and situation. Sometimes questions about context invite people to extend stories into new places and new situations. Context questions can also invite people to notice the role their culture plays in bringing forth and supporting preferred stories.

- Are there particular organizations or contexts that would support your new resolve?
- Where did this happen? What was going on at the time?
- Has your newly discovered competence shown itself more on the job or at home?
- Would you say the circumstances supported your doing this? How?
- Is this process you describe part of your culture? What is the knowledge from your culture about how one should meet these kinds of challenges? [11]

People

Most any story has more than one character. "People questions" invite individuals to re-collect the cast of characters contributing to an emerg-

---

[11]The Just Therapy Team in Wellington, New Zealand have worked extensively in helping people reclaim cultural stories and knowledge. See Law (1994), Tamasese and Waldegrave (1993), Tapping et al. (1993), and Waldegrave (1990) for accounts of this process.

ing narrative or to consider how particular people could play a role in the development of a story. These questions point to the importance of other people in alternate narratives. They also invite people "to consider the effects of their alternative stories in the lives of other people — family, friends, sometimes even strangers.[12] Since meaning is constructed in social interaction, it fits for stories to be "peopled."

- Who played a part in your taking back your life for yourself?
- Who will be first to notice that you've conquered this fear? How will it affect him?
- Has your correspondence with your mother played a part in this? What's the most important thing that she has written to you?
- How long do you think the rest of the family will have to see you following the rules before they relax about this change?
- If you keep your brother in your heart as you face this problem, what difference will it make?

Hypothetical Event Questions

We can also construct a story that builds on a unique outcome by adding details, process, time, context, and people from the realm of imagination[13] by asking about hypothetical events or circumstances. Future questions are always about hypothetical events, but they can be very important in constructing actual lives.

Diane Chisman, a member of the Evanston Family Therapy Center training team, pioneered a way to use hypothetical questions. After people make a distinction about themselves or their relationships that they find useful, Diane invites them to author a speculative history. For example, in a therapy conversation with Diane, Nadine and Hank realized that when they talked together about parenting they both were more confident about parenting. Because Renee had been born in Nadine's previous marriage, dominant ideas of what it means to be a "real" father had kept Hank from expressing his ideas about parenting. Dominant ideas about the responsibilities of motherhood had convinced Nadine that Renee was her total responsibility. The two did not collaborate, although each of them often felt overwhelmed and alone. When they realized that they would both like to share ideas and negotiate about their parenting of Renee, Diane asked them hypothetical questions to develop a speculative history. These were questions such as, "If you had

---

[12]Besides the importance of people who are part of stories, we recognize the importance of recruiting audiences for stories; that is, letting people in on the developments in a person's life. See Chapter 9 for questions that can be used in this regard.

[13]See Roth and Chasin (1994) for a description of narrative work carried out primarily in the realm of imagination through dramatic enactment, rather than questions.

known how well you could share and negotiate parenting ideas and how much you would both like it back when you first were married, how would things regarding Renee have been different between then and now?"

Once such a history is established, people can speculate on process, details, context, and people. These hypothetical pasts, once experienced, often have real effects on people's present lives.

The following are examples of "hypothetical event questions" that can be used in story development:

- If your mother had not died, how do you think growing up would have been different for you?
- If you were to take on such a project what would you do first?
- What do you imagine you would look like as a student? Would you change your style?

MEANING QUESTIONS

Through story development questions, people plot the action and content of their preferred stories. Through meaning questions, we invite people into a reflecting position from which they can regard different aspects of their stories, themselves, and their various relationships. These questions encourage people to consider and experience the implications of unique outcomes, preferred directions, and newly storied experiences. In naming the meanings of these experiences, they are constructing them.

When Martha came to therapy she described the problem as a sense of not fitting in or being cared about. She thought this had to do with two very significant life experiences. First, her mother died when she was 14 and she believed her mother was the one person who really loved her. Second, she was biracial. Her ethnic heritage was not obvious from her appearance, a fact which led her frequently to wonder what difference it would make in people's perceptions of her if they knew. She often felt that she didn't fit into either of her parents' cultures. To deal with the feelings of not fitting in or being cared about, Martha routinely made accommodations to other people's ideas. She often stayed involved in unsatisfying relationships because she thought they were better than being alone.

At one point she surprised herself at a job interview by basing her answers on what *she* thought rather than on her predictions of what the interviewer might want to hear. I (GC) asked her a meaning question about this: "What does it say about what's important to you that you said what you thought at the interview instead of what the interviewer might want to hear?" She thought about my question for several moments and then said, "I guess I only want to be hired for myself, not to play somebody else."

This was a significant performance of meaning for Martha. She said that *she would not have known this about herself* if she hadn't reflected on the interview in the way that the question invited her to. This self knowledge allowed her to identify other experiences where she had stood behind herself, and these, too were significant to discover. Through these discoveries Martha introduced herself to a different side of herself. We do not mean to imply that this performance of meaning was all that was needed or was even a turning point in the therapy. It was, however, a significant experience that helped Martha recognize how, although dominant ideas and practices in the culture had excluded her experience and her identity, she could choose to stand behind her own thoughts and identity and that this choice was personally rewarding.

We ask meaning questions about the answers to "opening space," "preference," and "story development questions." We also ask "opening space," "preference," and "story development questions" in relation to the answers to "meaning questions." Meaning questions are woven in and out of these other kinds of questions, especially story development questions.

In addition to asking about the general meaning and implications of stories as they unfold, we also ask about personal qualities, relationship characteristics, motivation, hopes, goals, values, beliefs, knowledge, and learnings that people derive from their developing narratives.

Meaning and Implications

Questions about *meaning and implications* are the most open-ended kind of meaning question. The answers may well speak of personal characteristics or values or one of our other listed categories. Through these questions people make meaning in whatever way makes sense to them.

- What does it mean to you that your partner would do this?
- If you were to apply this knowledge in your life now, in what context would it make the most difference? What difference would it make?
- What does this new perspective tell you about yourself?
- What is the significance for you as a family that you are here together talking about this new development?

Characteristics and Qualities

In asking about *characteristics and qualities* of people and relationships, we are focusing meaning on self-image or "relationship-image."

These questions are very helpful in updating the identity of a person or relationship to fit with a developing alternative story.

- What does it say about you as a person that you would do this? What characteristics does it show?
- In the light of having accomplished this together, how would your partner describe the kind of relationship you have?
- What qualities are evident to you about your son now that you've heard the steps he has taken to put temper out of his life?

Motivation, Hopes, and Goals

Questions about *motivation, hopes, and goals* invite people to notice how particular developments reflect larger life projects. Constructing the two as related adds to the significance of these developments.

- What do you think motivated him to take that step?
- Do you think the way that you two stuck to the task is reflective of what you hope for yourselves as a couple?
- We've just listed a number of things that you went ahead and did on this project. Does reviewing this make your goals in this area clearer? What would you say your goals are?

Values and Beliefs

Questions about *values and beliefs* can invite people to look beyond specific events and reflect on their moral, ethical, or spiritual dimensions. I (JF) consulted with a family for one two-hour meeting and six weeks later heard from Elizabeth, the daughter. The members of the family were white, middle-class Catholics of Irish descent. When Elizabeth became engaged to Jared, a Muslim engineering student from Iran, fear captured the family. The fear seemed to be fueled by the movie, "Not Without my Daughter" about an Iranian man married to an American woman. The Iranian man in the movie seemed to be a loving husband when in this country, but became an abusive stranger when the family visited Iran. The American woman barely escaped with the couple's child. A second phenomenon stoking the fear was a flurry of calls from family and friends, all of whom knew people who knew other people in American-Iranian relationships that had turned out to be disastrous. Thirdly, the church would not recognize a marriage such as the one Elizabeth was contemplating.

For the purpose of this illustration, I'll limit my comments to a brief portion of our phone call six weeks after the consultation. Elizabeth called to report that her parents were actually getting to know Jared, something they had not been interested in doing previously. I asked what she thought made the difference so that this could happen. She said that the most important thing was the way her parents answered a particular question. The question I asked was, "You've told me that you made up your mind to have nothing to do with this marriage; yet you're here, seeking a consultation. What do you value that has led you to seek therapy?"

"When they thought about that question, it was like they melted." Elizabeth said. "They had been frozen, turned against me for months, but when they heard that question, they started talking about how much they loved me, how they wanted to be part of my future, how they wanted the best for me, and it was like I had my parents back. After that, they began doing some things to actually get to know Jared. Now, Mom calls their house the United Nations."

With these questions we ask people how unique outcomes reflect their values and beliefs:

- Why does this new way of thinking suit you better than the old way?
- From what I've heard, what would I say you value in friendships?
- Now that we've reviewed what happened at your daughter's school, what do you think she must believe to have taken the stand she took?

Knowledge and Learnings

Since we often see therapy as an "insurrection of lost knowledges," we believe that it is important to bring forth people's specific local knowledge concerning unique outcomes and preferred directions in life. This is especially true when dominant cultural knowledge has played a hand in the constitution of their problem-saturated stories. Here are some questions we might ask to highlight learnings and knowledge that counter the problem:

- As you think back on that event, what did you know about your relationship then that somehow you have lost track of since?
- Is there something you can learn from this that might be important in other aspects of your life?
- When you see how far you've come what do you learn about yourself?
- As you reflect on this incident, what do you know as a result of it that "the friends of self-hatred" wouldn't want you to know?

STORY CONSTRUCTION

We could think of "story development questions" and "meaning questions" as our questions for story construction (rather than deconstruction or opening space). They build on unique outcomes, inviting people to use unique outcomes and preferred experiences as a basis for developing alternative stories and meanings.

Although we see the stories that develop in therapy as people's own, we have also thought about something that Karl Tomm (1993) points out in a discussion of Michael White's work. He writes that White picks the events he invites people to story and that the picking powerfully determines the kind of stories that will be constructed. The questions therapists ask clearly play a part in which events, both lived and imagined, will become storied. The unique outcomes that become candidates for story development are chosen by therapists when they ask more questions about them, but they are also chosen by the people we work with when they name them as preferred developments in response to preference questions.

Our values, the narrative metaphor, and our experience influence both our choice of questions and our decisions about which "sparkling events" to focus on. Since our choices have a hand in shaping the kinds of stories that are constructed, it is important that we situate ourselves; making our values, ideas, and the experiences that they are based in clear enough that people can understand that they are not neutral (White, 1995). We offer our ideas as ideas based in particular experiences, not as truth claims. We also invite the people we work with to ask questions about our questions and our intentions as we work with them. (See Chapter 10 for a more detailed account of this process.)

In therapy, particular strands of narrative are selected and thickened by weaving back and forth between story development and meaning-making. That is, as someone begins to develop an alternative story, we ask questions that invite her to perform meaning on that story. We may then ask what story developments result from the meaning that emerges, and so on, so that a tapestry of story developments and their meanings is woven. In Chapter 6 we will offer a transcript that illustrates this weaving process.

We'd like to point out that our terms "story development questions" and "meaning questions" are different from those adopted by Michael White from Jerome Bruner (1986). White (1991, 1995), followed by many other therapists, uses the terms "landscape of action" where we use story development and "landscape of consciousness" where we use meaning. He also uses a third category, "experience of experience" for questions asking people to adopt another's point of view.[14] Rather than putting these questions in a separate category, we have incorporated

---

[14]We have described using these questions earlier in this chapter under "point of view" when our intention is opening space.

them under "story development questions" or "meaning questions" according to our purpose in asking them. That is, we call these questions either story development or meaning questions, depending on whether they develop the story or its meaning from another person's point of view. For example, we would call the question, "If I had been there and seen you take that step, how do you think I would describe what had happened?" a story development question, and the question, "If I then were to tell someone what I saw in you that led you to take that step, what qualities do you think I would name?" a meaning question.

WHAT TO ASK WHEN

We worry that in presenting a list of types of questions in a particular sequence we might be giving the impression that these questions are meant to be asked in that sequence. It does seem to be helpful for some people to have a particular order in mind when learning and practicing how to use questions like these, and, as orders go, the order we have written them in is not bad. We want to emphasize, though, that other orders may work just fine.

We begin by getting to know people a bit as people, not in relation to their problems. As Vicki Dickerson and Jeff Zimmerman (1993, p. 229) point out, "This is an important step in understanding the family members as persons separate from the problem and as experts in their own lives."

Then, we've found it useful and satisfying to follow people's interests. Often, the conversation naturally moves to what brought them to therapy. If it doesn't, we can inquire. We then usually listen to a description of the problem, [15] and as we listen we begin at some point to ask deconstruction questions.

Recently, when we were presenting a workshop with a number of colleagues (Adams-Westcott et al., 1994), [16] someone asked, "How many deconstruction questions should you ask?" Jeff Zimmerman answered, "As many as it takes." We used to systematically ask deconstruction questions (especially "relative influence questions"), but now we are likely to start asking "story development questions" anytime there is an opening. We can always go back to deconstructive listening and questioning if the situation calls for it.

We may not use some types of questions at all in a particular inter-

---

[15] We discussed this under "deconstructive listening" in Chapter 3.

[16] Our colleagues were Janet Adams-Westcott, Vicki Dickerson, John Neal, and Jeff Zimmerman.

view.[17] We tend to use deconstruction and opening space questions in the early part of any conversation about a particular problem. We use preference questions throughout interviews, particularly in relation to unique outcomes. Once a preferred unique outcome is identified, we ask story development and meaning questions, often alternating between them or asking several story development questions and then a meaning question and then more story development questions. However, there are many exceptions to this generalized shape. For example, we sometimes omit preference questions, relying instead on voice tone, facial expression, and past statements of preferences for guidance.

If family members begin therapy by describing what they want and hope for, we usually respond to that as a unique outcome and begin inviting them to author that story—perhaps never listening to or deconstructing a problematic story. Alternatively, we might ask about a problematic story through story development questions that contrast the past with the present or future, so that the authoring of the alternative story and telling of the problematic story are interspersed throughout therapy.

Sometimes, we move between problematic stories and alternative stories in order to connect with people's experience. Perhaps a person begins to live an alternative story and then something stops him. He feels blocked or pulled back. In that situation, we can either ask about the alternative story, which may be enough to reengage him in it, or we can listen and ask deconstructive questions about what is pulling him back. For some people, the second choice is more fitting. They seem to reauthor a strand of story, then identify another problem, reauthor that strand, and so on, until they are fully immersed in the alternative stories.

In Chapters 8 and 9 we discuss ideas for developing stories even further and for recruiting audiences for stories. Once these processes are all underway, it is not uncommon for people to begin to use therapy primarily as a context in which to tell their developing story. We continue to ask questions, but our role becomes more and more that of a listener and scribe—documenting, witnessing, and performing meaning on the preferred story as it develops.

As people become more and more involved in living alternative stories, they generally decide at some point that they can do just fine without therapy. Often, instead of making a single definitive decision to "terminate," they want to leave the door open for an occasional consultation. Either way, since we negotiate one therapy meeting at a time at the

---

[17]There are also many kinds of questions that we haven't referred to at all. "Internalized other questioning," developed by David Epston and Karl Tomm (Epston, 1993b) and "Saying hullo again" questions, developed by Michael White (1988b) to use with people suffering from grief, are among them.

end of each meeting, ending therapy is usually a "natural" and easy process.

In "final meetings" we usually ask people questions that invite them to review the story as it has developed—especially questions contrasting the present and past. We also ask future-oriented questions. And sometimes we have a celebration!

Questions in Action:
Three Transcripts

Effective therapy must be continually re-created in the context of participant interaction. Otherwise it quickly deteriorates into a series of canned routines.

> — *Jay S. Efran and Leslie E.*
> *Clarfield, 1992, p. 211*

. . . client and therapist are seen as mutually creating meaning, and mind becomes a mutual intersubjectivity. . . . A new narrative, a new story is created.

> — *Harlene Anderson and Harry*
> *Goolishian, 1990a, p. 162*

To provide a feel for how the kinds of questions that we have categorized in the preceding chapter are actually asked in therapy, we offer three transcripts. This first transcript focuses on deconstructing and opening space, the second emphasizes story development and meaning, and the third shows how all five major types of questions — deconstruction, opening space, preference, story development, and meaning — work together.

LAZINESS? AN EXTERNALIZING,
OPENING SPACE CONVERSATION

This highly edited version of a single-session consultation that I (GC) did with Rick and his mother, Allison, shows deconstruction and opening space questions in action. Previously a good student, this year 13-year-old Rick had fallen behind in his homework. The authorities at school had tried various strategies to get Rick to improve in this area, all to no avail. A week before our conversation, they had called Allison in for a special meeting in which they explained that Rick was so far behind that it was seriously affecting his grades. If something didn't change he would probably have to repeat eighth grade. They highly recommended that she seek family therapy for the problems with Rick.

In the first part of this conversation, which does not appear in the transcript, Allison filled me in on the concerns that the school authorities had voiced. Our transcript begins at the point where I turn from Allison and begin to talk with Rick.

As you read this transcript, look for what is externalized, how it becomes externalized, and how the effects of the externalized problem are explored. What unique outcomes stand out for you? How were they brought forth?

GENE   It sounds like the school says you have an attitude problem. I'm wondering if you think you have a problem of any kind and, if so, whether you think it's an attitude problem, or whether you would say it's some other kind of problem.

RICK   I don't know how to even see the problem. I would say, I think I'm *lazy*, because I don't really do a lot of homework. And I think, my mom, she grounded me from the TV for the rest of the school year because I got put in this program. And I'm getting punished in the class, and now I'm grounded every day at home. So . . .

GENE   What do you think it is that stops you from doing your homework?

RICK   I don't really want to do it.

GENE   You used the word "lazy" before.

RICK   Yeah.

GENE   Do you think laziness is what it is?

RICK   Partially.

GENE   Or is it lack of desire? . . . I mean, how would you describe what it is that goes on?

RICK   I don't know. I'm lazy. I know that. I just don't want to do it.

GENE   Okay. Are there other places in your life, other than the homework, that the laziness causes problems, that the laziness enters in, or is laziness only a problem in regards to homework?

RICK   I would think just school work. I don't really know of any other places laziness would become a factor.

GENE   So, for instance, laziness is not something that causes you problems in terms of basketball?

RICK   (laughing) No.

GENE   You're perfectly willing to work hard and try to do better and put in a lot of time and practice and that kind of stuff in basketball?

RICK   Yeah.

GENE   Okay. . . . What's the difference? What is it about basketball that makes you be able to keep laziness from entering in?

RICK   I like basketball. I don't like school.

GENE   So it's hard to do stuff? So laziness kind of comes into the picture when something that you don't like to do is involved? Have there been times or instances in your life when there was something that you didn't like to do, but you knew you needed to do it, that the laziness didn't stop you from doing it?

RICK   (pause) Not that I can think of. (pause)

GENE   Well . . . for instance, it sounds to me like sometimes you *do* get some of your homework done.

RICK   Yeah.

GENE   So that would say to me that laziness doesn't totally take over, that sometimes you're able to take control of the situation and get something done. Is that true? Or not?

RICK   (with agonized intonation) It's like I don't want to be doing homework for three, four hours a night. Like last night, if I didn't have my homework done I was going to get detention. So, I was doing homework for three and a half hours! (pause, then in a calmer voice) Got it all done. I don't want to sit . . .

GENE   So last night, you got all your homework done?

RICK   Yeah.

GENE   Now was that just one day's homework or was that several days' homework?

RICK   Several days' homework.

GENE   Okay. So the three and a half hours was because it was more than one day's homework?

RICK   Yeah. It was probably about . . . it would have taken me, just for the regular day's homework, probably about two hours.

GENE   Is that your estimate of how much time you'd have to put in every day if you wanted to stay caught up with all your homework? About two hours?

RICK   Oh, I'd say . . . well, it really depends. Depends on what we're doing in the class.

GENE Yeah. But you know your classes and I don't. So I'm just trying to get some kind of rough idea of a . . .

RICK If I wanted to stay caught up every day?

GENE Yeah.

RICK (pause, then a long exhalation) Probably about an hour and a half. Two hours. Somewhere in there.

GENE So it sounds to me like if you really want to play basketball — and it sounds like you *do* want to play basketball — that that's going to mean . . . in order to play basketball, you're going to have to put in an hour and a half to two hours a day on homework. Am I understanding that correctly?

RICK Yep.

GENE Does it make any difference to you to think of it in terms of sort of maybe an extension of basketball practice, or what you've got to do to be able to play basketball? Does that in any way help you to stand up to the laziness?

RICK (hesitantly) Ye-ahhh-uh.

GENE I can't . . . that was one of those "yeahs" that I can't be sure whether you're saying it because you really believe it or because it seemed like it was a good idea and you didn't want to disappoint me.

(Allison smiles and laughs.)

RICK Oh no. (laughter) Well . . . I believe it . . . sort of.

GENE You believe it, but you're not sure, even though you believe it, that you'll be able to put it into action?

RICK Yeah.

(We skip to later in the conversation. Rick has explained about a special detention program he has been placed in.)

GENE So it sounds to me like this laziness — for lack of a better word — right now, one of the effects it's having in your life is that it's making you be in this special program. Right?

RICK Uh-huh.

GENE What do they call this program?

RICK Resource.

GENE What all's involved in being in Resource?

RICK You got to have your homework done.

GENE And if you don't have your homework done, then . . .

RICK Every three assignments that you don't have done, you get a 20-minute detention.

GENE So the laziness also is getting you detentions?

RICK Yep.

(We skip ahead again. Rick has explained that he is only one assignment behind now. He is in the middle of explaining how far behind he was before. His teacher had listed all his missing assignments on the chalkboard, and . . .)

RICK . . . I took up half the chalkboard in missing assignments!

GENE (laughing) Wow!

RICK From before I was put in the class.

GENE So you've actually caught up a lot then if you're only like one . . .

RICK I'm missing one, and I'll try to do that tonight.

GENE And how long have you been in the program?

RICK (looks to Allison)

ALLISON This is your second week. Right?

RICK Yeah, I think I've been in for ten days or something like that.

ALLISON Yeah, it's the second week.

GENE Wow.

RICK I don't really want to say how many I've missed in front of my mom, but I was missing 26 assignments!

ALLISON (taking a deep breath) Oh my.

GENE Can you see how that's kind of a surprise to me? I mean, I've been sitting here talking to you like . . . I mean, you had me convinced that laziness had so taken over that you still weren't working very hard. But, if I'm hearing you right, in addition to all your daily assignments that you've been getting every day since you've been in the program, you've also caught up 25 other assignments!

RICK Uh-huh.

GENE Is that right?

RICK Yep.

GENE Well, can you see how that gives me sort of two different pictures of you?

RICK One of the reasons I did it, was because for every three of those assignments you get a 20-minute detention, and there was 26 assignments, so that's about nine times. . . . That's 210 minutes of assignments! So, I did a lot of those and it took me four days to make all those up. And then, I'm still behind one, but I have to do that tonight.

GENE Well, what do you think? Do you think you're going to do it tonight? Or do you think laziness is going to take over and keep you from doing it?

RICK I was doing it on the way over here, in the car.

GENE Hmmm . . . So, does that surprise you? That you've been able to get that much done in that short a time?

RICK (grinning slyly) Yeah.

This was the only time I saw Rick. In a consultation with Allison on another matter six months later, she told me that Rick was still caught up in all his homework and he was the starting power forward for his school's eighth grade basketball team.[1]

WHAT A DIFFERENCE A YEAR MAKES: AN ILLUSTRATION OF STORY DEVELOPMENT AND MEANING QUESTIONS

The couple in this example first came to see me (JF) one year before this meeting, having already filed for divorce. Their marriage had deteriorated in the two years since their first child had been born.

Maggie's description of the situation was that after Matthew was born she began to see Richard in a new light. She had almost total responsibility for Matthew's care, while Richard's life had changed very little. Maggie began to see him as selfish and irresponsible.

Richard experienced Maggie as the one who had changed. Before Matthew was born he found her to be enthusiastic, energetic, and sup-

---

[1]Although we did not talk about this explicitly at the time, Allison later told me that the expectations that accompanied her to the therapy meeting included the strong possibility of mother blaming. Assuming that the problem was the problem, rather than that Allison or her parenting practices were the problem, made a difference in Allison's story of herself as a parent.

portive. Although he continued doing what he had always done, he experienced her as having little but anger and criticism for him. She had wanted a child and he had helped her make her dream come true, but it seemed to be backfiring for both of them.

Through deconstruction questions Maggie and Richard began to see the role that patriarchal patterns in the culture had played in shaping their relationship. Although they had resisted many of these patterns in the early part of their marriage, after Matthew was born these patterns took over, determining their roles and responsibilities as mother and father and robbing them of much of what had been unique in their relationship. The roles especially did not fit for Maggie—there was less room for her voice and desires than for Richard's—and this lack of fit encouraged blame and anger to come between them.[2] The blame and anger led to distance and fear.

As Maggie and Richard unpacked this sequence of events they decided that they wanted to be in charge of their relationship, rather than relying on the patriarchal gender roles that were clearly not working well for them. They did a lot of talking about how they would like their relationship to be and a lot of renegotiating about tasks and responsibilities. This was not easy. The habits that they now thought of as bad had made quite an inroad in their lives, and they sometimes found themselves pulled back into old ways of relating, in which anger and fear took over.

At the time of the following conversation, the couple had seen me once every three to five weeks for a year. Although they had stopped all divorce proceedings, a point of contention that continued to come between them had to do with Richard's family. When they visited, Richard's family paid lots of attention to Richard and Matthew, and very little to Maggie. Feelings of being a nonperson or invisible dominated Maggie's experience. Richard was more easily pulled back into old ways of relating to Maggie in the context of his family, and worry about how she would be treated kept Maggie from relaxing at all.

There had also been disagreement between Richard's parents and Maggie about how they should treat Matthew and about what they would encourage him to do. Much of this disagreement centered around differences in religious beliefs and practices. In visits to his childhood home, old habits, including religious practices, seemed to capture Richard. This involvement with old ways of doing things kept him from supporting Maggie to the extent they both thought would be fitting, and the lack of support paved the way for anger and distance between them.

Because discussion about visiting Richard's family resulted in insecu-

---

[2]See Zimmerman and Dickerson (1993) and Adams-Westcott (1993) for a discussion of the concept of "fit" in couples therapy.

rity, worry, frustration, and anger, the couple decided that Richard and Matthew would go without Maggie. They prepared for the visit by deciding together what Matthew could and couldn't do, and Richard was determined that through him the couple's desires for their child, rather than the ideas his parents had, would be honored.

During the visit, in a telephone conversation, Maggie learned that Matthew had taken part in a religious ritual that did not fit their beliefs. The discussion about this quickly gave anger and feelings of being misunderstood an opening to take over their relationship.

The transcript begins with Maggie's description of what transpired several hours after Richard and Matthew arrived back home. As you read it you may want to focus on the use of story development and meaning questions.

MAGGIE   I was ready to kill him on Sunday. I was absolutely ready to kill him. And I asked him to leave the house. And I was just livid and I knew I was livid. I just said, "Get out of the house. Go! Go! Just leave me alone. Get out of the house. I mean we first got Matthew to bed, and. . . . It was a trying night. The flight was late. He'd scheduled the flight really late. It was late. I had a very tired, cranky child on my hands. Then he lost one of his bags. Richard left it on the shopping cart and it fell off the cart. I had to wait with a very cranky kid in the car while he spent 45 minutes looking around the airport for it. So it was finally like two hours later, we get home, and I was just livid. I was getting madder and madder, and I told him I wanted him to leave. I wanted him out of my life. I wanted him out! I wanted him to leave, and specifically I wanted him to leave the house at that point in time. (She begins to direct her remarks to Richard.) And I knew I was very angry and I just thought, "Get out of here!"

The point at which I started hitting you at home was when you started defending the fact that your mother wasn't whining. I just . . . I mean it was like, defending your family was about the worst thing you could have done at that point.

JILL   So then . . . (pause) Now did you leave then, Richard?

RICHARD   No, I didn't.

MAGGIE   Well, what happened is (turns to Richard), you decided that you were going to bed and I decided . . . I slept on the couch. And I went to bed. And I had been up most of the previous night because I was so upset from Saturday night about this whole thing. And (turning to Jill) then we sort of agreed that he would stay out Monday night and I was teaching Tuesday and Thursday. He had a study group Wednesday so we wouldn't have to see each other.

JILL   Uh-huh.

MAGGIE   And then what happened is Monday, during school, Matthew had a real difficult time. I went on a field trip—Matthew is in nursery school now—I went on a field trip with him. And because of having gone on a field trip I was in the classroom, and at one point we were leaving the classroom and I walked back in for a minute to help another child get his coat on and Matthew just screamed. I mean he freaked out the minute I left him for a minute. And . . . he was very tired, and he was very upset, and he probably had some sense that Richard and I were fighting in the car, although the worst of the fight occurred after he had been put to bed and he was asleep. And we were in the kitchen, and we were just pretty far removed from his bedroom. But he just freaked out the minute I left the room and the teacher said, you know, "What's wrong with him?" I mean, you know, the teacher was upset. And Matthew hadn't had a nap in three days, and I realized that this whole thing was having a really bad effect on Matthew, so I called Richard up and said, "Look, you can come home tonight. I'll learn to live with this. You know what's important is Matthew's welfare, and we have to stop fighting." And so I told him he could come home Monday night. I mean come home at dinner time as opposed to staying out 'til I went to bed. And also, it sounds really crazy, but I realize that 95% of the time he does a good job. He's a wonderful parent. He does a lot of work around the house. He's done so much better in keeping up his end of things. It's just this one thing. *I freak out.*

JILL   Uh-huh.

MAGGIE   Vis-à-vis his family. I had tried so hard. Before he left, I gave him a list of 13 things I wanted him to do. I said, "Now you know Matthew's got medicine," because he has a little lung infection so he is on medicine. I said, "I want his medicine given to him. I want him to take naps. Make sure he has his chewing gum for the plane flight." (turns toward Richard) Actually, I forgot to mention the chewing gum, but I did give you some. And I was doing fine on Friday. I drove him to the airport. I went bike riding. I went out to a wonderful dinner. I worked all day Saturday. I went over to a friend's house Saturday night for dinner. I was doing fine on my own. I was taking care of myself. I thought I was doing okay, I really did. And I think I would have done OK on Sunday if he had just protected me from this whole incident that went on in New York. Umm . . .

JILL   Well, look. Can I just stop you for a minute? (Maggie nods.) Now, would you have said when you first came to see me . . . you said that 95% of the time that Richard is doing great. What would you have said before? What percentage would you have given before the 95%?

MAGGIE   25 to 30. (pause) Part of it was that he wasn't doing so great around the house. He wasn't doing so great with Matthew. He wasn't as attentive. I mean his behavior has changed a lot.

JILL   Yeah, that's a tremendous amount. And when you look back at that difference, what does that tell you? . . . (pause, Maggie looks puzzled) Well. let me just ask a different question. What do you think made it possible for Richard to go to 95%?

MAGGIE   Oh! I presume he wanted to stay in the marriage.

JILL   Uh-huh. Okay. So, the marriage was important enough that all those changes could happen, and knowing that, what implications does that have for you?

MAGGIE   Oh, I'm content to stay in this marriage, too. It's just . . .

JILL   Okay, wait. Before you go on . . . (to Richard) Were you aware of that? That Maggie is content to stay in the marriage, too?

RICHARD   Well . . . she wasn't content Sunday night, but by the next day she'd changed her tune.

MAGGIE   See, a year ago I would have been angry and angry and angry. Now I can say, "Okay, I really lost control. I got horribly upset. And I know what I got upset about, but it's a relatively small part of my daily life."

JILL   Okay. (turning to Richard) So, according to Maggie, you've changed 75% for the better. What percentage would you give her, over the same period of time?

RICHARD   Uh . . . (long pause) Gee, I don't know. I haven't really thought about it. . . .

JILL   Well, she just gave an example now that seemed really true to me, that a year ago this would have been something that would have lasted a long time and required all sorts of things to make a difference. So there are probably a lot of other things . . .

RICHARD   Just her recovery from that . . .

JILL   Right! Well, wouldn't you say . . .

RICHARD   It was definitely a remarkable change, and I don't know if it could have happened a year ago.

JILL   Okay. And what other things do you think are different about Maggie? That couldn't have happened a year ago?

RICHARD   Well, I think she's showing more appreciation for me and what I do, though I suppose that's . . . that's maybe because I'm doing more to be appreciated *for* rather than necessarily her changing. I don't know. I think she's . . . she's also been very supportive of me as I've gotten more active in my job search lately. And I don't know, she might have done so a year ago, but I'm feeling now she has a genuine interest in supporting me to help get a job that will be more satisfying to me.

JILL   The thing that seems really different to me is just how much. . . . It seemed like she was on guard more a year ago, and that she's really relaxed and warmer and more open. Do you agree with that? (Richard nods his head yes.) Okay. So, what percentage would you say that she has changed?

RICHARD   Uhh . . . I don't know . . . I'll give her 75 too.

JILL   Okay. Now . . .

MAGGIE   That's higher than I would have given myself.

JILL   What would you have given yourself?

MAGGIE   40.

JILL   What do you think . . .

MAGGIE   I think he's actually changed more than I have.

JILL   Uh-huh.

RICHARD   Actually I was going to say 50 but, I thought well . . . why be a piker? (All three laugh.)

JILL   But 50 is still more than she would give herself. (to Maggie) What do you think that he sees in you that you may not have recognized in yourself, that he would give you a larger percentage?

MAGGIE Maybe the warmth.

JILL Uh-huh.

MAGGIE I sort of think that just because he's doing so many more things I'm less hard on him. And I don't perceive that I'm warmer. I just perceive that he is getting into trouble less. Because I was always coming down on him because he was doing so little. And I was always having to say to him, "Now you've got to diaper Matthew, you've got to do this, you've got to do that." You know, now . . .

JILL Okay. I want to come back to how much Richard is doing in a minute, but I want to just ask you a different question first. Which is, umm . . . if you owned the warmth that Richard experiences in you for yourself, what difference would that make for your future?

MAGGIE If I owned the warmth?

JILL If you felt it, experienced it, believed it about yourself, the way that Richard experiences it in you. What difference would that make for your future?

MAGGIE My individual future?

JILL Well, whatever. Your individual future, your future together. . .

RICHARD If she believed that she had the warmth?

JILL Uh-huh.

MAGGIE I suppose it would give me more power.

JILL Hmm.

MAGGIE (musing to herself) If I felt I had this ability to be warm. (to Jill, louder) Actually, I *do* feel I have the ability to be warm and loving.

JILL Uh-huh.

MAGGIE And I am sometimes that way.

JILL Well, what kind of power exactly?

MAGGIE Well, it just gives me a wider range of tools I can use in dealing with people. That sounds awfully manipulative but . . . I mean, I could choose to be warm or I could choose not to be warm.

JILL You mean you'd have more flexibility, more range of possibility?

MAGGIE Yes. I guess.

JILL   And what difference do you think having more flexibility and range of possibilities would make within the relationship?

MAGGIE Well, it probably would help me adjust better, be more . . . bounce back better.

JILL   Uh-huh. Which is something you are already doing. So there would be even more of that?

MAGGIE Probably. Yeah.

JILL   Okay. Great. Now, so you said that . . . you already started to answer this question but you were a little bit ahead of me. How do you think that the changes that Richard has made support and contribute to your changes?

MAGGIE Well, the one thing that comes to mind is he has this habit now of calling me. . . . He calls me every day from work. And you know, usually it is five minutes. It's "How are you doing?" And it's like this really nice "I care about you" message. I remember that the first time I mentioned feeling bad about the fact that he never called me was when Matthew was eight months old, but it took a year and a half for it to sink in, and for some reason about a year ago, less than that, you started calling me every day. And um . . . now I got off the track. Where was I? What was your question again?

JILL   What is it in Richard that's been coaching the changes you've made?

MAGGIE Oh, Okay. I was using that as an example of, I thought that was a really sort of an "I care about you" message, which would make me more trusting of him and perhaps less guarded.

JILL   Right. Okay.

MAGGIE Do you want more examples?

JILL   Do you have more?

MAGGIE Well . . . he does very well in carrying out his projects. It is just incredible. (She turns to Richard.) I mean you haven't bounced a check. (She turns back.) The bills get paid on time. I haven't heard from the creditors. The cars get repaired. I mean, it's amazing. The cars even get washed and cleaned out. It's like magic! Matthew gets bathed three times a week, and that used to be a big thing. I'd have to say, "You know, c'mon, he hasn't been bathed in five days. You're responsible for bathing him and he smells." And now he gets bathed. And Richard's very reliable about picking up Matthew. A year ago I picked up Matthew on Tuesdays and Thursdays. I wasn't teaching as much, and I was doing much more then.

JILL Uh-huh.

MAGGIE We sort of shifted some of those duties. And so I don't have to worry about things. I don't have to worry about the money. I don't have to worry about the income taxes. You even said that we've got to review the budget. I was stunned! And it's such a relief not to have two part-time jobs and a two-year-old. I mean, it's wonderful that I have a three-year-old now. I mean, I just had so much more responsibility last year. And even more the year before that. And the responsibility was just so disproportionately allocated. And just because I think he's taking all these balls and running with them, makes me happier.

JILL Uh-huh. Yeah, I see what you mean. So, Richard, it sounds like you've become a much more active person who's doing a whole lot of initiating and also is more responsible. Do you feel that way?

RICHARD Yeah, I do feel more active and engaged. Taking a wider variety of responsibilities and fulfilling them. I feel good about that.

JILL Yeah.

RICHARD I'm glad to help ease the load on Maggie.

JILL And how do you think Maggie's changes support and help facilitate those changes in you?

RICHARD Well, by expressing warmth to me she makes me feel that the whole thing is worthwhile. So that's a great motivator right there.

MAGGIE Plus, I also compliment you when you do these things. I'm always you know, "Thanks for giving him a bath," and, "Gee, you got the car cleaned. It looks great!" I mean, I say a lot of those things.

RICHARD Yes, you're very good at that, and I do appreciate it.

JILL So this question is for both of you. Knowing all these new things about yourselves — (to Maggie) that you've really taken on warmth and become a person of flexibility and trust, and (to Richard) you've become a lot more responsible, active, and engaged — knowing those two things about yourselves and each other, how do you think that those things can begin to make a difference in the future about this 5% that is still problematic?

Maggie and Richard then began to develop a speculative future about relating to Richard's parents differently. They began to live this story a little bit at a time in the following months.

HEEDING THE TRUST, HAVING A VOICE: QUESTIONS IN ACTION

The transcript that follows demonstrates using all five types of questions we described in the previous chapter — deconstruction, opening space, preference, story development, and meaning questions.

It also records an important episode in Hollie's story. Hollie originally sought therapy more than seven years before this conversation. She first went to individual therapy and then she and Robert went to couples therapy because of feelings of uneasiness and distrust that plagued Hollie throughout most of their 19-year marriage. My (JF) understanding of the previous therapies were that they focused on Hollie changing her feelings. I met with Hollie and Robert as a couple twice before this conversation. I tried to listen deconstructively and understand the feelings of uneasiness and distrust — their impact on the couple and what may have contributed to them.

After these two meetings, while Robert was on a business trip, Hollie went to his office and went through his desk. She discovered that he had regularly been giving presents and very large sums of money to a woman, and that he was buying this woman airline tickets to the locations he had been flying to for "business meetings."

Hollie called the woman, who pleaded with Hollie to let her keep the car that Robert had bought her, and said, "You don't think that I'm the first, do you?"

Robert denied Hollie's discovery until the evidence became undeniable. Then there was crying, pleading, and silence between them. At the time of this meeting they were living together but discussing whether they would stay together.

Robert chose not to come back to therapy. Hollie came alone. This meeting took place two weeks after her discovery. During those two weeks we had met and talked about the discovery and what it meant to Hollie.

JILL Did the conversation we had last time leave you with any new thoughts or . . .

HOLLIE I was just thinking . . . thinking about when I was little and growing up and, you know, how things were. And I had a discussion with my sister after I saw you. We were just talking about the family as a whole. You know, she said that she escaped, and she thinks I didn't. And I don't think it's just because my marriage is in bad shape, but she said to me, and this was very strange, because I said, you know, that you and I were talking about how I grew up in such a sexist situation all around, you know? And I'm not sure how it tied in, but she brought up a situation and I said to her, "I don't know why very often this particular scene pops into my mind." And she said the same thing. This one time, our family—there's three of us kids, my mother and father. . . . When I was getting dinner, putting it on the table, I can't remember what was going on at that minute. My brother, my little brother and I always would be verbally fighting at the table. And all I can remember was that my father stood up at the table, took the entire table—food, dishes, everything, chairs—and knocked it over. Things were flying all over the place and there was broken glass everywhere. Everything was a wreck, and my mother just stood there and didn't say a word. And then, I don't know what happened. I guess she just cleaned everything up. It was just weird that we both said that we remembered this. What a scene.

JILL What significance did that have for you?

HOLLIE That my mother, when you think about it, she didn't like say anything, you know? She didn't take any stance, like say, "What the hell? What are you doing?" You know, "What's your problem? I know the kids are fighting," or whatever it was. But that was nothing. And it was like . . . it was bad. It was real bad. But she took it. She just tolerated it.

JILL What do you think must have been going on for her to just take it?

HOLLIE I guess, I don't know, she must have been scared. It was pretty scary.

JILL What do you think would have happened if she did take a stance?

HOLLIE I don't know. Maybe it would have been worse.

JILL Do you think there are ideas in the world that would keep her quiet that way?

HOLLIE I do. She probably thought she was supposed to calm everything down, protect us kids.

JILL So you think there are dictates in our culture for women not to take a stand, to put other people first?

HOLLIE I do.

JILL How do you think that model has affected you?

HOLLIE Well, I think it's made me. . . . When I think back in my relationship with Robert there were some situations where I never said a word, when I should have. I'd say to myself, "No, don't say anything because he's entitled to do this." I remember a situation years and years ago. We were married just over a year. And I heard him speaking to his brother on the phone. His brother wanted money. We didn't have any money. I was working and I'd pay the rent. We had no extra money. And he gave his brother money, and I remember thinking to myself, well, don't say anything. It's his brother. He should be able to give his brother money. But this was something that my husband was deciding without me, you know? He could say, "Holl, I know we don't have any money but, what do you think? Should I loan him or should I not? Can we not afford it?" I should have been able to say something, but I said, well, it's his brother, it's okay that he does this. But he never spoke to me. So I guess I feel like, seeing my mother as this model didn't make me say anything when I should say something. When I would not have been doing anything wrong in saying something.

JILL I wonder what models your mother had that put her in that situation?

HOLLIE Yeah. I'm sure it was even more than today.

JILL What do you see that encourages these ways of being?

HOLLIE Well, like we said last time, and that's what I was talking to my sister about, you know, these men's attitudes of women being like property and their being in charge and whatever they think . . .

JILL And what situations take women's voices away, given those attitudes that our society supports in men?

HOLLIE It's that whole model about relationships. That men are in charge, and you know, women can't say anything.

JILL   And how do you think that model has affected you?

HOLLIE   Well, I mean, I've done everything. All the things that I've done, you know, given, done, or what not. I've always been the one to give and, I mean, it feels good to do and give of yourself. I don't feel good about it now because I feel like I was just kicked in the face . . .

JILL   Do you think that model of relationships where you do all the giving and doing and he has the say — is that what you want for yourself?

HOLLIE   No. I don't. I just thought I was being loving . . .

JILL   Do you think that model of the woman always giving and the man having the say tricks people into not behaving in ways that suit them, by thinking that's what you have to do to be loving?

HOLLIE   Yeah, I guess. I didn't think of it before but, it looks like it.

JILL   Um-hum. Okay. So you said that model of relationships sort of left you without a voice?

HOLLIE   Yeah.

JILL   Do you see that in other areas of your life, or is it mostly just in your marriage?

HOLLIE   Um, I see it sometimes, you know, where I won't say anything or I won't. . . . You know, maybe I'm better at it now than I used to be, speaking up when I think I should. But it's still difficult.

JILL   When you say that you're better at it, where do you see . . . does any particular incident come to mind where you've been able to break out of this model?

HOLLIE   Yeah, I mean, I'll be in situations sometimes where, you know, something might go on and I'll just . . . instead of letting it pass completely, I notice I'm being taken advantage of. I might let it pass for a little while and think about it more, and then go back to it. Whereas before I would just let it ride and forget about it. Still, sometimes, I think I get frustrated. Maybe I do let it ride and I forget about it. But I think I . . . I think I seize the opportunity more now.

JILL   Good. Okay. Do you have a particular time when you have seized the opportunity?

HOLLIE   Um . . . well, I can think of a few situations, but I think one that has a lot of bearing is when my mother invited this disgusting uncle I have for the holidays.

JILL   Yes.

HOLLIE   And it took everything out of me to say to my mother, "If you have him," I said, "I'm not going to be around, or if it's going to be at my house, I don't want him there." Maybe it was . . . I don't know what holiday. I said, "If you want him here, you have him at your house or we'll have the holiday at my house the first night. Tell him not to come in until the second night, because I don't want to be around him." It took everything out of me to tell her that.

JILL   But you did it.

HOLLIE   I did it.

JILL   How did you get yourself to do that?

HOLLIE   Um, I don't know.

JILL   What went into that?

HOLLIE   Well, this was tough. I kept thinking, um, okay, now he's sick, you know? God knows, I don't know exactly what his health problems are. And I thought, well, you know, being very ill, well, okay, can I tolerate it for an evening? And then I kept . . . the other side of me said, "No way. He's there every holiday . . . I have to listen to this disgusting. . . . He's just an out-and-out jerk. As sick as he is, do I have to really tolerate this? Does every holiday have to be a disaster because of this person?" And I just said, you know, "I can't listen to this man. I just can't." First I talked to my father. I don't know why, because you know, he finds these dirty jokes and insulting digs humorous, too. I said, "Dad, I can't take it." My father said, "Well, I'll talk to him," you know. But he didn't, and so I just finally told my mother, you know, "I don't want to be around him."

JILL   Do you think, like if we would be able to sort of look back in time from now to then, that there might have been some sort of turning point that made you think that you had the right to have a voice in that situation?

HOLLIE   I'm not sure I . . .

JILL   Well, I mean, do you think that there was sort of a gradual building up to feeling like you could say, "No, I'm not going to be with this person"? Or do you think it happened just right then? I guess I was wondering, like with the things going on in your life, what sort of helped you build up to this point?

HOLLIE   Yeah, I . . . I can't pinpoint and tell you what, but I'm sure . . .

I'm sure there was. . . . I don't think it was just that instant that I decided that.

JILL   So you have this sense that there were other things that made you think that you really didn't have to tolerate this?

HOLLIE   Um-hum.

JILL   Okay. How long ago was it?

HOLLIE   It was last year.

JILL   Last year.

HOLLIE   Yeah.

JILL   But this feeling that you have a right to have a voice, has that been increasing? Or would you say it's just . . .

HOLLIE   It has. It really depends, you know, on the situation. It really does.

JILL   So there's some contexts in which this is developing and other contexts in which it hasn't started yet?

HOLLIE   Right.

JILL   So, which context, where do you feel like it's developing the most?

HOLLIE   Um, I think I'm able a little better now, you know, when I talk to my father. Like the other day I said to him, "You know, what is wrong with Mommy? She's just . . . I mean, I know she's unhappy."

And he says, "Well, do you have time?" And I said, "Well, you know, what is it? I talk to her and she's nasty to me on the phone. She knows there's problems and the reason I told her I'm unhappy is so she wouldn't nag me, and you know, she's nasty. Is that, you know, the reason you moved back from Florida—to see the kids more?" I said, "You know, Dad," I said, "I've got enough of my own problems just now. You know, you're nagging me with like this heavy stuff."

I mean, my father's constantly saying there's something wrong with the kids in our generation. They don't like families, and they're not family-oriented. When they were our age they used to go to their parents' every Sunday, it was an all-day family thing.

And I just said, "Hey Dad, there's a difference these days." I said, "Our generation is, you know, not nine to five. They work, you know. I have a husband who works his ass off. He travels, he's never around. Sundays at home, I've got to be honest with you, he doesn't want to sit in your house all day.

Neither do I. You know? We want to relax. We want to be with you, but we want to relax."

So they, my father, just can't see the difference today. So I think this voice is developing. It's helping me say it like it is a little more. I don't get through, though. I'm speaking, but I don't think the message is conveyed. But at least I'm speaking better.

JILL Yeah. Well, I'm glad that you can notice that you're speaking, even if it's not always heard.

HOLLIE Right.

JILL So, one area is with your parents. You're being able to have a voice more with them.

HOLLIE Um-hum.

JILL Are there other areas you've noticed where you're having a voice more?

HOLLIE Um, I think I do have more of voice with Robert. Definitely. But again, it's frustrating because I don't think it gets through. In my own little ways I'll try to make him aware of things, financial situations . . . I'll say, "Now Robert, do you realize . . . " and I tell him this over and over again, you know, "You keep taking money that we don't have and giving it away." You know, one day, I said, "We'll have nothing. Nobody's going to be there handing you checks. I mean, I try and make him, in some ways, see some light maybe from a different perspective but. . . . So my voice is there, but it doesn't really have any weight.

JILL But, okay. Now, what do you think it means about you, to know that your voice is there in more situations?

HOLLIE Um, I'm glad it's there. I think it was . . . it used to be there, but just in my mind. I used to think about it but never, you know, verbalize it. I think it also shows, you know, your opinions. I take a stand, you know. Hey, this is what I'm saying! This is what I believe!

You know, as petty as this might be, oh, what's the name of that one store? (pause) Barney's. I happened just to see a pair of pants that I had bought there on sale. I brought them back just a few days later because they needed to be altered. So I showed the saleswoman and she said, "I'm sorry. There's nothing I can do."

I thought, wait. I'm getting the run-around here. I told her,

"This isn't right. You can take these back." And she looked at me and she said, "Well, I'll talk to the manager."

And I thought, you know, it was just like . . . I stood there for a minute, and then like, not in a million years would I have ever done that! But I just . . . something just said, "This is not right."

And she came back and she said, "We'll give you your adjustment."

As I said, I like really surprised myself. Maybe this was like a petty thing, but I never . . . I don't know, I just don't think I would have made a fuss before. I'd have said, "Well, it's my hard luck." You know? So, I guess it made a difference.

JILL Yeah. It also sounds like you were heard in this instance. Now, you were saying that you would have never said that before?

HOLLIE No, I don't think so.

JILL So, what's different now about you that you did this?

HOLLIE I don't know. I . . . I don't know. I mean, I hope. . . . I don't want to think I'm turning into like a big jerk. I mean, I hope it doesn't come across that way, but I just, inside I just said, "You know, I just don't like this. It just doesn't sit well with me."

JILL So, would you say that when it feels to you like something's not right, that now you're not going to stand for it?

HOLLIE Yeah.

JILL Whereas you were sort of standing . . . before, you were standing for it . . . because you thought even though it didn't feel right, there was that model saying what you were supposed to do?

HOLLIE Yeah, I guess so. Yeah. I mean, I think before, if she would have said, "Well, you know, that's our policy," I would have said, "Well, I guess, you know, my hard luck," you know? So, yeah, it . . . even though . . . what you just said. It didn't feel right.

JILL And you're trusting that?

HOLLIE Um-hum.

JILL Okay. Do you think that's important?

HOLLIE Oh, yeah.

JILL How might it be important, beyond this example?

HOLLIE I think I trusted myself before, but I didn't heed the trust because of that—what do you call it? That model. So, the importance is, when I know, you know, when I feel something, that I really have to act on it, instead of suppressing it.

JILL   Is this something that is becoming more . . . a real part of the way that you operate?

HOLLIE   Um-hum.

JILL   What kind of difference do you think that it will make in your life—to know that you can act on what you know about what feels right?

HOLLIE   I think I'll feel a lot more confident than, you know, second-guessing or being ambivalent or not doing anything. You know, I think it's kept me at a standstill.

JILL   Yeah. So you can see yourself moving forward in your life instead of being at a standstill?

HOLLIE   Um-hum. Absolutely.

JILL   Well, that seems to be significant to me. I just keep feeling like asking you more and more about this. I want to make sure. . . . Is there something, is this okay, that we're talking about this?

HOLLIE   Yeah.

JILL   Does this seem on target to you?

HOLLIE   Yeah. This is fine. I guess, you know, as you talk about this, though, and I know, like you said before, that, you know, when you talk about what's going on, like with Robert and how . . . how what's happened, you know, isn't my fault but, somehow I feel like I've just been so stupid that, you know, I trusted and got lied to and, I don't know, I feel like I was made such a fool of, and I feel so stupid that I have such faith and didn't trust what I felt inside.

JILL   What do you think is important for you to know or do to be able to look back on that without feelings of stupidity coming in? I mean, what would it take to be able to look back on that and say, "I'm glad that that's behind me"? Or, you know, "I've learned something"? Or whatever? Do you know what I mean? (pause) Or maybe, what would have to happen for you to feel like, in your present life, or in your future life, that that wouldn't happen to you?

HOLLIE   I guess I have to make sure I trust what I feel inside and go for it, at whatever cost. Because I think I've suffered too much not heeding the call.

JILL   Um-hum. Can you see how, to me, when you're telling me that in the store . . . you were saying, "This isn't right. I'm not going to do this." And you were willing to give them back the pants. Can you see how to me that's directly related to what you're saying you would need to do to feel more confident about your future?

HOLLIE   Um-hum. Yeah.

JILL   What are you learning about yourself as we look at this stuff that you've been doing?

HOLLIE   I can trust myself.

JILL   Yeah. Are you finding something out about your qualities as a person?

HOLLIE   Well, I always knew I was, you know, a trustworthy friend or a trustworthy wife. I guess I'm learning I can be trustworthy to myself.

JILL   So what do you think will be the next thing that will happen with this to move it more into different aspects of your life?

HOLLIE   You mean, heeding this trust?

JILL   Um-hum. Yeah. Like, where else could you see it occurring?

HOLLIE   Um, I don't know. Maybe it would spread out, you know, into other relationships or, you know . . . you know, maybe once I'm working, you know, that it would be felt there. That . . .

JILL   Um-hum. So how could you imagine it being there? Like, what would be an example of something that maybe you wouldn't have done five years ago, that you think that you might begin to do now in one of those other contexts?

HOLLIE   Well, I remember a situation which was longer than five years ago, when I was at this job I was working at. And I remember I went in and talked to this guy about . . . it was time for my review and to get a raise, and I talked to him about, you know, my review, salary increase, whatever, and I remember him saying to me—this guy was the same age as Robert, and he knew Robert very well—and he looked at me, and he said, exact words, "What do you need a raise for? Robert makes enough money." And I remember thinking to myself, this guy's the biggest jerk in the world. And I remember thinking, there's nothing you can do. And I don't want to cause waves. And I thought, it's not right. This has nothing to do. . . . Robert could be, you know, Donald Trump. This has nothing to do.

. . . But I didn't do anything. I didn't take it one step further. I just left it as it was.

JILL   And what do you think you would do now?

HOLLIE   Oh, now? I mean, now I would have caused trouble. I would have gone, you know, to the next person. I mean, I would have filed a harassment suit if I needed to. I don't know if you'd call it harassment, but . . . whatever—a grievance.

JILL   You would have filed a grievance?

HOLLIE   Right. Of some sort. Yeah, I would have caused trouble. Because that . . . that type of statement and his actions were just intolerable, you know? So, I think today I would have made a point of doing something.

JILL   Um-hum. Okay. So, it will be interesting to see how . . . where this leads.

HOLLIE   Yeah.

A year following this conversation, Hollie is heeding the trust and using her voice regularly. She has begun a new career that she is finding very satisfying. She and Robert are in the process of divorcing and Hollie is trusting herself in new relationships.

Reflecting

[T]he power of the reflecting idea is not in the switching of
rooms, but in the switching of perspectives.

— *Judith Davis and William Lax,*
1991, p. 1

The use of the reflecting position . . . is in essence a political
act whose function is to distribute power among all the different voices in the discourse, dominant and nondominant.

— *James Griffith and Melissa Elliot*
Griffith, 1994, p. 166

The notion that there are multiple ways to describe a particular event or
relationship comes to life in the practice of reflecting from different
perspectives. Including time and space for reflection in therapy promotes
experience of experience, and it is through the experience of reflecting
on our experience that we make meaning of it. While the practice of
reflection may occur even when we don't formally encourage it, such
"natural" reflection does not necessarily focus on the preferred experiences or new narratives that are developing in therapeutic conversations.

Ever since the 1950s, when therapy teams began to observe from
behind one-way mirrors, a reflecting *position* — by which we mean a
relatively out-of-the-fray, listening position from which one can reflect
on events as they unfold — has been available to therapists. Writing about
the one-way mirror, Lynn Hoffman (1981, p. 4) notes,

> The late anthropologist Gregory Bateson speaks in *Mind and Na-*
> *ture* of the advantages of a bicameral format — the jump to a new
> perspective or emergence of new possibilities that follows the plac-
> ing together of two eyes, two hands, two chambers of the brain.

This format applies also to the one-way screen. The screen turned psychotherapy into a bicameral interaction that offered a similar chance to explore a new dimension. One had two places to sit. One could take a position, and have somebody else take a position commenting on or reviewing that position.

When we first began to work with behind-the-mirror teams, we used the reflecting position in at least two ways—as a vantage point from which to phone in directives or suggestions to therapists, and as a place from which to gather information. Sometimes we would discuss the information we had gathered with in-front-of-the-mirror therapists after interviews. At other times we would take a break during the therapy session to formulate strategies, messages, or interventions that the "designated therapist" would then deliver in front of the mirror while the rest of the team stayed out of sight.

Many teams still use this practice and, depending on the team's philosophy, there may be free-form discussion to arrive at a hypothesis from which the intervention emerges or there may be a rather standard format, such as first offering compliments, then composing a list of exceptions to the problem, and finally delivering an assignment that has to do with noticing, cultivating, and performing more of those exceptions. In this sort of format, toward the end of a session the therapist comes behind the mirror, leaving the family in front of it. The team then engages in a conversation that the family is not privy to, composing a single message—regardless of whether there is initial agreement among the team members on what that message should be[1]—and delivering the message through the therapist, who rejoins the family in front of the mirror after the team meeting.

The reflecting team format, first developed by Tom Andersen (1987, 1991a) in collaboration with team members in the north of Norway, is radically different. Andersen had studied for years with the Milan team, and we first heard of this innovation from Luigi Boscolo and Gianfranco Cecchin.

In the reflecting team format, the therapist and the people meeting with the therapist (whom we call the family in this description) talk together in front of the mirror, with the team observing from behind the mirror. At some point in the meeting the therapist and family switch places with the team so that the team is in front of the mirror, observed

---

[1]This statement is an oversimplification. Team messages may reflect more than one possibility. For example, a message may be worded, "The women in the team think . . . and the men think. . . . " or "Some team members predict . . . while others aren't so sure." Often these kinds of splits are used for strategic reasons. They generally describe two possibilities, usually geometrically opposed, rather than multiple possibilities.

by the family and therapist, who have gone behind the mirror. The reflecting team members then discuss their ideas, questions, and thoughts in response to the conversation they have just heard among family members and the therapist. In the team's discussion there is no attempt to reach a single conclusion. When the team members finish their "reflections," the family and therapist again switch places with the team, assuming their original positions. Once they are settled in front of the mirror, family members have the opportunity to comment on what they heard from the team.

By coming in front of the mirror and letting each of their individual voices be heard, reflecting team members put the postmodern notions of multiple perspectives, horizontal, collaborative relationships, and transparency into action. Literally changing places with clients and talking openly about multiple ideas may be the most dramatic example so far of the difference it makes to bring a postmodern worldview into the therapy room.

Consider these comments by Tom Andersen and by other people who have begun using their own variations of his idea:

Reflecting processes . . . are characterized by the attempt to say everything in the open. Everything the professional says about the client's situation is said so that the client can hear it. (Andersen, 1993, p. 306)

Our reflecting team members' conversations attempt to model open inquiry and frank discussion of life dilemmas for families, but do not attempt to instruct specific choices for how dilemmas should be resolved. (Griffith & Griffith, 1992b, p. 50)

The reflecting team has to bear in mind that its task is to create ideas even though some of those ideas may not be found interesting by the family, or may even be rejected. What is important is to realize that the family will select those ideas that fit. (Andersen, 1987, p. 421)

Reflecting team members can be discouraged from engaging in the time-honored structuralist and functionalist truth discourses of the psychotherapies, and encouraged to respond to those developments that are identified by family members as preferred developments, or to speculate about those developments that might be preferred. (White, 1991, p. 38)

These quotations underscore what has been for us a tremendous change — from the invisible teams of our family therapy training to the reflecting teams that we have adopted as a more fitting practice for narrative ideas.

The first time we had the opportunity to participate on a reflecting team we had no idea what to reflect. We were part of a group of beginners. Within eye- and earshot of the family, all of us were too uncomfortable to be able to replicate the kind of lively conversations we had participated in behind the mirror. Besides, those conversations, in which we suggested things for strategic reasons or argued about what we thought was "really" going on, seemed inappropriate when we knew the family was listening. We had begun to be uncomfortable in the position behind-the-mirror teams required, but we didn't know what else we had to offer. An awkward silence reigned until someone haltingly began describing his observations. We each then began to speak, but we did so in a state of discomfort, subjecting ourselves to critical second thoughts and editing furiously as we went along. We were quite relieved when at last we could retreat behind the mirror.

Later, when Michael White was consulting at our center, he set up a structure for reflecting teams and discussed kinds of participant responses that he had found useful in his work. As always, we found his ideas quite helpful. They gave us an orientation for how to watch interviews as team members and how to reflect out loud in ways that fit with the rest of our work.

Now that we have been using reflecting teams for a number of years, we wish we could use them in every therapy interview. Later in this chapter we will discuss ways that we use reflecting practices and a reflecting position even when we don't have the luxury of working with a team. But first, let's take a look at our current reflecting team practices.[2]

REFLECTING TEAM PRACTICES

Lynn Hoffman (1992) has said that her only guidelines for reflecting teams are that participants are encouraged to take an affirmative and affiliative stance and to have "relentless optimism." Six months after we heard her statement, as the therapists in our training program were reflecting on their learning over the previous year, we were vividly reminded of it. Al Ross articulated something that met with enthusiastic agreement from all the other team members. He said that he learned over and over again that it is attitude, not technique, that is central to this

---

[2]In true postmodernist fashion, different people and different teams have developed different ways of reflecting. See, for instance, Penn and Sheinberg (1991), Madigan (1991), and Furman and Ahola (1992) for ideas about different ways of structuring interviews using reflecting processes.

way of working. Comments like Lynn Hoffman's and Al Ross' give us pause when we start to share guidelines for reflecting teams. Perhaps in offering ideas about what to *do* we will divert you from the more important issue of how to *be*.

On the other hand, our own early awkwardness and confusion made us glad to try out the structure that Michael White offered. That experience led us to continue trying to articulate what seems to work for our team. We offer these ideas because we have found them helpful in our own team work. We believe that they help us keep awkwardness and confusion out of the room so that we can cultivate the affirmative, affiliative, genuine curiosity and wonderment that are more important than any technique or guideline.

There are three primary tasks that we suggest reflecting team members orient themselves to: joining with the family, supporting the development of new narrative, and facilitating deconstruction of problem-saturated descriptions. Team members then, listen to therapy sessions (1) to develop understanding (so that they can join better with the family), (2) to notice differences and events that do not fit dominant narratives (so that they can support the development of new narratives), and (3) to notice beliefs, ideas, or contexts that support problem-saturated descriptions (so that they can invite the deconstruction of those descriptions).

Which of these tasks is most immediately relevant changes over the course of therapy. Their relative importance also changes from family to family and from person to person. Generally, joining is most important at the beginning of therapy. The first time a team reflects — or whenever new members join in the reflections — members begin by introducing themselves and briefly situating themselves, mentioning what their work context is and why they are on the team (e.g., "I'm Ann Kogen. I work with children and their families in a day program and also have a private practice. I'm here as part of the Evanston Family Therapy Center alumni team that meets once a month for peer consultation."). If, as often happens, new team members and/or new family members have met briefly behind the mirror before the "formal" interview started, introductions need not be repeated.

The team's initial comments should include acknowledgment of what has led people to seek therapy and a brief statement of what one or more team members understand the present situation to be — something like, "I hear that both George and Luisa are very concerned about the suicidal thoughts that have been plaguing Maria, and I understand that she is glad to be home from the hospital and would like to put this time behind her."

We suggest that the bulk of a reflecting team's questions or comments focus on supporting and thickening new narrative developments. Team members are encouraged to recount things people did, said, or described in the interview that do not seem to fit with the problem narrative. If an event that interests a team member has not already been acknowledged in the interview as a preferred development, the team member may tentatively offer it, as long as she remembers to wonder aloud if it could be a preferred development. Once an event is recounted, team members — including the original speaker — pose questions about it, particularly questions about how it occurred and what it means. As the conversation develops, other team members may join in the conversation, either to raise a new event or to wonder about the one raised by the original speaker. In this way events are highlighted and questions are raised that invite people to perform new meaning on and develop new narrative around those events.

We believe the team should be careful to play only a supportive role in performing these meanings — wondering about them or making tentative speculations, but not trying to "sell" them. As Michael White (1995) has stated, this process is quite different from pointing out positives. Our intention is to notice unique outcomes and wonder about their significance, not to compete over which team member was most blown away by which incredible event. However, the curiosity and wonderment evoked by this process are often contagious, and we certainly hope that people try on and take home some of the new meanings that team members glimpse in the events of their lives.

In our early experiences using a reflecting team, we limited ourselves to the two tasks described above: (1) joining and (2) supporting the development of new narratives. People generally found these teams helpful. However, in a few instances where people laid bare extreme suffering, we later learned that they had experienced the team's focus on "sparkling events" as either disrespectful or not understanding of — sometimes even completely disregarding of — their experience.

For example, we saw a family consisting of Annette and her four children, who ranged in age from sixteen to eight years. In the initial meeting the therapist invited each participant in turn to describe how he or she saw the current situation while other family members listened. We heard that Alex, the eight-year-old boy, had raised a teacher's concerns by talking about suicide, Robbie, the ten-year-old boy, had been suspended from school for violent behavior, and Annette had been invaded by feelings of being overwhelmed and not up to the demands of mothering. A long history of many psychiatric hospitalizations for depression supported the ideas of unfitness. At the time of the interview, worry about the work she had ahead of her in finishing a master's degree, holding down a job, and taking care of her children dominated her experience.

The other children complained that the oldest child, 16-year-old Sam, was telling them what to do and enforcing his orders with threats and shoving. The children were spending more and more time at neighbors' homes; while Annette experienced this as a relief, it also confirmed (to her) her inability to care for her kids. Annette had divorced some years before, and the children's father lived in a distant state. He had only very occasional contact with the children, but Arlene, the 15-year-old girl, wondered if she could go live with him.

The conversation concerning these many problems was somewhat hard to follow from behind the mirror, as the two youngest boys made jokes to each other and raced around the room.

When we switched to the reflecting team, team members introduced themselves and made a brief joining statement. One member said something like, "I can see that the family has been through a lot." Other team members nodded in agreement. Then the team moved into a discussion of possible openings to new narrative.

This began with one team member noting that the whole family had made it to the session together and on time. We then speculated and wondered what this meant about Annette's parenting skills and the strengths of the family. Someone else noted that many people found raising four children to be more than a full-time job. She wondered how Annette managed to be doing that along with working towards a master's degree and holding down a job. Another woman on the team told of how she had reluctantly decided to cut back on work once her child was born, even though in her prior planning she had thought she could continue with everything. She wondered how this mother did it and what it said about her that she did. Someone else noted that all the children were spending time with neighbors and that one of the children had talked to a teacher about his frightening and unhappy thoughts. He talked about how, even though many people became isolated when difficulties took over, members of this family seemed to know how to reach out and connect with other people. Other team members wondered how the children had learned to reach out and if it had been helpful to them in the past.

When the family members reconvened after the team, they seemed quite subdued and made very few comments on the team's reflections. The next day, Annette called the therapist to tell her she was doubtful about the usefulness of the team. She said that it was obvious to her that the team did not understand the seriousness of the problems. She wondered why we were spending our time talking about how the family got to therapy on time when one of her kids was suicidal, another was suspended from school for being violent, and another was suggesting breaking up the family by going to live with her father. She thought the team had no appreciation at all for how overwhelmed she felt.

Experiences such as this have led us to include deconstruction as a possible reflecting team task. As reflecting team members, we follow the lead of the people who have come to consult with us. If they and the therapist spend most of the conversation describing and deconstructing problematic narratives, the reflecting team will focus more on deconstruction questions.

In the example just given, the family might have felt better understood by team members if we had talked about the problems that the family talked about. For example, someone on the team could have mentioned Annette's struggle with feelings of being overwhelmed and wondered if those feelings were playing a part in some of the other problems people mentioned. There could have been questions about the effects of those feelings. Some team members could have wondered about particular contexts that left the door open for these feelings. Team members might have wondered what contributed to this. Someone might have told a story about her own experience of the impossibilities of living up to a "superwoman" image.

Other problems could have been addressed specifically as well. For example, a team member might have wondered about the effects of the suicidal thoughts that had been voiced — not only on Alex but on everyone in the family. Someone else could have wondered how much those thoughts had taken over and what particular situations or people coached them. Another team member could have speculated that often such thoughts are spurred on by images and words, and wondered if Alex had found such images or words encroaching on his thoughts. Questions such as these would have acknowledged the family's problematic narratives while inviting their deconstruction.

If they had been interspersed with these kinds of questions, questions inviting construction of alternative stories might have been more welcome. For example, after a conversation about feelings of being overwhelmed, team members might have been able to wonder about whether Annette ever escaped the effects of these feelings. We could have wondered whether getting the family to the center that night was an example of not letting the feelings rule her. Such a question might have been more welcome in the context of deconstructive questions.

GUIDELINES FOR REFLECTING TEAMS

In our supervision program, we have begun reflecting on our reflections. That is, after the conclusion of a therapy meeting, everyone — the therapist, the supervisor, the team, and the individuals and families we work with, if they so choose—reflects on the entire process.[3]

Reflections on our reflecting team process have produced the list of specific guidelines that follows. These guidelines are not entirely original. The current list started as a distillation of suggestions from others that we followed as we began to learn about reflecting teams. The reflections of our training teams and the people who have consulted with us over the years have refined them and will continue to refine them so that they fit for our local culture.

We think that for many people guidelines such as these are especially helpful in their early experiences as reflecting team members. The guidelines are intended to help people embody particular attitudes and postures, and they are just *ideas*, not *the* way to use a reflecting team. Once the attitudes and postures are learned the guidelines may no longer be so relevant.

Here, in the form of an annotated list, are our current guidelines:

1. Reflecting team members participate together in a conversation.

When we first began using reflecting teams, people tended to each write down several ideas as they were watching the interview and then wait eagerly for a chance to put each one of them into the reflecting "conversation." What was supposed to be a conversation became a series of discontinuous ideas. Even worse, comments often came across as jarring or competitive.

Some team members tried to speak through the mirror—to the family rather than to each other. If the reflecting team took place in the therapy room, they looked directly at family members, ignoring the members of the team.

We've found that having a real conversation with each other has a number of advantages. Probably most significant of these is that the family has a sense of being able to "eavesdrop" on a compelling discussion about them. People from the behind-the-mirror vantage point have told us that a real conversation is much more intriguing to listen to than a series of statements, and that protracted discussions of a few well-chosen points are much more inviting than what was often experienced as being bombarded with many points.

When team members truly engage each other in meaningful conversa-

---

[3]At other times after therapy interviews we ask questions inviting the therapist and reflecting team members to situate and deconstruct their work (Madigan, 1993; Neal, in press). We invite the family to join in the questioning. This process is described in Chapter 10.

tion, family members have the choice of being able to respond or not to whatever is said. A direct gaze, on the other hand, can be experienced as pressure to respond (Hoffman, 1991).

Another wonderful advantage to having a real conversation is that ideas develop and new ideas are born in the interaction of team members. Team members who felt pressured to "come up with something" when reflections consisted of a series of disjointed statements now relax and trust that they will be able to contribute to the evolving conversation as the team develops ideas and questions around a few observations.

2. Team members don't talk behind the mirror.

There are at least three reasons for this guideline. First, it helps keep our conversations fresh and reflective of multiple possibilities. When an idea is mentioned behind the mirror, it can grab everyone's attention and focus the way that people listen, so that instead of a multi-voiced team we go in front of the mirror with a single voice. Such a voice offers no choice.

Second, we want the family to be the privileged authors of their own stories. If we were to comment to each other throughout the interview, we would tend to develop our own private version of the story and become invested in it. The team's only choice with such a story would be either to offer it to the family or to abandon it. It would be hard to offer a story that all team members were invested in without "selling" it. If we chose to abandon it rather than sell it, we would have nothing left to offer. If, instead, each idea brought to the team's conversation has been kept private, members can speculate about it and wonder about it, leaving the family the choice of whether to use it to weave a story or not.

Third, behind-the-mirror talk can all too easily become disrespectful or pathologizing. Conducting all our conversations in front of the family helps us practice respectful and nonpathologizing ways of talking and thinking. These practices of language bring forth a reality that we prefer.

3. We try not to instruct or lead the family.

We strive instead to bring forth a variety of perceptions and constructions, so that family members can choose what is interesting or helpful to them. We ask questions or offer ideas *tentatively*, talking about what we are wondering (*I was wondering if . . .*) or using the subjunctive mood (*could, might, perhaps*). We strive to keep our comments nonevaluative. We wonder about differences or new occurrences around which family members might choose to perform meaning.

4. We base our comments on what actually occurs in the therapy room.

We wonder about and give our personal responses to things that have actually happened in the interview. We begin new topics by referring to something that we observed ("I noticed that Ernestine said . . . "). If someone has an idea but does not know what cue the family gave her that the idea might be so, the team is encouraged to speculate about what in the therapy conversation could have led to the idea.

5. We situate our ideas in our own experience.

We describe what in our personal and professional experience supports our ideas and makes particular events stand out for us. Team members speak as individuals, not as representatives of "knowiedge" or "authority." This allows family members to understand where we are coming from and to freely adapt our ideas to fit their experience (White, 1991). Our situating comments help flatten the hierarchy and contribute to the transparency of the process. As Davidson, Lax, Lussardi, Miller, and Ratheau (1988, p. 77) write, "Rather than providing a framework for clinical neutrality, the reflecting team highlights an awareness of personal subjectivity."

6. We try to respond to everyone in the family.

Experience has taught us that people are more interested if some of the team's comments are about them.[4] And we don't want anyone to feel left out.

7. We aim for brevity.

Especially if there are small children in the family, it is important to keep comments short, interesting, and pithy. Even with only adults observing, it seems to work better for team members to err on the side of brevity rather than holding forth for too long at a stretch.

REFLECTING TEAM PRAGMATICS

We are quite flexible about the number of people on a team. If there are just two of us working together, the therapist who interviews the family interviews the other therapist about her reflections. We have seen teams with as many as a dozen people go quite well, although not every-

---

[4]In the first therapy meeting with a large family, the training team at EFTC failed to mention the seven-year-old boy in the reflections. As far as we could discern, he never listened to the team's reflections again.

one speaks each time such a team reflects. Tom Andersen (1987) has written that he has found a team of three people to work well because while two people discuss an idea, the third may come up with a different idea to contribute to the conversation. Our teams usually include from three to six people.

The team can be used for one particular meeting, throughout therapy, or occasionally. We find that families almost always find reflecting teams very valuable. In fact, we understand that Michael White (1993) has asked families how many meetings a meeting with a team is worth, and the average answer is four meetings!

Before the meeting begins (this could be at an earlier meeting, or for a first interview, it could be over the phone), we suggest the possibility of a reflecting team and describe it. If the family agrees with the idea, we proceed. We would favor using reflecting teams every time we do therapy, but economics and scheduling conflicts prevent that. Instead, we use teams (1) when people request them (this request usually has to do with a past experience or a description from a friend), (2) for learning, (3) when we have therapist guests who also use narrative ideas, and (4) for consultation.

If the team is going to sit in the same room as the family, we introduce the family to team members as the first meeting begins. If the team is behind the mirror, we generally ask if family members would like to meet the team before the meeting begins or when the team reflects. Some people are more comfortable if they have seen the people behind the mirror before the interview. Others prefer not to meet team members until they reflect.

Although in consulting with the family about whether to have a team we have already described the reflecting process, at the beginning of the first meeting we orient the family to the process again. The therapist who interviews the family says something like, "The team is next door watching us through this one-way mirror. At some point during our conversation, maybe at several points, we will trade places with the team. We will go behind the mirror and they will come in here." Or (if there is no mirror, and the team is in the same room as the therapist and family), "As we talk, the team members will be paying attention to our conversation. Let's pretend that there is a one-way mirror between us and them, so that we don't have to pay attention to them, but they can pay attention to us. In a while, we will reverse things so that it will be as though we are behind a mirror watching and listening to them. They will be talking to each other and we can listen in. They will have a conversation about what they noticed in our conversation. They may have questions or ideas. After their conversation, we'll change back again and you'll have a chance to comment on their conversation. I'll ask you what stood out for you, what fit or didn't fit, or what ideas you had while you were listening to their conversation."

Either the therapist, the family, or the team can suggest that it would be a good time for team reflections. Our usual practice is that thirty or forty minutes into an hour interview the therapist suggests that it is time for the team to reflect. However, the therapist is free to suggest reflections at any time. This freedom is particularly helpful for therapists who are just beginning to learn to use narrative ideas. If uncertainty threatens to tongue-tie them, they can simply suggest a reflecting team.[5]

On occasion, members of families who meet regularly with a team have said, "I wonder what the team would say about that," which we take as a cue to switch places.

The team may also suggest that it is time to reflect. In our center, the team can do this by knocking on the mirror. If the therapist and family agree, then the team reflects.

The team generally reflects for ten to fifteen minutes. (We aim for ten, but all too often take fifteen.) At our center the signal to end the team is a knock on the mirror from the therapist sitting with the family. We like the conversation to end with the sense that there is a lot more that could be said, so the therapist tries to knock while conversation is still active. The therapist could decide to knock earlier than usual if he senses that family members have had enough or are finding the reflections overwhelming.

We are often asked whether a reflecting team can practice without a one-way mirror. In fact, some teams choose to do so even if a mirror is available (Wangberg, 1991). We prefer using a mirror because it seems to help people stay in a reflecting position more easily. However, if a mirror is not available or the people we are working with prefer it, we find it works quite well to stay together in one room. In that case, as we mentioned earlier in the chapter, we preface the team's reflections by saying, "We are now going to be talking with each other as though there was a one-way mirror between us and you. It's as though we can't see you, but you can see us and are free to listen to our conversation or to think about whatever seems most relevant to you. After we finish talking you'll have a chance to let us know what stood out to you from our conversation—what fit or didn't fit or any ideas you had while we were

---

[5]Joyce Goodlatte, who participated in our training program, told us that in the past, when she worked with a (nonreflecting) team, she often had feelings of being scrutinized and evaluated by the team. With a reflecting team, though, she felt like the whole team was there to help and work with her. "If I missed something," she noted, "I knew someone on the team would ask questions about it. I didn't have to get everything, so I could relax."

talking." Then the reflecting team members make eye contact only with other team members during the reflections.

Another question that often occurs to therapists when they are learning about reflecting teams is whether the idea can be used without a team. In other words, can a therapist serve as his or her own reflecting team? In describing how he does just that, Finn Wangberg (1991, p. 4), an original member of one of the teams that first developed the idea of the reflecting team, writes

> I tell them that I will give them more than just my reactions to what they tell me, but also the thoughts behind the reactions. Whether I am seeing only one person or several, I will then lean back to create a bigger distance, I will either look at the ceiling or out of the window, and talk *about* them rather than to them.

On the same subject Tom Andersen (1987, p. 424) writes,

> When the team consists of only one person, this person may leave the room for a while; it could be minutes, or it could be days or weeks. On returning, she or he might say, "When I was away from you, I had these ideas that I would like to share," and then give the speculative reflections, saying afterward, "Were some of these ideas worthwhile? Would you like to talk about them?"

We, too, find that we often act as a single-member reflecting team. Our version is usually quite casual. We might say something like, "Thinking back on what we've talked about so far, several things stand out for me. Would you like to hear them?" If the answer is yes, we begin to recount something that was said in the therapy conversation and what we wonder about it. We then situate our comment in our own experience. We may wonder about several events before asking, "Are any of those events or ideas interesting to you too?"

EXAMPLE OF A
REFLECTING CONVERSATION

Imagine that a family comes to therapy because Adam, the nine-year-old boy, has been stealing. In the interview he agrees with his parents that stealing is not a lifestyle that he wants for himself, but he says that he can't help it. In the course of the interview, it is discovered that that very morning he saw several dollar bills sitting on his father's dresser. He could have taken them but he didn't.

If we think of the problem-saturated story as one of stealing taking over Adam's life and tricking him into leading a stealing lifestyle, then this event may refer to a unique outcome, an opening to an alternative story. Let's imagine that this sparkling event was mentioned in the conversation but there was no discussion during the interview of whether this was a preferred event and no meaning was made of it. In such a case, the team might speculate about it and wonder if it was a preferred development.

After introductions and joining statements, a team member may bring up the event by saying, "I was a bit surprised to hear that just this morning Adam noticed some dollar bills on his father's dresser but he didn't take them."

Another member might ask the first, "Why was that surprising to you?"

"Well, when they were talking about how Adam was leading a stealing lifestyle and when he said he couldn't help it, I began to form an idea that whenever there was an opportunity to steal Adam found himself doing it. Did other people form that picture?" Several team members may agree that they did. "Now I'm wondering if Adam had that same picture of his life. If he did, I'm wondering what it means to him to see that just this morning stealing could have taken over but he didn't let it?"

Someone else might add, "You know, as you were describing that picture I began to wonder whether Joe and Amelia (Adam's parents) also saw that picture or did they already know that at times Adam was able to keep stealing out of the picture?"

Another team member might then say, "Yes, I wonder if they see what happened this morning as a hopeful sign?" These questions invite Adam and the family to decide what the meaning of this event is and whether it is a preferred one or not.

If this ground was already covered in the therapy conversation and the family did recognize this event as a preferred development, the team would probably be interested in raising questions that would invite family members to story the event. For example, one of the team members might say, "As the interview went on I kept replaying over and over that moment when Adam realized that just this very morning he saw that he could take some money and he didn't, and he saw that stealing did not have such a strong grip on him as he thought. As the interview went on I was wondering: did Adam know all along that he could beat stealing like this, or is this a new development?"

Someone else might have joined in saying, "Yeah, I'm curious about that, too. I wonder if there are other times he could tell us about when he was in charge of his life rather than stealing being in charge."

"Hmm," someone might add, "What would be interesting to me about those times would be how he did it . . . how he did it and what it means to him that he could do it."

The first person might say, "In that light, I guess I'm wondering if he could look back and see a turning point, something that turned the tide, so that this morning he was stronger than stealing and stealing was weaker than him?"

"Oh, I see what you mean. If there was something leading up to this, I wonder if Joe and Amelia noticed any differences that might have had something to do with it."

At the same time that this is going on, team members work to situate their comments in their own experience and imagination and make their thoughts and intentions transparent. Doing this helps flatten the hierarchy. Ideas are seen as coming from personal experience rather than being "truth." This helps family members know how to take comments and feel free to reject those that don't fit. Situating questions and comments are interspersed as part of the conversation.

Putting these elements together, the reflecting team will sound something like this:

One team member might say, "As the interview went on I kept replaying over and over that moment when Adam realized that just this very morning he had the opportunity to take some money and didn't, and he saw that stealing did not have such a strong grip on him as he thought. As the interview went on I was curious about whether Adam, in fact, has been more in control of his life all along than he realized or if this is a new development."

Someone might then ask, "Why are you so interested in that?"

"Well, yesterday I was talking to someone who was trying to quit smoking and it reminded me of my own experience. I smoked for years. I finally quit twelve years ago, but that was the third time I quit. The first two times were miserable and I ended up going back, so I thought that when I tried again it would be unbearable. Instead, it was painless. It was almost like I had been doing it bit by bit without realizing it. When I heard how Adam passed up the money this morning I wondered if he too had been doing it bit by bit without noticing it. I don't know . . . "

Someone else could join in saying, "Yeah, I'm curious about that too. I wonder if there are other times he could tell us about when he was in charge of his life rather than stealing being in charge."

"What do you have in mind when you ask that?" someone might ask.

"If his experience is like Randy's (the team member who quit smoking), and it is happening bit by bit, I thought it might be useful to notice the bits. It might add to everyone's confidence that things are going in a new direction."

"Well," someone might add, "What would be interesting to me about those times would be how he did it and what he thinks it means about him that, at that moment anyway, he tricked stealing instead of letting stealing trick him."

"Why are you interested in how he did it, Michele?"

"One reason is that I work at a school and this is not an uncommon problem for the kids there. I think it might help me to help them if I know something about how one person was able to beat stealing."

The first person might say, "In that light, I guess I'm wondering if Adam could look back and see a turning point, something that turned the tide, so that this morning he was stronger than stealing and stealing was weaker than him."

"I see what you mean. Do you have any speculations about what it might be?"

"No, I really don't know, but I wondered if maybe something happened that convinced him that stealing wasn't his friend."

Another team member might then say, "If there was something leading up to this, I wonder if Joe and Amelia noticed any differences that might have had something to do with it."

Perhaps at this point the conversation would turn to a different preferred event or a possible opening to an alternative story. A number of such events are usually discussed during the course of the team's reflections.

After the reflections, the family and team change places again so that the family and therapist are in front of the mirror and the team is behind it.

Then the therapist asks family members one at a time for their responses to the team's reflections. The therapist says something like, "What stood out to you from the team's reflections? Were there particular questions or ideas that were most interesting to you?"

Sometimes children or teenagers say they don't remember what the team said. Briefly reminding them sometimes helps (Lax, 1991).

We have found that most people do comment on the team's reflections and that some even refer back to team reflections at later meetings.

As a family member refers to a particular comment, the therapist might ask more questions, such as "What about that was interesting to you?" "What thoughts and ideas did you have in relationship to it?" "Did you learn something about yourself or the situation or reach some conclusion in thinking about it this way?" "How do you think these ideas will play a part in your life?" It is important that all family members get a chance to respond, so the therapist should be parsimonious with follow-up questions.

The therapist can also comment on what stood out to him in the reflecting team and mention what about those comments caught his attention.

REFLECTING WITHOUT A TEAM

A characteristic of our therapy — and probably of the therapy of most therapists using narrative ideas — is a movement between direct experience and reflecting. Even when we work with a single person, we move between the "landscape of action" (direct experience) and the "landscape of consciousness" (reflection on that experience). This movement between direct experience and reflection is characteristic of our work, whether or not we are using a reflecting team.

Inviting Reflection on Others[6]

When we first began doing family therapy,[7] we learned to have family members talk directly with each other so that we could either gather information about their "interactional patterns" or let them rehearse a new way of interacting. This way of working made sense when we believed that we could identify or find what was "underneath" a problem and when we emphasized changing behavior. When we asked people to talk with each other in therapy we were setting up a context either for gathering information that we would use to make assessments to guide our interventions or for intervening by suggesting that people try out new behaviors. In this sort of therapy, people were either doing something active or listening to us. They usually did not have the opportunity to voice their reflections in therapy.

When we studied the Milan approach, instead of asking people to talk with each other, we learned to ask one of them at a time circular questions that focused on interactions between other family members. In our first way of working, if a child was refusing to go to school we might have asked the parents to demonstrate how they would talk to him to get him to go to school (either with or without coaching from us). In the Milan approach we would have been more likely to ask a sibling of the

---

[6]We have some hesitation using words such as "self" and "other" because of their common usage as designations of essentialist entities. We think that reflecting processes can be significant and effective precisely because of the multiple possibilities that emerge when people interact. In other words, the practice of reflecting is a particular and powerful instance of the social construction of selves and others.

[7]These comments are based on our past experience. We know that if we revisited the people we studied with in the past, their ideas would be different. Gianfranco Cecchin and Luigi Boscolo, for example, now use reflecting teams.

child a series of questions such as, "Who is most upset that your brother won't go to school? Who next? When your mother is upset that your brother won't go to school, what does your father do?"

Milan-style circular questions invite people to become an audience to themselves, their families, and situations. In listening to other people's answers, they can learn how other family members see them; they can reflect on the relationships among other family members as well as on those between themselves and other family members.

In our current work, we still interact with one person in a family while the others listen. Influenced by the idea that, rather than uncovering what is already there, we are cocreating experience and meaning through social interaction, we hope to ask questions that will open space for new, preferred narratives.

So, given the problem cited above, we might now ask the boy, "On the days that you do go to school, how do you get the best of the fear? What have you done to ready yourself to stand up to the fear in this way? How have other family members supported and encouraged you to be able to do this?"

This way of working again makes people an audience to each other, themselves, and their relationships, but we now go a step further. We ask people to reflect on what they've heard. We might, for example, simply turn to the father and say, "What thoughts were you having while your son was talking?" Or we might ask the mother, "Were you surprised to hear that your son had made these preparations to stand up to the fear? Now that you know that, how does it change your picture of him?" Questions like these invite people to reflect on a new narrative as it is evolving. Their reflections then become part of the narrative and other family members may reflect on the "thickened" narrative, thus making it both more substantial and more complex. This process is a vivid example of the social construction of reality.

When we work with groups of people, we generally have a fairly lengthy conversation with one person at a time. We invite the other people to listen from a reflecting position and we invite them from time to time to voice their reflections.

In inviting this sort of reflecting, the first and most important task for the therapist is to insure that people stay in a listening position. Sometimes this is easily accomplished by speaking and making eye contact with only one person at a time and, if the conversation includes reference to others in the room, speaking about them in the third person. This mode of conversation invites the people not being addressed to listen reflectively.

Often in problem situations the dominant story influences people to be very invested in their own perceptions and descriptions of the problem and the events that surround it. This in turn may push them to use therapeutic conversations as an arena for getting others to consider and accept their versions of reality. A conversation used this way can end up with everyone talking and no one listening. In such a situation, the deck is stacked against recognizing openings to new possibilities that might build new narratives.

Also, family customs of many people speaking at the same time or previous therapy instructions for people to talk directly to each other may conspire to make the task of setting up a listening position more difficult.

We have found that telling people how we would like to proceed is the simplest way of avoiding these difficulties. We usually address our explanation to the person or people we would like to be in a listening position first. We say something like, "What I'd like to do now is talk to Fred about this situation for a while. Then I'd be interested in hearing your thoughts about the conversation that Fred and I have. Later in the hour I will talk with you and Fred will have a chance to reflect on our conversation. Does that sound all right?"

This is a genuine question. If people have other ideas about how they would like the conversation to go we are interested in knowing about them. For instance, I (GC) recently worked with a man and woman who had been divorced for several years and their seven-year-old child, who had been experiencing some difficulties at school. Scott, the child's father, requested a single meeting of the parents without the child. At that meeting, Scott, who is African-American, began by saying that he wanted to tell Brenda, who is Anglo-American, how he had come to the realization that racism played a part in their divorce. He said that he had not talked with her about this at the time because he hadn't understood it, but so that they could trust each other now, as co-parents, he wanted to talk about it. He said that he did not want to tell me about it with her listening, as previous conversations had been structured, but wanted to talk directly with her in the context of another's presence. In this instance, following Scott's request, I sat back and listened while the two talked, only later adding my reflections.

Most of the time, though, people agree on a structure in which we talk to one person at a time while the others take up a reflecting position.

Even when people have an idea of the proposed format and have agreed that it sounds like a reasonable way of proceeding, old habits may continue to take over, getting them to interrupt and offer their description or evaluation of a particular event. When this happens, we let them know we are interested in what they have to say and that they will have a chance to respond a bit later.

An alternative that we learned from Harlene Anderson, which is particularly useful when old habits continue to take over, is to invite those participants who are initially to be in a listening position to listen from behind the mirror. When the appropriate time comes, they can then switch places with the person initially talking and offer their reflections.

Setting up a structure for the conversation seems to loosen the grip of problem-dominated narratives. Perhaps because there is no opportunity for those in listening positions to bring up dominant narratives while another speaks, they seem freer to hear other descriptions, which allows them to make meaning of events at odds with the problem-dominated story.

The second major task for a therapist interested in inviting reflecting on others is to ask questions to encourage the reflections. In this context we ask questions with two purposes in mind. The first is simply to invite general comments on the conversation. In such comments, people bear witness to each other's realities. The second purpose is to invite reflections on specific events, usually events that we think might open onto a less problematic strand of lived experience.

To invite general comments, we usually turn to someone in the listening position and ask something general, such as, "What thoughts were you having while Fred and I were talking?" The simple act of witnessing that this invites can have very profound effects.

For example, I (JF) am currently seeing two women who were a couple for 14 years. Karen broke up with Diane rather abruptly six months before I met them and she almost immediately became involved with someone else. Gradually over the six months, larger and larger waves of unhappiness and confusion swept through Karen's life. She began to wonder if her decision to end the relationship had been a mistake. She asked Diane to work on the relationship with her to see if they could resolve the problems that had led Karen to leave.

Karen described the most significant problem as "almost no sex, which was driving me crazy, and Diane seemed totally uninterested except when she thought I might leave."

Diane had been experiencing tremendous grief since Karen had left. She was quite interested in exploring the possibility of their being a couple again, but each time they talked, so much distrust, anger, and jealousy came between them that the possibility of ever being together was nearly washed away by feelings of despair. This was particularly true when Diane heard allusions to the fantastic sexual relationship Karen had been having while Diane had been grieving. All these feelings were so powerful and threatening that they sought out therapy as a safe context in which to talk.

Although they had attempted many times to have conversations with each other, both at the end of their relationship and in recent weeks, it was only in the first therapy meeting that Karen told her story of ending the relationship and beginning a new one. She described how Diane had wanted to make love with her at the beginning of their relationship but that had faded rapidly. This had brought on insecurity about Diane's feelings for her. It led her to think of herself as unlovable and unattractive. These experiences made Karen's vision of the future "colorless and barren." She thought she "would dry up from lack of love and just get old," even though other parts of the relationship were very satisfying and wonderful. Karen's repeated and continual inability to get Diane to talk about their sexual relationship came to mean to her that nothing different could ever happen.

When another woman showed romantic interest in Karen, she saw it as her last chance to be loved. She reveled in the new sexual relationship, but as time went on she recognized that it was all she had. She saw that sex didn't equal love, and for the first time in years she could look back and recognize all the ways that Diane had loved her. Now she regretted having given up. She hoped that she hadn't thrown away the best relationship she ever had.

In her listening position, Diane wept throughout Karen's conversation with me. When I asked her what she was thinking as Karen and I talked, she said, "I never knew how hard it was for her. Every time she has tried to tell me, I've thrown the other relationship in her face and talked about betrayal. I couldn't stand it that she was with someone else. I never understood what it was like for her all those years not to be with me in that way."

Karen was intensely grateful that Diane was willing to witness her pain and despair. As Diane and I reflected on the new understandings Diane had about Karen, Karen, now in the listening position, became more and more visibly relaxed. My maintaining a focus on Diane helped Karen to witness Diane's feelings of pain and betrayal without moving into defensiveness. This experience was so important to Diane that it paved the way in later meetings for her telling of the sexual abuse she had suffered as a child and its effects on her, which included difficulty with sexual feelings as an adult. Karen's witnessing of Diane's story in turn allowed her to reinterpret the difficulties in their sexual relationship.

For our second purpose, inviting reflections that acknowledge and develop openings or new narrative, we might begin by asking questions designed to draw attention to events that don't fit with the problem-saturated story. "Were you surprised by what Karen said?" or "What stood out as new or encouraging for you in the conversation we were just having?" are examples. We could then ask questions to develop the story or reflect on the meaning of whatever stood out or was surprising. Questions such as, "Why did that stand out for you?" and "What have you learned about Diane that you might not have known if this event hadn't come to light?" or "Which of Diane's characteristics seemed to shine through as we heard how she was able to leave the past behind in so many ways?" are possible questions to invite meaning-making.

In addition to asking people in the reflecting position general questions that are designed to draw attention to things that don't fit with the dominant story, we might more directly point out a possible unique outcome and say, "I had a picture that the lack of sex had colored Karen's view of your whole relationship. To me, hearing Karen say that she has recognized that love doesn't equal sex doesn't fit with that picture. What did it mean to you to hear her say this?"

Once people respond to initial questions like these we may ask more questions to expand ideas that have been mentioned or to invite reflection on other aspects of the conversation. Then we can ask the person with whom we were originally speaking to reflect on the reflections— "Karen, what is the effect on you of hearing Diane recognize these things about you?"

Inviting Reflection on People's Own Emerging Narratives

People can also reflect on their own emerging narratives. They can do this with or without the presence of other people in the meeting. Questions such as, "Thinking back over today's conversation, what new developments stand out for you?" and "When you compare how you would have handled this problem six months ago with what you are now doing, what do you learn about yourself?" encourage this process.

These kinds of questions invite people to evaluate their experiences and the therapy, rather than letting therapists do the evaluating. By this we don't mean that we encourage self-criticism. Rather, we ask people to decide whether and how events are meaningful and we ask people to decide if the work is taking them in helpful directions. This practice reflects a change in ideas about the balance of power in therapy. As the expert position of the therapist is deconstructed, voices of the people we work with take a more prominent position.

When we invite people to reflect on their own emerging stories, we usually intersperse such reflection throughout a conversation. Thus, we invite people to move in and out of reflecting on personal narratives as they unfold. Reflection is for us a more separate and distinct activity when we ask people to reflect on others' stories than when people reflect on their own developing narrative. Self-reflection may occur as a response to one question at a time, asked amid a flow of other kinds of questions. In self-reflection, then, the conversation flows among deconstruction, openings, preference, story development, and reflection.[8] It moves among these domains without any of them being separated out or necessarily highlighted.

When people move from being in a conversation to reflecting on it, they become an audience to themselves. This puts them in a better position to perform meaning on their own emerging narratives.

We have the same purposes in mind when we invite people to reflect on their own experiences as we do when we invite people to reflect on others' experiences. That is, (1) we are interested in offering them the opportunity to make general comments on the therapy conversation and what emerges during it, and (2) we are interested in hearing their ideas about possible openings and the meaning they make of them.

"What do you think the most significant thing is that we've talked about today?" and "If you look back and see how far you've come since you began struggling with this problem, what do you notice about yourself?" are examples of somewhat open-ended questions that we might use to invite reflection.

More specific questions include, "What have you learned about yourself in accomplishing this?" "Can you see how to me this new development means that you have taken a big step forward? What do you think I see?" and "What qualities have you shown in accomplishing this?"

A way of inviting verbal reflections from children that we learned from Michael Durrant is for a therapist to make a distinction and then ask a child if he ever thinks about himself in that way. For example, on hearing that a child has slept the night through, rather than letting fears keep him awake, a therapist could comment, "It sounds like you are getting braver! Is that right?"

In working with young children, we ask fewer and simpler questions, relying more on tone of voice and facial expression to invite them to make meaning of a developing narrative. We also give broad hints. That is, we might communicate delight or excitement as we witness new developments a child is making and only then invite her to respond with her own feelings about it. We understand that, in one phase of his practice, Michael White was famous for falling off of chairs as a way of punctuating new narratives!

We have also found that there are some adults and teenagers who initially don't seem to respond to questions that invite reflections. With them, we first offer our own reflections and only then ask for their comments on our distinctions. We do this by asking what Michael White

---

[8]As you may have noticed this list matches our list of question types except that meaning is replaced by reflection. Meaning questions do invite reflection as do other more open-ended questions, such as, "When you think back on what we've been talking about so far, what stands out for you?"

(1988a) calls indirect questions. These are questions like, "Can you see how to me this means you have taken a big step in standing up to the worries?" We would follow this question with something like, "What do you think I noticed that led me to think that?"

Another way we deal with a seeming lack of responsiveness to our questions is to offer choices. For example, we might ask, "Do you think this development has more to do with your determination to solve this problem or with your creativity in responding to what life offers?" Happily, many times people reject our choices altogether and offer their own ideas instead!

The Plot Thickens

... the words in a letter don't fade and disappear the way conversation does; they endure through time and space, bearing witness to the work of therapy and immortalizing it.

— David Epston, 1994, p. 31

It is in the performance of an expression that we re-experience, re-live, re-create, re-tell, re-construct, and re-fashion our culture. The performance does not release a preexisting meaning that lies dormant in the text. Rather, the performance itself is constitutive.

— Edward Bruner, 1986a, p. 11

After attending our first workshop with Michael White[1] we decided to use his ideas with a family we were seeing. The family had come to therapy because of worries about 11-year-old Liza. Jan, Liza's mother, and Margaret, Jan's partner of eight years, described Liza as fearful and insecure. She seemed reluctant to go to school and to socialize with friends. Liza concurred with Jan and Margaret's description of her. She sat looking down, quietly fidgeting and speaking in monosyllables only when spoken to during the first interview.

It was between the first and second meeting that we attended the workshop with Michael White. We decided that at the second meeting we would try to externalize the problem using relative influence questioning. We were delighted with how well this interview went. Family members were all talking about fears coaching habits. The conversation brought forth a story of how the fears were having effects on Jan and Margaret as well as on Liza.

At the third meeting, Margaret continued to talk about how fears had

---

[1]In this one-day workshop White interviewed a family and talked about some of his ideas. It was meant as an introduction to narrative therapy, not a skill-building workshop.

coached habits between meetings and how she had begun to have glimpses of how she could avoid some of the habits fears had coached in her. Jan was back to talking about Liza as being fearful and insecure and wondering how as a mother she might have done something wrong. Liza was silent.

We had no idea how to proceed. After stumbling around for a bit we dropped the externalizing conversation and went back to what we would have done before we met Michael White. By the end of the meeting, Margaret dropped the externalizing conversation as well.

Looking back at that therapy now, we are amazed that the one conversation in which we used some narrative ideas went as well as it did. We didn't understand that these ideas work in the context of a worldview and set of attitudes. The least important part is the technique. We also didn't understand how persistent problematic stories can be. People have usually been living them for a long time. Often their local culture includes attitudes and practices that support the problem-saturated story. It is not at all unusual for an alternative story to fade between therapy conversations.

Having said that, we've also found that there are things that we can do to keep the story going. In this chapter one of our two purposes is to describe those ideas that have been most helpful to us in keeping stories alive, both during interviews and between them.

Our second purpose is to describe possibilities for helping people make the stories they are authoring thicker and more multi-stranded. Some of this seems to happen automatically. Bruner (1990), for example, suggests that as we construct self-narratives we search our pasts for small stories that can help explain or account for these narratives. In addition to the way this process happens automatically, we have already described how through asking questions we invite people to thicken and add complexity to an emerging alternative narrative by connecting it with stories of past events and hypothetical future events. We think of these supporting stories and their meanings as adding strands to and thickening our narratives. We have found that repetition and thoroughness — especially in terms of (1) asking about detail, (2) inclusion of more people, and (3) inclusion of various perspectives — are extremely helpful. In this chapter we describe a number of practices that can work together with the story development ideas that we described in Chapters 4 and 5.

We want to emphasize that none of these practices are standard or routine for us. With some people, we've used many of them; with others we've used none. The first idea we describe, for example, is to begin therapy conversations with a summary from the previous conversation. Recently, as we were seeing a couple together, one of them asked us to start the conversation with a summary, saying, "It's been so helpful when you've done that before. That way we can take off from where we were

·with what has happened since, and relate that to our ideas about what's important right now." Other people come in quite focused on how they want to use the time that day. In that situation, a summary of the previous meeting can feel like it's hampering the process and closing things down. So it goes with most of these ideas. They are only useful when they are useful. We ask people if they seem like good ideas and only proceed if they are interested.

BEGINNING INTERVIEWS WITH A REVIEW
OF THE PREVIOUS MEETING

We have asked ourselves what would have happened if, when we met with Liza, Jan, and Margaret the time after our "narrative" conversation, we had begun the interview saying, "Last time we met we talked about the habits that had been coached by fears and how those habits have affected each of you and your life together. Have you had any other thoughts about that or noticed other effects in your life? . . . Since we met have you noticed a time where one of those habits could have taken over, but you were able to resist it?"

When a person enters into an alternative conversation, her perceptions about herself, her relationships, and the dilemmas she is struggling with can sometimes shift so that she very quickly is living a new story. In the situation we've been describing, Margaret's perceptions shifted so that after our externalizing conversation she noticed things in this new way. Between meetings she saw fear coaching habits and she had glimpses of how she could avoid some of the habits that fear coached in her. She had begun to live an alternative story that suggested alternative meanings and solutions. As she lived this alternative story she was not seeing Liza as fearful and insecure. And she was not seeing Liza as the problem.

Although Liza and Jan had participated in the same conversation as Margaret, they did not experience this same kind of perceptual shift. We think that they were seeing things differently as they talked with us, but those different perceptions didn't last. There may have been stretches of time in which one or both of them did live an alternative story, and had we inquired, we might have been able to find out about those times. But we did not inquire, and the story faded.

For many people, in the beginning of therapy there are moments and contexts in which they are living the alternative stories that they have begun to construct in therapy and other moments and contexts in which they are immersed again in problematic stories. For other people, although they may have had glimpses of alternative stories during a therapy interview, these glimpses, in their judgment, have had no impact between meetings.

In both situations we have found it helpful to begin interviews with some reference to the sparkling moments of the previous meeting. Sometimes a review of the narrative that has emerged over the course of all our work is useful. Beginning in this way orients the conversation to the reauthoring process and offers an invitation to continue redescribing and reliving alternative stories.

The reference to previous meetings can take a number of forms. Sometimes we ask, "I was wondering if any of the ideas or accomplishments we talked about last time have figured importantly in your thoughts and life since we last met. Have you had more ideas about them or have they been important in some way?" We may add something more specific, such as, "I particularly wondered about the notion you called 'a new kind of parent.' Was that name and the ideas that go with it helpful?"

Alternatively, we can offer a more extensive summary of the previous meeting, inviting people to reenter the conversation with us, filling us in on how things have continued.

Often, from the vantage point of such a summary, people can look back at the time between meetings and discover that there were indeed unique outcomes. Summaries of the emerging narrative remind people how to situate themselves within it. From inside the new narrative they can see life events that had gone unnoticed. Therapy can then continue with the storying of these events. If people do not discover unique outcomes in this process, they very likely can name different aspects of the problem. These aspects of the problematic story can then be deconstructed.

Even for people who have thoroughly begun to live alternative stories, beginning sessions with references to or summaries of earlier meetings can continue to be useful. As aspects of alternative stories are retold, they thicken and take on new strands, allowing people to feel their impact and understand their meaning more thoroughly.

The following is a transcript of the beginning of an interview between John, who was taking his life back from bulimia, and me (JF). My contribution to this conversation was to offer a summary of a previous meeting. John used the summary as an opportunity to develop the story he was already authoring. This conversation was so relevant, and John had so much to add, that the summary and his additions ended up comprising the entire meeting.

JILL   I was reading over my notes over from last time and some very exciting things are happening.

JOHN Um-hum.

JILL The thing that stood out to me as I was reading this all over, you were telling me you went to this wedding in Kansas City . . .

JOHN Oh, yeah. Oh, yeah, oh, yeah. Okay. Maybe you should bring back . . .

JILL Okay. I'll just read it to you, Okay? You were saying that you were really surprised at how well you had bounced back.

JOHN Oh, yeah.

JILL Even though you had gone through this whole thing and put a stop to the bingeing, and even though it wasn't that long since you had put a stop to it, you felt like you were sort of back in the same place you had been before the bulimia took control. And then you gave me a bunch of examples . . . some things that were sort of remarkable that tested how committed you were to stopping the bingeing. Like even though there were four sheet cakes in your refrigerator for 24 hours . . .

JOHN (laughter) Yeah!

JILL . . . you didn't . . .

JOHN That's true! For my birthday I baked a cheesecake to take to work and I didn't binge on that either!

JILL Wow! And the bulimia didn't talk you into bingeing on this sheetcake that you had overnight. And so I asked you how you were able to do this . . .

JOHN It was huge, too.

JILL And you said that the way you did this was with willpower. You said that something in your mind says, "No," and then you just don't . . .

JOHN Yeah, which, to me, doesn't seem as much like willpower, because willpower. . . . You said that I said I did it by willpower and when I think of that, it makes it sound as if it was a struggle that you had to keep fighting.

JILL Um-hum.

JOHN You know what I mean?

JILL Yeah, I think so.

JOHN Willpower implies that it was an ongoing struggle that you . . .

JILL So what would you say it was? Instead of willpower?

JOHN Well, even then what I said was if the idea pops into my . . . do you know what it is? Not willpower, but self-protection.

JILL Self-protection.

JOHN It's self-defense. Because for some reason I've been able to get it to this point that if it comes up, you just, your mind just shifts. And so it's not willpower, implying struggling like that. It's more self-defense, like — *no, I can't* — and, you know, *that's not an option. I don't even want to think about it because I can't deal with that.*

JILL Um-hum. Well, that's interesting to me.

JOHN It's more like self-defense, more so than willpower, because it doesn't have as much to do with willpower.

JILL Okay. Yeah, I think I see.

JOHN Having to rely on willpower isn't what it's like.

JILL Okay. And last time I asked you how you thought that self-protection got built in?

JOHN You know, actually I think it had a lot to do with staying at Ted and Anna's because it's almost like I turned my back on bulimia by living there for a month and I began to accept that *I can't do it.* You know, I put myself into that situation.

JILL Well, you mean when you say, "I can't," you mean that it's not an option?

JOHN Yeah.

JILL So it was like you created this habit of it's not being an option?

JOHN I created an environment that it wasn't an option for me.

JILL And then you were no longer in this environment, but it had become built in by being in the environment. Is that what you're saying? Because . . .

JOHN Well, since I was with Ted and Anna . . .

JILL Right, but I understand you created the environment by spending a month with Ted and Anna, so that you knew that there was no opportunity for bulimia to take over . . .

JOHN No. That's when that self-defense mechanism kicked in, I believe. Since I created this environment where that wasn't an option, I think that's when the thought came into my head, it's like *I don't want to do it.*

JILL Right.

JOHN Because at that point, it's like, why fight it? *I can't do it.*

JILL Right. Okay. Now, what I . . .

JOHN So why torture yourself with these thoughts? Why say, "I want to do it," when you can't?

JILL Um-hum. You'd say no to those thoughts?

JOHN I think so. I think that's when that actually kicked in.

JILL But what my question is, these other examples were after you had moved back on your own. So how come it was still like that? That's why I asked, did it become a habit, to have this self-protective — is that how you described it?

JOHN I think it's reinforced just by the fact that . . . well, it's kind of snowballed because I've been able to do some things that I thought were really good — you don't want to lose that — and I think this time around I was just able to get a good feeling real quickly from stopping the bingeing because in the past, when I've stopped, when I've become . . . when I've gotten back in control, instead of bulimia being in control, it wasn't always real easy.

JILL Uh-huh.

JOHN And I wasn't even able to derive a good feeling about it. Maybe because it was such a struggle all the time.

JILL Okay.

JOHN You know, you don't feel as good about it. It's like you don't even have the ability to feel proud of yourself because it's like such a damn struggle all the time. It's like, how can you feel good about having to struggle all the time? You know?

JILL So, I just want to make sure I understand this. It's like when you're in a situation where there are like . . . where bulimia talks to you and says, "You could binge," like there are cheese-cakes in the refrigerator, you, at this point, would say "No." And you'd be aware that you'd done so much and you feel so good about that, and it's important to keep that going. And feeling good about it and seeing how much you've done and the self-defense kicking in give it a kind of ease. Is that sort of how it works?

JOHN Yeah. Well, I guess, see, yesterday was kind of a struggle, but I mean, it wasn't a major struggle, but it was kind of a struggle. And it's not like I just said "No," and didn't think about it anymore, because I think it was a little harder yesterday. It just was.

JILL But you did it anyway?

JOHN Yeah, I did.

JILL Okay. Well, do you want to talk about that? I'm interested in what went into your keeping the upper hand even though it was a struggle, or do you want me to finish this?

JOHN That's fine (pointing at the notes).

JILL So you said, after you had given me all these examples, you said that you were proud about how well you were doing. And you told me about going to this wedding in Kansas City where you shopped . . .

JOHN Oh yeah.

JILL . . . walked around, enjoyed unstructured time by yourself.

JOHN Um-hum.

JILL And I asked you what conclusions you drew about yourself by being able to really enjoy spending this time alone and structuring it without the bulimia pulling you in. And you said . . . the conclusion you drew was *this was a person who likes himself.*

JOHN Um-hum.

JILL You could have gotten into putting yourself down because bulimic thinking got you into counting calories and trying to be . . .

JOHN I was a little obsessive.

JILL What you said to yourself, though, is, "This is going to ease off. You're doing really well." And you allowed yourself to feel good even though your attention was pulled to calories.

JOHN Yeah, um-hum.

JILL And that seemed like a bit of a breakthrough because in the past you might have been more down on yourself about that. Is that right, or not?

JOHN Yeah, yeah, I guess. Or I could have just let it continue . . .

JILL Yeah.

JOHN . . . thinking, oh geez, this is a real bummer and you know, that's how I was sitting around feeling that way. But when I let myself realize that geez, it's only been a month, you know, and I was able to just be proud of the fact that I was doing what I was doing after only a month. Yeah!

JILL Is that pattern of being able to recognize how well you are doing in a particular context instead of letting perfectionism sort of take over, is that a new kind of triumph for you?

JOHN   I guess it is, actually. Yeah, I guess it is. I guess so because, yeah, I mean, I'd have to think about it, but yeah, I think it is.

JILL   Are there other contexts in your life where that would be a useful new way of dealing with things?

JOHN   Well, yeah, because remember when I was talking about exercising? I was trying to get myself back into being a little consistent with it and even if that meant if my energy was. . . . I'll tell you what it is. It's trying to get out of the rut where I think I have to do this he-man workout and, you know, just kind of drag myself out, you know, wear myself down by forcing myself through this workout that's more than I really care to do and probably not all that healthful. I don't know. And just say to myself, "I'll do what I can." And if that means doing less than what I'd like to do or less than what I normally do, at least I've done something . . .

JILL   Well, you're already doing it, in the context of exercising!

JOHN   I'm trying to. And sometimes, even though . . . yeah, I've done somewhat less at times than I would have in the past. Because in the past I got into this thing where if I didn't work out for an hour and a half and drag myself out and I didn't lift X number of pounds X number of times, then I hadn't really done anything, you know? And now, if I'm sitting there and saying, "Well, I don't feel like doing anything," then I just do a little bit. At least you've done something.

JILL   Yeah. Do you think the way you're doing it is more your way or bulimia's way?

JOHN   My way.

JILL   So it really is a way that you're talking to yourself, isn't it? You're saying some things to yourself to really acknowledge what you are doing?

JOHN   Oh, yeah. And Saturday I went out with a friend and we went to this neat place and I kind of told myself that I was going to relax and not try to be so uptight and have something that was something I wouldn't normally have, you know, that wasn't real restrictive. And, you know, on the menu they had salad, and it would have been just like me to have a salad. That's what I would have done. But instead we had appetizers at the bar and we had sweet potato fries. I was so hungry. I really was. And then we got to the table and we liked those so much that we got another order of sweet potato fries and split them. We got a small, but we split an angel hair pasta with chicken, you know? And for me that was good, because fries are something I wouldn't have had. A pasta dish is probably something I wouldn't have had. Like I said, there were salads on the menu, and I had to just about force myself not to take the salad, because I always do that.

The conversation goes on. We continue to weave the summary from the time before and new developments together as John re-authors his life.

RELATING THERAPY CONVERSATIONS TO PROBLEMS AND PROJECTS

In re-authoring their lives, many people have told us that naming problems and projects or plots and counterplots has been helpful. Once they are named, people more easily recognize when the culprits are around and when they themselves are moving into preferred territory. With this recognition people more often experience themselves as being able to choose what to do.

The questions we use to ask people to name the plot and counterplot or problem and project are quite straightforward. Questions such as the following ask people to name the plot:

- This problem you've been telling me about, what can we call it?
- Would you say that it's *misunderstanding* that comes between the two of you? Is that a fair thing to call it?

If a person's story is less straightforward, asking about restraints is sometimes helpful in naming problems:

- What keeps you from realizing the dreams that you mentioned?
- What gets in the way when you set out to find a job?

It is also useful to name the counterplot. This naming often comes later in the process. The following are examples of questions to ask people to name the counterplot:

- You escaped the temptation of the problem on at least two occasions in the last week. If you were to give a name to this new direction you are taking, what would you call it?
- These new developments in your life seem like a project you're taking on, is that right? Does the project have a name?

Once meaningful naming is agreed upon, much of therapy can be organized around it. As events are recounted or performed in the therapy room, people can be asked questions to sort them by plot or counterplot.

- Was that behavior more on the side of fighting or on the side of intimacy?
- Do you think that was self-doubt talking or confidence?

Even if people have not explicitly named the problems they are struggling with and the projects they are engaging in, we can refer to problems and projects by offering candidate names. For example we can refer to "pro-fear" and "anti-fear." Over time, as a person responds to these candidate names, they might evolve and be refined to "living in a war zone" and "harmony." Having names enables us to ask people whether particular events are on the side of the problem or on the side of the project.

In our first meeting, William described growing up with a large trust fund. He thought that the trust fund created a breeding ground for procrastination and other habits that had lured him into inactivity. The inactivity, in turn, created a lot of room for misery in his life. We talked about the role of cultural and family expectations in making none of the choices William thought about seem good enough. In this environment, procrastination often seemed to be a desirable way of avoiding competition. At the age of 38, William was recently divorced and had not worked in the several years since his company went bankrupt. Lack of direction seemed to be a main feature of his life. He named the problem "old habits luring me into inactivity" and the project "taking my life back from the habits."

Between our first and second meeting William moved from an apartment to a house. (The plan for this move was underway before therapy began.) At the beginning of the second meeting, in talking about the move, William said that his kids were coming to spend the weekend with him and he hadn't yet bought a television. I (GC) asked, "Would buying a television be on the side of old habits or on the side of taking back your life?"

William thought about the question and then answered, "TV anesthetizes me. It disables me." He went on to contrast what he had accomplished around his house the night before with what he would have done if he had a television. Although he had originally mentioned not having the TV as something that would be disappointing to his kids, he now began to wonder if not having it would create possibilities for a different relationship to begin with them. Television, he decided, was on the side of old habits. Although procrastination had a part in his not buying a television set earlier in the week, at our meeting he decided not to buy one as a way of taking his life back for himself.

What could have been simply a report of his move became the occasion for discovering a unique outcome by asking, "Would buying a television be on the side of old habits or on the side of taking back your life?"

As David Epston (1989b) notes, our questions can offer people the choice of aligning themselves with problems or projects. When people decide to align themselves with projects, they are constructing alternative stories in which they experience personal agency. Karl Tomm (1993) argues further that these questions (which he calls "bifurcation questions") mobilize people's emotional responses, aligning positive emotions with the project (assuming a person commits to a project) and negative ones with the problem, which can be helpful in opposing it.

Posing dilemmas between problems and projects keeps both therapists and the people they are working with on a re-authoring track. If someone launches into telling the story of an event that the therapist feels is tangential, he can ask, "Would you say that this event you are describing is on the side of depression or against depression?" In order to answer, the person must relate the event in some way to the story of her struggle with depression, and the re-authoring process can proceed.

Another benefit of asking people if events, thoughts, feelings, and the like are on the side of the problem or on the side of the project[2] is that the answers offer opportunities to thicken developing narratives. As people sort conversations, television programs, comments, books, activities, and so on, into these categories, the tension between the plot and the counterplot extends into the nooks and crannies of their lives. The activities of daily living become decisions by which they must align themselves either with alternative stories or problematic stories. This makes life an opportunity for the dramatic performance of preferred narratives.

The posing of dilemmas also alerts people to possible traps the problem may set and to steps they may take toward solutions. Often people adopt this process as their own and ask themselves questions such as, "Would going on this date be pro-intimidation or anti-intimidation?" or "Is this really what I think or is this the voice of self-hatred talking?" As

---

[2]These questions seem to be most effective when they match the wording the people we work with use to describe their alternative relationships to problems. Here we are using language assuming the person and the problem are on different sides. We could use language suggesting the person could transform his relationship with the problem. For example, we might say, "This new music you're listening to, would you say that it supports your learning from the messenger of fear or does it promote fear turning into panic?" See Freeman and Lobovits (1993) for a discussion of the impact of the use of different metaphors for relationships with problems.

people begin to ask themselves and answer questions of this type they tend to choose behavior supporting their preferred narratives, and in so doing create new supporting events for those narratives.

For example, a family came to see us because the school recommended therapy for nine-year-old Jeremy, who was repeatedly sent to the principal's office for angry outbursts. At the third interview Noreen told us that the afternoon before Jeremy had burst into the kitchen 45 minutes earlier than he was expected home. When she saw the look on his face, Noreen was immediately overtaken by negative expectations. These expectations convinced her that temper must have gotten Jeremy in trouble again.

"Mom!" Jeremy exclaimed. "That game the kids were playing was on the side of temper. You should have seen it!" When Noreen asked Jeremy to explain he said, "No one could agree on anything! Everyone was shouting at each other and calling names. That game was on the side of temper, so I just left." This delightful turn of events became the focal point of the therapy conversation. It was a turning point in Jeremy's relationship with temper. The family now saw that temper was something that Jeremy could turn his back on. Inspired by Jeremy's performance of this alternative relationship, Noreen decided that she could turn her back on negative expectations about Jeremy, thus adding another strand to the story.

NOTETAKING

One of the things we've noticed (and copied) in watching both Michael White and David Epston work is the way they utilize notetaking to record and repeat not their own ideas but some of the important-seeming words that people they work with say.

Let's use this hypothetical example as an illustration: Through techniques of intimidation a woman has been kept, even in her thoughts, from voicing any rights to her own opinion. At the third meeting she hesitantly says, "Since we last met, I did have an opinion that I thought to myself." The therapist might say, "In the face of all this you actually had an opinion and you allowed yourself to know it?" The woman might then say, "That's right. I did." The therapist might then say, "Is it all right if I write this down? I'd like to get the exact words." The woman says "Yes," and repeats, "I had an opinion that I allowed myself to know." The therapist then says, "I want to get this down right (taking notes and speaking slowly). You had an opinion and you allowed yourself to know it." The woman nods and says, "I did."

In this process a single event is stated four times. It seems to us that this repetition alone is valuable in making a story more real.

The people we work with tell us that it is a different experience to hear something than to say it. This process affords both perspectives. There may also be different accompanying thoughts and associations with each repetition; so each repetition thickens the story. The notes that we take in this process become an "official record" of the counterplot.

Once, as we sat behind Michael White's mirror at Dulwich Centre, we heard a woman contrast the experience of reading White's notes about their work together with that of reading a case file from the hospital where she had been an in- and outpatient for years. She said that when she read her hospital chart she felt old and small and stuck. She felt like a chronic mental patient with no hope, not even like a person.

Then she talked about reading Michael White's notes. She said that the more she read the more alive she felt. She could see movement in her life. She felt like a valuable person who was making her life better every day.

From our vantage point behind the mirror, the woman looked like two different people as she made this comparison. As she talked of the hospital chart she talked and moved slowly and seemed somehow shriveled and dull. When she talked about White's notes, we saw a transformation. She glowed.

The "permanent record" comprised by our notes on people's projects can become a sacred text that enshrines a person's preferred story, making it canonical and "real." (See pp. 209–210 for details about notetaking.)

TAPES

With people's permission, we sometimes videotape therapy conversations. When we do, it is with the understanding that the tapes belong to the people we are working with as much as they do to us (or more in the sense that they can revoke our use of them at any time). People sometimes watch the tapes and then return them. Sometimes they keep them. We've worked with people who have watched every conversation, others who have asked for a particular tape, and others who have chosen not to watch the tapes at all.

For those who do watch the tapes, the experience is a more expanded version of hearing a statement read back to them. They might spend more time thinking about a particular question. Or they might mull over the meaning of something that they hear themselves say as they review the tape. The authoring that begins in the session is often taken a bit further as they watch the tape. Not infrequently, people come to the next meeting with ideas and questions that developed as they watched tapes.

At times, people have found it helpful to watch a tape from one of our early meetings. In doing so they often reflect on the difference in the person they see on the tape and the person they now experience themselves to be. They can recognize how far they've come, giving their developing story a sense of movement over time.

Much as we'd like to report that the people who see us always steadily move only forward, our actual experience is that many people move in and out of new stories. For someone experiencing a backslide, watching a tape that documents their living in more preferred ways can be very helpful. Hearing and seeing themselves talking about how to constitute preferred versions of themselves is more empowering than any report of what they were doing mediated through someone else could possibly be.

Although we haven't used them, audiotapes could be used in the same ways.

LETTERS

According to Michael White (1995), David Epston has done an informal survey of people who have worked with him in which he found that on the average they thought a letter was worth 4.5 sessions of good therapy. David Nylund (Nylund & Thomas, 1994) also did a survey of 40 people who had worked with him. His results showed that the average letter was worth 3.2 interviews. It would seem, then, that letters are useful in continuing stories and thickening them.

Letters from therapists have been used for some time and with many different purposes (Elkaim, 1985; Pearson, 1965; Selvini Palazzoli, Boscolo, Cecchin, & Prata, 1978; Shilts & Ray, 1991; Wagner, Weeks, & L'Abate, 1980; Wilcoxon & Fenell, 1983; Wojcik & Iverson, 1989; Wood & Uhl, 1988). The only limit is the therapist's creativity.[3]

Letters not only thicken the story and help the people we work with stay immersed in it, but also involve us more thoroughly in the co-authoring process, giving us an opportunity to think about the language and the questions that we use. We find that in writing letters we have ideas we might not have had otherwise. This may be because we write letters from a reflecting position. We are removed from the actual therapy conversation but thinking back and referring to it.

For us, letters serve three main purposes: (1) to summarize and recap our meetings, (2) to extend ideas or stories that were initiated in a therapy conversation, and (3) to include people who didn't attend a meeting.

---

[3]For ideas about using letters and documents in therapy we highly recommend White and Epston (1990), Epston (1994), "Therapeutic documents revisited" in White (1995), and Nylund and Thomas (1994).

Summarizing Meetings

We write letters directly from our notes. Therefore, the summaries we offer in letters are very selective and edited versions of therapy conversations. Since the narrative metaphor guides our work and we consistently check with people about their preferences, letters can offer an advantage over tapes, in that they highlight those aspects of the conversation that build and reinforce preferred stories.

Writing this kind of letter effectively requires taking very good notes.[4] We organize our notes in terms of the narrative metaphor, keeping track of the plot and the counterplot. On the left side of the page we note things that have to do with problematic story (or plot). We keep these notes in externalized language. That is, as someone says, "We can't get along. We disagree about everything. It's embarrassing to have people over because we're always fighting," we write down

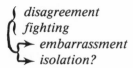

These notes make it easier for us to ask deconstructive questions, such as, "So disagreement and fighting have taken over your relationship, is that right? And this leads to embarrassment at times? . . . Were you also saying that the embarrassment encourages isolation?"

On the right hand side of the page we keep track of the alternative story that is developing. When we note something that may be a unique outcome we put a star in front of it. We are more likely to take down people's exact words on the righthand side of our paper so that we can go back and ask about them or refer to them in suggesting word choice that seems fitting in naming the project. Recording people's exact words also allows us to quote them in letters.

In the above example, when the couple tells us that they do have some good friends, Bob and Sophia, who they regularly go out with we might record

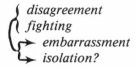   *good friends, Bob and Sophia*

---

[4]We assume that remembering very well would also facilitate this process, but since neither of us does, we can't really speak to that possibility.

We can then ask questions about how they are able to maintain the relationship with Bob and Sophia, rather than ending it under the influence of embarrassment and isolation. As the details of the story of their relationship with Bob and Sophia are told, we record the highlights on the right side of the page.

When we write a letter, it is with our notes in front of us. We write with the idea of helping people immerse themselves in a new story or thicken and add strands to a developing story. The following is an example of a letter I (JF) sent to Rhonda, who is 15 years old, after our first meeting.[5]

Dear Rhonda,

It was good getting to know you at our first meeting. Here is my understanding of what we talked about. Please let me know if I have something wrong or if I've left out anything important.

You told me that an "overwhelming feeling of loneliness" had come over your life and tried to talk you into believing that you were not wanted or that you didn't belong. This feeling at times had convinced you that no one wanted to be with you. It did this by putting thoughts in your mind like: "They're not going to like me" or "They're going to think I'm annoying" or "Why don't they talk to me?" These thoughts made you stand back and keep to yourself. They've kept you from talking to people and they've even kept you from believing in yourself and appreciating yourself. These thoughts seem to have gotten a stronghold on your life when you were doing sports after school and your friends spent time together without you. The thoughts started telling you, "They've been close. You're on the outside."

You may have been vulnerable to these thoughts because of many experiences earlier in school of being made fun of and put down by boys who have called you fat and ugly. It isn't all boys who have done this or who you think would do this. When I asked how you thought boys could get pulled into having the kinds of attitudes that would make this behavior possible, you said, "Magazines, TV shows, billboards. Everything shows thin women. That's what we've been raised on." But you can see and I agree with you that these images are unreal and unattainable. Even if they were attainable, would that be an excuse to treat someone else this way? What attitudes do you think talk some boys into treating girls this way?

---

[5]It is not necessary that letters be as long as this one to be effective and worthwhile. Many of the letters we write are briefer than this. We have chosen this one because it thoroughly summarizes the preferred events in a single interview.

The unreal perfectionistic images have turned your opinions against yourself. They have nurtured a critical voice that tells you, "I'm ugly. I'll never get a boyfriend." What it all comes down to, you said, is the "importance of someone wanting to be with you." And these perfectionistic images and the accompanying thoughts and feelings have made you think, "No one will ever like me."

What you would like is to "get back your opinion about yourself." You named the project you will work on with me, "To feel better about myself and stop putting myself down."

You already have some things on your side when it comes to this project. First, although the thoughts are telling you, "I'll never get a boyfriend," you've said, "That's stupid." Somehow you've been able to be the one to evaluate the thoughts instead of the thoughts always evaluating you. Do you think evaluating the thoughts is a good idea?

You said the thoughts were stupid because "boyfriends aren't the most important thing. Liking yourself is." How do you think girls and women get convinced that relationships with boys and men are the most important thing? How have you been able to see through this way of thinking and decide that liking yourself is more important?

The thoughts haven't blinded you to knowing that you have friends and family who like and love you. Meagan, for example, calls you on the phone. If I were to interview Emma she would say, "You're nice. You're pretty. And you're smart!" I would be interested in finding out more about your friends' role in your project to feel better about yourself and stop putting yourself down. Since I'm quite a bit older than you I'm sure there are things that I will get wrong and that I won't understand as we work on this project. I'm excited about what I may learn from you about teenagers' knowledge (but please don't think it's your job to teach me). But do you think we should invite another teenager to join us to make sure that teenagers' knowledge gets full representation in our meetings? Would Meagan or Emma be a candidate for this?

Another thing that you have going for yourself in this project is that these perfectionistic images haven't fooled you into thinking that looks are important in a guy. There are many invitations to talk about how guys look, but you don't take them. And sometimes you've even suggested that other people not talk about looks! Where did you get that idea? In fact, you told me that you thought you deserved to be a candidate to become a card-carrying member of the "Fighter for Social Justice and Good Feelings Team."

Others have told you that "you're the nicest person." You think what they mean is that you are really there for people and you

*always try to have a good outlook. I'm quite interested in hearing
about a time when you were there for someone else. I'm particularly interested in hearing about just what you did and how you got
in the frame of mind to do it. Is it all right if I ask you about that?
Do you think that that experience would qualify you to become a
card-carrying member of the Fighter for Social Justice and Good
Feelings Team or are there other memories you can add or is there
more to do first? Is getting this card part of the project to feel
better about yourself and stop putting yourself down? You did tell
me that looking at the card and reminding yourself that that's who
you want to be would helpful. At what point do you think you
should get the card?*

*I have two more notes about steps you have already taken for
your project. One is that you discovered that bad feelings are more
likely to take over if you don't speak your feelings. Speaking feelings with me is part of telling people what is going on and a step in
feeling better about yourself and stopping putting yourself down.
I'll be interested in finding out the effect of our conversations.*

*The second note is that you have determined to not let the
thoughts sent by loneliness and perfectionistic images be in charge.
Instead you want to think for yourself. You decided to tell yourself
a counter-thought: "I may not have the perfect body but I have lots
of things going for me. I'm doing well in school and I have lots of
friends and family." I'll be interested in finding out what difference
this thought makes.*

Looking forward to seeing you next time,
Jill

The letter to Rhonda follows the flow of the conversation we had,
highlighting parts that seemed most important in terms of the problem
and the project and adding questions to further the story. However,
letters need not refer to a single therapy conversation. There have been
occasions when we've written letters to summarize a number of meetings.

The following letter is to Julie. When I (GC) wrote the letter, I had
been meeting with Julie for about three years, and she was still in a
life-and-death battle with self-hatred and self-doubt. For as long as Julie
could remember, the feeling that she wasn't really a human being had
strongly colored her life; she had never experienced the sense of belonging that "real" people seemed to feel. Julie wondered if, in part, this
feeling was connected to being adopted.

For most of her childhood, Julie's adoptive father had a stronger
bond with alcohol than he did with her, and neither parent had ever had

much experience with warmth or intimacy. When Julie was 12, she had an illness that kept her home for three months. Fearfulness about returning to school coupled with lack of insistence or guidance from her parents conspired to keep her out of school with a home-bound teacher for two years. When she reentered school, Julie felt alone and out-of-phase.

In her senior year of high school, Julie became involved with a man who, after six months, began to abuse her violently. She remained in that relationship for four years, convinced that she was unlovable and that she deserved the abuse.

Since that relationship ended she has lived "like a stranger, a boarder" in her words, in her parents' house. She finished college and worked at a series of (her words again) "dead-end jobs." She is now forty years old.

The "reparenting" project that I refer to in the letter was progressing fitfully, and Julie was seriously considering taking a break from therapy. I thought it was her perfect right to decide whether and when to meet with me, and I wanted to support her in making decisions for herself. However, I wasn't sure who was actually in favor of the break—Julie or self-hatred. At times she talked as if the break would be a vacation that she would use to practice relying on herself. At other times it seemed that self-hatred was convincing her that her situation was so hopeless that talking with me or anyone like me was futile. At those moments it seemed that self-hatred might be close to convincing her to take a break from life itself.

I wrote this letter to support her in deciding for herself what to do. As part of that process, I hoped she might reflect on the story of her struggle as we had thus far constructed it in our meetings. To that end, I acknowledge the story of her struggle with the "old feelings" of doubt, self-hatred, and hopelessness, gently inviting her to deconstruct them as I recount and connect many of the sparkling moments she has told me about.

Dear Julie,

At the time of our last visit, it seemed that some of the old feelings that you have been struggling with for so long had gotten the upper hand. I know that those feelings are powerful and very familiar, so powerful and familiar that they very easily overshadow less familiar feelings.

My intention in writing is not to act as if the old feelings are unimportant or to try to convince you that they are less formidable than they are. They are both formidable and important. However, it seems to me that if you are still interested in the project of reparenting yourself, an important part of that project would be the care and feeding of new feelings and ideas about yourself. So I thought I would review some of the things that have come up from time to time in our talks that seem to be exceptions to the old familiar thoughts and feelings.

In a meeting we had in February 1993, you talked about two relationships in your life that were enjoyable, one with your horse, Angel, and the other with your cousin, Margaret. We have talked about these relationships at other times since then, as you know. In that same conversation, you talked warmly about being on a farm in Minnesota at age 11. Then you said that graduating from college was a big accomplishment that you felt good about. You also said that around 10% of the positive comments that people make about you actually get through and make some sort of difference in your self-perception, and you said that you would like to give up the habit of self-criticism. This leads me to wonder if you could let the positive comments from Margaret get through, what would they be?

In March, you talked about how you were looking at people around you at work and saying to yourself in a believable way, "I can do what they're doing." In April, you talked about realizing that your co-workers couldn't all be better than you in every way, and you said that your bosses' behavior did not define who you were. (If they were insensitive, it was a comment about them, not you.) There were some feelings about your own worth and qualities you were recognizing in yourself that went with these experiences. You chose not to name them to me but would it be helpful to name them again to yourself?

In May you had an apartment of your own, you had completed a course in an MBA program and were getting ready to start another, and you joined a group for single people. You followed through on assignments to talk to group members on the phone, go to movies, etc. You went to a health club and started swimming lessons. You talked about how having your own apartment helped you see yourself as "grown up, competent, and adult." You said that having more adult feelings reduced your susceptibility to fear. In June you talked about how you were learning to rationally counter negative self-talk and catastrophizing. I know that when the old feelings get the upper hand it is hard to see through them to some of this knowledge you have gained, but I'm wondering what the you from that time would advise now.

In August, in spite of some setbacks, which included a disappointing relationship and a broken ankle, you finished a marketing course. You said that you had considered suicide, but when faced

*with that decision, the alternative of pursuing a career as a respon-
sible person suited you better. In October, even though the going
was very rough, you clung to the knowledge that you could work
and support yourself. You talked about how being able to work
and support yourself was the essential step in being a responsible
person. Through the fall and winter, you struggled with feelings of
shame, badness, and unlovableness. Can you see how what stands
out for me about that time is that you continued to struggle, that
you didn't give up?*

*Even during that hard time, you were able to enjoy, at least a
little bit, your brother's boys. You talked of spending time with
them over the holidays and appreciating that they were "real," not
phony or hypocritical. You applied for nursing school. You talked
about how great it was to see your cat in the evening. You said you
really liked to blast your car radio on the way home from work.
You talked about positive memories: burying your head in your
horse's neck, being in the back of a haywagon at dawn.*

*You went into the hospital rather than give in to the voices of
self-doubt and self-hatred. You used the break that the hospitalization afforded to decide not to continue in a job that had become
very demoralizing and ugly. You almost immediately talked about
how great it was not to have to go in to "that job" each morning.
We talked about the pervasiveness and power of ideas of badness
and shame and habits of passivity—how they were family traditions that you were choosing to oppose.*

*When doubts about finding a new job arose, you talked about a
memory you had of once being one of the three people out of 500
who got hired for a certain job. You also remembered that recruit-
ers had told you that you are in the top 5% of hireable people.*

*In February of '94 you talked about how you had gotten yourself
into an "I don't care" attitude at the health club rather than allowing yourself to be overcome by self-criticism. You went on to talk
about being able to imagine yourself at work with that same sort of
"I don't care" attitude. Later in February you said, "It's not impossible to change, it's only difficult." You said you wanted to transcend the fear that you learned from your family's way of living
and to find the affection and approval that your parents couldn't
give. Can you see how these statements, in my mind at least, fit in
with your reparenting project?*

*That winter you got the highest score in your class on an ac-
counting exam. You took that as proof that your brain was still
capable of functioning. In looking back at your old job, you began
to see how lousy they had treated you, and said that you were*

seeing quitting that job as a positive step. You talked about how
you had no regrets about leaving, no second thoughts, and that this
was a first for you.

In April you had a day in which you played racquetball, bought
textbooks for new classes, did an exercise tape, and went to an AA
meeting. You still felt good about all of that at our meeting the
next day. In that meeting, you said that the idea that feeling bad in
the present doesn't have to stop you from moving toward a better
future was helpful and motivating to you. Later that month you
said that you believed that you were more mature, more assertive,
and more outspoken than you had been.

In May, you were able to appreciate yourself for working full-
time at _____ for four weeks, for eating right, and for having
conquered urges to binge and to drink. You said that you were
paying less attention to how you looked and more attention to
what you thought about yourself and less to what other people
thought of you. You were practicing talking with people and stay-
ing out of black-and-white, either-or thinking.

In June, you said, "I've learned how to function in a work
situation." "I can at least be more responsible than my brother."
You appreciated that you had chosen a responsible lifestyle.

In July you talked about how you were feeling more in control,
less bad. On the Thursday before our conversation, you had con-
quered the temptation not to go in to work. You said that you had
come to realize that facing other people's opinions at work wasn't a
life-threatening situation. You spoke of learning to detach, to let
go of expectations concerning your parents, and you also said that
you were talking to yourself differently. What can you remember
about that shift? How might you be able to continue to build on
the things you learned back then?

Later in July you continued to talk about shifts in your thoughts
and feelings. You said you were even more able to talk yourself
through a bad day at work, that you knew that when you felt
negative vibes that it didn't necessarily mean that people were really
thinking that you were bad. You said that you were becoming less
reactive to others, not giving them so much power over you. You
spoke of some positive changes in your relationship with your fa-
ther—how you were trying to be less reactive to him and how he
saw you as more capable and dependable.

By August, you were talking about getting positive feedback at
work. People were telling you that you should be looking for ways
to move up within the company. You said it felt good to get such
feedback, that it was good to get some "grounding in reality." You
were realizing that it was never as bad at work as you sometimes

*feared that it was going to be, and you spoke of how the positive
messages had you entertaining the notion that you could survive if
you moved out on your own.*

*That pretty much brings us up to the things I've written about in
letters since November. I wonder what thoughts and feelings you
are having as you read this highly edited sampling of things you
have told me about your life. Can you see how I might read it as a
story of progress? One thing I know about your past history is that
it has been helpful from time to time for you to withdraw from
therapy for a while until you felt ready to take some further steps.
From my vantage point, it seems that achieving the success that
you have at _____ and beginning to establish yourself in your
new place have been big steps. You certainly deserve some time to
savor them and consolidate your gains before taking on any new
tasks. What do you think you can do to most effectively counter
the old habits, doubts, and fears as you settle in to your new
situation? Does reflecting on some of your past progress and enjoyable memories help? I trust you will let me know when the time is
right.*

   Warmly,
   Gene

Julie is still consulting with me. For a while after the time of this
letter, she was making steady progress at distancing herself from self-
doubt and self-hatred. (See the letter I wrote to her in the next section,
"Extending Ideas and Stories that Began in a Therapy Conversation,"
for some examples of the alternative story that she was beginning to
author at that time.) Then two disasters happened at once. The company
where she had finally found a job that seemed tolerable, with humane
policies and a boss she found reasonable, was taken over by a bigger,
meaner corporation. Julie's boss was replaced by someone she characterized as "a heartless young automaton." People were fired right and left.
The old employees who remained were abused and overworked, creating
an atmosphere of anger, submission, and hopelessness. Julie hung on to
her job for months before deciding to quit. Although her quitting was a
decision not to subject herself to a dehumanizing atmosphere, it left her
jobless.

   On top of this, a relationship with a man that had seemed promising
fell apart. What I saw in the end of that relationship was Julie standing
up for the kind of relationship that she wanted. What she saw was an
example of a man who couldn't be trusted and further proof that she was
not lovable.

   These events let self-doubt, self-hatred, and the belief that she wasn't
a whole human being come back into Julie's life. She gave up her apart-

ment and moved back into her parent's house. She isolated herself from people, working for a "temp" agency where she never stays long enough at a single placement to make friends.

At the time of this writing, things are touch-and-go for her. She has signed up for some post-graduate courses that could lead to a better job in a few years. She is very cautiously exploring some group-type activities. She has started reading very actively, and one focus of her reading is to attempt to find a spiritual/moral/ethical path that might suit her. She has begun to have a different kind of relationship with her father, one in which she feels they treat each other like real people. But she is still leading a pretty isolated, separate existence. Ideas that she is fundamentally lacking in something that other people have — some social skill or feeling of belonging or social grace — oppress her most of the time, making any step toward connection slow, scary, and painful. Much of the time the belief has her convinced that she will never get out from under it in this lifetime.

When we were compiling the manuscript for this chapter, Jill, who consults with Julie and me, suggested that we could invite you, the readers of this book, to write to Julie. I thought this was a great idea! However, the problematic story had such a hold on me that it kept me from talking to Julie about the possibility for weeks. It had me convinced that Julie would either reject the idea out of embarrassment or scorn me for suggesting anything so foolish.

When I finally did mention that we could, with her permission, ask readers of this book to write to her, Julie was doubtful that anyone would respond, but curious about what people might say if they did write. Her willingness to hear your thoughts, feelings, and responses to her as you read my letter and description of her story mean to me that she has a growing willingness to connect with people. In the light of her life experience to date, I am humbled by her bravery in being open to letters. Besides your general responses, are there things that you wonder? Have you had experiences, personally or with other people, with extreme forms of self-doubt and self-hate? What did you or other people that you know find helpful in getting through such experiences? Might some of the people who consult with you want to form an "anti-self-hatred, pro-connection-with-people league" (see pp. 252–255) with Julie? You can reach her by writing to:

> "Julie"
> c/o Gene Combs
> Evanston Family Therapy Center
> 636 Church St., #901
> Evanston, IL 60201

Extending Ideas or Stories that Began in
a Therapy Conversation

Letters need not follow the sequence of a therapy conversation or
series of conversations. They can focus more on amplifying ideas or
stories that started in an interview. In the following letter I (GC) group a
number of statements Julie made together because I hoped that taken
together they would have greater weight.

> *Dear Julie,*
>
> *As I look back over my notes from our last meeting, I find a*
> *smile growing on my face and in my spirit. To me, it feels really*
> *good to hear you saying things like these:*
> *"I don't think I'm as bad as I think I am."*
> *"I don't think I'm as helpless and incompetent as I think I am."*
> *"I can't be as bad as I think I am."*
> *"I might be bad, but I'm not that bad."*
> *"I'm feeling more that my life is important. I count as much as*
> *anybody else."*
> *"It was time to let go of my parents a long time ago. I need to*
> *do things for myself. There's nobody there [at her parent's house]*
> *to support or encourage me in these things—it's more lonely there*
> *than it would be on my own."*
> *"I've decided I've got to go ahead and do some of these things.*
> *I'm tired of being my own worst enemy."*
> *You certainly don't sound like your own worst enemy to me in*
> *any of the above statements, and everything that I have put in*
> *quotes is something that's as close as I could copy it down to*
> *something you actually said in our conversation. I wonder how it*
> *feels to read your words back in this edited and concentrated form?*
> *Does the experience tend more to arouse old habits of self-doubt*
> *and self-criticism or more to further you in your project to "go*
> *ahead and do some of these things"?*
>
> *Warmly,*
> *Gene*

We might also help people thicken a story by a much shorter letter
that perhaps asks a question about one unique outcome or asks a question that invites the person to take a new step.

> *Dear Susan and Mel,*
>
> *After you left I was looking back at my notes. I had written*
> *down that you decided together what to do about the difficulty*

Raymond is having getting into school. I wondered if this was a situation that could have been dominated by conflict and bad feelings but wasn't? Can you fill me in on how you did this when we meet again?

Jill

Including People Who Didn't Attend a Meeting

When someone who has been attending therapy misses a meeting, we often write a letter to keep that person included in the story and updated on its developments. At the same time we can use the letter to ask questions that might thicken the story. The following is an example of such a letter written by the Evanston Family Therapy Center training team.[6]

Dear Maria,

Roberto, Juan, and Rosa came to see us on February 14 and we wanted to write you a letter to include you in what happened. There were a couple of things that stood out for the team during this conversation. First, Juan said that he was able to go to school for nine days in a row—the team considers this a nine-day winning streak. Would you agree? We understand that heaviness and worry may pull your attention to the Friday when this winning streak was interrupted. However, we are still curious about this accomplishment (the largest all year). Would you consider discussing these questions with the family?

Juan said that the first Monday was the hardest day to go to school. What do you think Juan did to overcome the difficulty that day? Do you think it took a special effort? He says it got easier towards the middle of the week. Roberto said Juan seemed more relaxed at that point. Did you notice a lightness or ease in Juan during those days? Was there a lightness or ease in other family members?

Juan mentioned that it was easier to go to school on Friday if he was completely free (from detention and grounding) for the weekend. Did you realize that Juan was thinking before acting, weighing the consequences before deciding whether or not to cut classes?

---

[6]Dina Shulman was the therapist working with this family. The team included Michele Cohen, Marsha Azar, Gene Combs, and Jill Freedman.

What do you think it says about him that he's thinking this way? Is it at all surprising to you that being grounded makes a difference to Juan?

In the first meeting, Rosa told us that anger had come between her and Juan and had gotten her to watch what he was doing and try to set him straight. During the last conversation she mentioned "not paying attention" to Juan's actions. Do you think it is a good thing that Rosa is no longer being so affected by the problem?

If we're understanding correctly, Juan has given up sneaking out. Does this mean that something new is sneaking into his life? If so, we're curious as to what it might be. One team member was wondering if it was in part out of consideration for other family members. What do you think?

See you next Tuesday!

Sincerely,
Dina and the team

Clients' Writing

We've been considering letter writing here from the standpoint of therapists writing to the people they are working with. Peggy Penn and Marilyn Frankfurt (1994) have written about asking the people they work with in therapy to write between meetings. They (pp. 229–230) write,

> Our clinical experience soon taught us that writing slows down our perceptions and reactions, making room for their thickening, their gradual layering. And that this process, which could be described as poeticizing, encourages us to develop many different readings of our experience. Finally, the writing, something to keep, to study, to revise, to show, enables us to hold our many stories in tension. . . . The participant text as the vehicle for therapy transfers new knowledge from the inside of the session to the outside, as well as from the outside to the inside. This movement has an integrative function, sowing possibilities between our lives and our therapy, and giving voice to our many-faceted selves.

We too have worked with people who have used writing as part of the therapy. Sometimes the writing was their idea and they brought letters and notes for us to see. At other times, we asked if they were interested in writing.

Documents

Because there are multiple possibilities, infinite strands of experience, and countless ways of interpreting any idea or event, important intentions and even accomplishments can get lost. When people make important commitments or when we get ready to celebrate significant achievements with them, we think of documents. Before we prepare a document we ask if they would be interested in having one to declare their position or mark their accomplishment.

Typically, we cocreate documents. The person whose document it will be has the final say about wording.

Susan is a 24-year-old woman who has missed out on some of life because of fear's longstanding domination of her life. Fears have made Susan avoid a number of experiences, such as going away to camp and going to college. They have made her an easy target for drugs and alcohol, which she thought helped chase away the fears. She has now realized that they blurred years of her life and she feels as though she missed growing up and learning social skills. She says that it's like she's "at the back of the bus." She wishes she could move up but is overtaken with confusion about what this would mean. For example, confusion keeps her from knowing whether it's in her best interest to continue living with her parents. Other people's ideas of who she should be pull at her, keep her from having her own ideas, and lead to comparisons with others that pave the way for bad feelings about herself. She wants to be the one to decide who she will be. She has named this project "Standing Tall."

After the conversation in which she named the project, she found that guilt, second thoughts, and habits kept her from moving ahead with it, especially around her family. She said, "I am so unused to saying how I feel it's like someone is squeezing the air from my lungs when I try to talk." She decided that a declaration would help her fill people in on what would be helpful to her and help her remind herself of her chosen direction. She could either give it to people or read it aloud to them. The document that we (Susan and JF) created is shown in Figure 8.1.

After the meeting in which we wrote the document, Susan read it out loud at the family table during Passover. Although her parents said nothing when she read it, her mother put it up on the mirror in her bedroom. Susan has found herself referring back to it to explain her thinking and behavior to her family. She's told me that the declaration seems to have created more room for her to stand tall in. Consequently, she has more air to breathe. She has been able to know and say what she thinks in difficult situations.

Documents don't have to be elaborate or pretty to be meaningful. I (GC) often jot things down on the same legal-pad paper on which I take

SUSAN'S DECLARATION OF STANDING TALL

1. In order for me to grow up I need to stand tall.

2. Standing tall means that I will form my own ideas and opinions.

3. This does not mean I don't like you or that I disrespect your opinions.

4. It does mean that I am interested in finding my own opinions and living by them.

5. I hope you will support me in standing tall because I think I could be taller with your help.

Figure 8.1

my clinical notes and give them to people to underscore or make more tangible some new experience or idea that has emerged in our conversation. An example of this occurred in my work with Emma, whom you may remember from Chapter 4. Emma was talking about how her whole family—parents and siblings—treated her like she was "adequate," but not really good at anything. This attitude coached her to believe that she should live her life for *them*, not for herself. She told me about a confrontation she had had with her brother in which she stood up and walked out when he threatened to fire her. She said she felt very strong and worthy as she walked out, and she was saying over and over in her head, "It's not my job to keep him from being an asshole."

Earlier in the meeting, Emma had told me how important her college degree was to her. It was proof that she was better than adequate. It symbolized her ability to achieve and to do things for herself. She framed it and hung it on her bathroom wall where she would see it every day. This story demonstrated how meaningful a document could be for Emma, and it rang in my head as she told her story about walking out on her brother.

I wrote,

IT'S NOT MY JOB TO KEEP HIM FROM BEING AN ASSHOLE

on a page of my legal pad and handed it to her. I asked her if she thought it might be useful to hang this phrase on or near her bathroom mirror for a while. She was delighted with this idea.

She did hang the phrase on her mirror, and looking at it on Sunday morning motivated her to read the job ads in the paper very carefully, type out a resume, and send it out to five different places. That's how she got the job we mention in the transcript in Chapter 4.

Other documents mark achievements, especially those that signify accomplishing projects. These may take the form of certificates, cards, awards, or the like. Figure 8.2 shows Rhonda's card that you read about when it was still in embryo in the first letter in the "Letters" section of this chapter, under "Summarizing Meetings."

SYMBOLS

Although the school had indicated that nine-year-old Erica would be seen weekly by the school social worker, his caseload and Erica's class projects seemed to get in the way all too often. Grant and Diane, Erica's grandparents, worried that Erica might be "depressed." They decided to take matters into their own hands and brought Erica to see me (JF).

In a phone conversation before the first meeting, Ron, Erica's father, told me that he thought Erica needed something because she seemed to "always be cowering and not speak up" and her grades had plummeted.

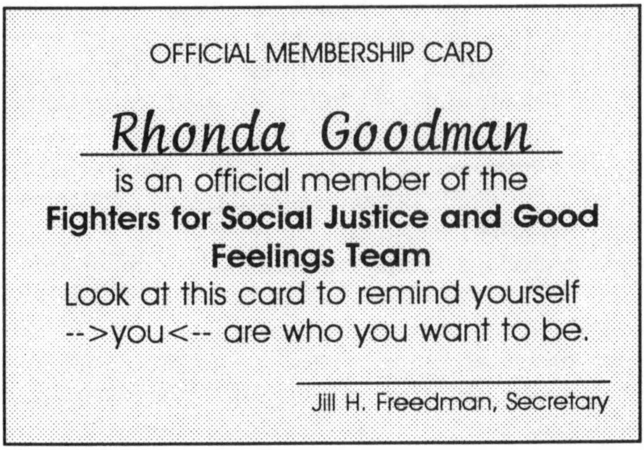

> OFFICIAL MEMBERSHIP CARD
>
> ## Rhonda Goodman
>
> is an official member of the
> **Fighters for Social Justice and Good Feelings Team**
> Look at this card to remind yourself
> -->you<-- are who you want to be.
>
> Jill H. Freedman, Secretary

Figure 8.2

However, he and Erica's mother, Clarisse, and Erica's younger sister, Hannah, could not regularly attend our meetings because the couple worked different shifts, they were already in couples therapy, and Ron was in individual therapy and night school. The family had tried family therapy once and believed that it didn't work. Ron said that it was okay with them if Erica came to see me with his parents. We agreed to stay in touch by phone and Ron indicated that the family would consider coming to occasional meetings.

The First Meeting

At the first meeting I began by asking Erica what she liked to do. She mumbled, "I don't know," but did not disagree with her grandparents' list, which included art, drawing, singing, working on the computer, ice skating, swimming, and rollerblading. Erica did volunteer that she didn't like her seven-year-old sister, Hannah. She didn't know if there was a problem, but listened quietly as Grant said, "She doesn't give herself credit for anything. She never brags. She's always saying she's sorry — for nothing." Diane added, "She's very quiet. Hannah tells all of Erica's good news. Erica has nothing of her own because Hannah is always in on it."

I asked Erica what she thought about what her grandparents said. She said she didn't know. With several more questions she finally said that she guessed she didn't give herself credit. I asked if she would be interested in making a picture to show what she didn't give herself credit for. She quietly drew on a large piece of newsprint a framed picture to represent her art, a report card, a bell to represent the bell chorus she is part of, a Taekwondo uniform because she takes Taekwondo, a math book, and six friends (Figure 8.3).

I asked her about each of the elements of the drawing. She reluctantly told me that her grades in math are pretty good. Her grandparents agreed. She said that she didn't know whether the six kids she drew really were her friends or not, but in answer to questions she decided it was better to think they were because that would make her "act on the other side," acting friendly instead of shy.

Erica did not seem interested in conversation about what kept her from taking credit for these things, so I asked her, "If you could wave a magic wand that would help you start taking credit, what do you think you would notice that you are not noticing now?"

Erica quickly answered, "I would be thinking on the happy side." She explained that she would be seeing brighter colors, like a rainbow. She added a rainbow to the picture.

With further questioning she said that she'd feel better about going to

*Figure 8.3. Erica's drawing of what she doesn't
give herself credit for.*

Taekwondo and would be saying to herself, "I'll do better than usual."
"I'll get my pattern right."

Erica seemed to know so much about this that I asked her if the words
she would say to herself were familiar ones. It turned out that just two
days before she played a whole song in bell chorus without messing up
once! She had said to herself, "I'm going to do good," and she did. She
thought that saying to herself, "I'm going to do good," helped set the
mood that would make her chances for "doing good" great!

Erica's grandparents were delighted to hear that Erica already had
taken a step toward giving herself credit. They knew she could do it,
because she had in the past. To back this up, they recounted some
experiences that they were delighted to hear about when Erica told about
them in past years.

As they were getting ready to leave I asked Erica if she wanted to take
the picture home to remind her of what we had talked about. "No, I
want you to keep it," she said looking down. "But could I borrow the
magic wand?" On my desk, she had spied my telephone companion, a

clear tube full of glittering confetti suspended in a thick substance. I gave it to her.

The Second Meeting

At the second meeting Erica was much more talkative. She told me that after our meeting, at first she had forgotten about our conversation, but when she saw the magic wand she remembered. Then she reminded herself to take credit. The forgetting and remembering happened a few more times and then she decided to carry the wand with her. She found out that " . . . it could make life better to give yourself credit. Then you won't always be mad at yourself."

She named the problem "self-blame" and the project "feeling better about yourself." Erica saw that she was getting the best of the self-blame already. Giving herself credit made it possible for her to keep doing what she already could do, but to feel good about it. The result of this was that she was happy and she discovered that she was really good at Taek-wondo. She thought that giving herself credit also helped her write a biography of her grandfather. She thought her teachers saw a difference because they had commented that she was working harder. She thought maybe her parents noticed because she had been happier at home, but she wasn't sure.

Diane and Grant noticed that when they picked Erica up from school she was smiling and talking to other kids instead of standing quietly by herself.

We all wondered about where this project would make itself known next. Erica thought it might be with her sister. She told me, "I might not always fight with her. I might stop getting mad at her for stuff she doesn't do."

"So do you think the self-blame turns into blame against others some-times?"

She nodded.

"And it gets you in fights too, huh?"

She nodded again.

"Wow. I didn't know it was so powerful. And you've already turned it around this much?"

Again she nodded.

"Do you think as you turn this blame around even more you'll be more in touch with loving your sister?"

Erica nodded.

"Then what will happen?" I asked.

"Well," she confided, "Probably my parents will stop telling me I'll get coal in my stocking." (It was December.)

I wondered if maybe the blame was messing up Hannah's life too. Diane and Grant thought maybe it was. We all agreed that it would be good for the whole family to know about how Erica was turning self-blame around and feeling better about herself. We agreed I would phone Ron and Clarisse and invite them and Hannah to the next meeting. We agreed that we would show them the picture and fill them in on Erica's "feeling better about yourself" project.

The Third Meeting

Erica, Hannah, Clarisse, and Ron attended the third meeting. I had expected Diane and Grant to come as well but the family worked it out for just the four to come.

After I got to know Hannah, Clarisse, and Ron a bit, we unveiled Erica's picture and together described what the different images meant and what she had accomplished on the "feeling better about yourself" project.

Ron had already noticed a big difference in Erica that was consistent with the project. "Erica has always tried hard," he said, "but now she seems to be taking big steps." He noticed that she had become more involved with kids her own age, whereas before she seemed to always be alone or with younger kids. He noticed her interacting more at the bell choir practice and Taekwondo. She began having guests over for the first time. Both he and Clarisse were happy about these developments.

I asked Ron what he thought this said about his daughter. He answered, "She's becoming more mature." He then added that she was also standing up for herself. He noticed her standing up for herself both with other kids and with Hannah.

Clarisse agreed in part but said that she still hoped that the fighting, arguing, bickering, and whining between Erica and Hannah would stop.

I turned to Hannah and told her that Erica and I had had a conversation about how Erica thought that blame had come between them. She agreed. I wondered what effect the blame had on their sisterhood and whether this was something they might work on together.

Erica blurted out, "I don't want her coming. This is for me."

"Would it be okay if you fill Hannah in on what we talk about that has to do with her and the two of you see how you could work together?" I asked.

Erica nodded.

The Fourth Meeting

At the fourth meeting with Erica, Grant, and Diane, Erica updated me on her "feeling better about yourself" project. She got promoted to a green belt, got an 89 on a report she did, and she felt happy most of the time! She updated her picture because there was now more she was taking credit for. She added a stage for being in a play, a snowflake for sledding, and "NUBS is the best and so am I!" NUBS was the name of a group she belonged to at her church.

I asked a number of questions to fill out the story of how all of these changes were happening, what steps Erica was taking, what the turning points were, and how she was advising herself.

Erica shrugged in response. "I still carry the magic wand. I remember the picture."

"What do they mean to you?" I asked.

"That I can do it," she said. "That I can turn self-blame around."

Since Erica was very interested in the ground she was gaining on self-blame and less interested in how this was happening, I asked her if she would like to show me how much ground self-blame had before and how much it had now. I said, "First, you could draw a box that would hold all the self-blame from before. . . . "

She drew an oblong box.

"And what would be in it?" I asked. Erica filled in:

Getting bad grades.
Pictures aren't good.
Fighting with sister.
My parents fighting.
Because I don't have any friends.

"So those are all the things that self-blame blamed you for?"

"Yes," said Erica, writing "Before" in the box.

"How big of a box would it take to hold the self-blame in your life now?"

Erica drew a much smaller box.

"What's in it?" I asked.

"Fighting with my sister," she answered, filling the words in and adding "Now." She then drew a line through "Getting bad grades," "Pictures aren't good," "My parents fighting," and "Because I don't have any friends," in the first box, leaving only "Fighting with sister."

I showed the representation to Grant and Diane. "Did you know Erica had shrunk self-blame this small?"

They had wondered but hadn't known for sure. We all speculated about the relative sizes of the two. The change had happened over the course of nine weeks, so we wondered how long it would take to shrink the "now" box or if it was okay to leave it the size it was.

The Fifth Meeting

The fifth meeting took place three weeks later. In a phone call with Clarisse before this meeting I discovered that Erica and Hannah were getting along much better and that Grant and Diane were on vacation. Clarisse volunteered to bring Erica to the meeting. I assumed we would meet together, but Clarisse dropped off Erica so I saw her alone.

Erica told me that the most important thing that happened in her project was that she made a lot of new friends. We made this list of new friends:

Alison	Morgan	Dawn	Sam
Emily	Mara	Yukiko	Matt
Ilana	Heather	Christina	Aaron
Brooke	Vera	Ginger	Hayden
Enid	Stephanie	Demetria	Frank
Natalie	Hannah	Antonio	Robert
Shannon	Melissa	Reed	Sean

Erica was able to make all of these friends just by being herself. What she learned was, "Don't act like you're somebody else." The self-blame got her to try to act like somebody else. The "feeling better about yourself" project helped her be herself.

The main differences she identified between this year and the last were that now she felt better about herself, she appreciated herself more, she had better grades, and she had more friends. She said that her parents and teachers noticed and that her grandparents would notice when they came back from vacation.

When I turned the conversation toward the relationship with Hannah, Erica said, "But I told you. Now she's one of my friends."

I hadn't realized when she listed "Hannah" that she was talking about her sister.

Erica was very matter of fact about the old news that blame no longer was coming between her and her sister.

She thought that the project was finished. We decided to meet one more time with the whole family to celebrate. I felt confident in making this suggestion because of my previous conversation with Clarisse, who had confirmed that Erica was doing great.

The Sixth Meeting

At the sixth meeting I announced that we were there to celebrate Erica turning around self-blame and achieving the project of feeling better about herself! Erica showed the picture again, describing it and pointing out the additions. She then read the list of her friends' names. Hannah beamed when her name was read. After the reading was completed, Hannah confirmed that blame was gone from their relationship. She thought that Erica was mostly responsible because she had been "nicer and happier." Everyone agreed this would make a big difference in family life.

Ron added that at the time the therapy began the school was very concerned about Erica's performance. There had been talk of her possibly repeating the year. This prospect had been extremely distressing to Ron. He and Clarisse had contacted a Catholic school about the possibility of Erica going there. They hoped that this would forestall her repeating a grade and that in a more structured program she would catch up. The Catholic school was not willing to admit Erica at grade level unless reports improved. Ron was relieved that at a parent-teacher conference just two days before, Erica's progress was characterized as excellent. He wondered if the therapy was responsible.

I said that we hadn't talked about school problems. I had known that Erica's grades were lower than in previous years but I hadn't know the extent of this. I had spoken to the school social worker twice, but he had not mentioned academic problems. I said that it sounded to me like Erica was responsible for turning this around all by herself! She beamed.

We all had cookies that Diane supplied and congratulated Erica.

As the family was getting ready to leave Erica handed me back my "wand."

"You can keep that," I said.

"I don't need it anymore," Erica told me. "The magic is here now," she said, patting her heart.

This story illustrates the use of a number of symbols that emerged from the therapy—the picture, the wand, and the boxes showing the shrinking of self-blame. For some people, particularly children, but not only children, symbols and concrete representations of portions of the work seem to make it more real and graspable (Combs & Freedman, 1990; Roberts, 1994).

For example, near the end of therapy, one couple created a collage representing their hopes for their relationship. They phoned three years later to say that everything on the collage was happening! When we asked what the role of the collage was in achieving their dreams, they said that it kept them focused and reassured each of them that they were in it together. They said that the collage also made their dreams seem more real and clear.

THE STORY OF CARRIE

In this chapter we have presented documents, letters, certificates, and the like as aspects of therapy that serve to thicken and develop stories. We've thought of them as very important, but important in a supportive way—not the main work. So we were intrigued when our colleague, Virginia Simons, told us about her therapy with Carrie. In this work what we had thought of as supportive or adjunctive took center stage. This was not by design at the outset but in response to what Carrie was willing to talk about and become involved in. Carrie, her family, and Virginia gave us permission to tell you their story.

June and her six-year-old daughter Carrie came to see Virginia because June was concerned about her daughter's fearfulness. She described Carrie as timid and shy. Except around family, she was reluctant to speak. She had few friends. These problems were exacerbated when she started first grade. Carrie's teacher reported that she refused to stand in line in the lunchroom to buy milk because she was worried she wouldn't be able to find a place to sit if she didn't take a seat immediately. Carrie was not joining in on class activities that required any focus on her at all and refusing to go out for recess. She would go to the nurse's office or sit in the school library.

Virginia asked Carrie if she agreed with her mom that these things were a problem. Carrie didn't answer. In fact, over the course of the therapy, Virginia attempted three times to engage Carrie in naming the problem. By the third time, the relationship between Virginia and Carrie was well established and it was clear that Carrie enjoyed talking to Virginia. In that context she confided to Virginia that "talking about problems grows them. I don't want to." Therefore, the problem was never named.

At the first meeting, June identified some developments in Carrie's life that she found encouraging. With Carrie's permission and input on word choice, Virginia listed these three developments. They were:

1. Speaking up for yourself when someone yells at you.
2. Sitting with a grown-up and talking about the sneakiness of fears. [This refers to the therapy conversation itself.]
3. Going to school each day.

Usually when unique outcomes or sparkling events such as these are named, we ask questions about them to develop the story. In this situation, although Carrie agreed for achievements to be written down, she wasn't happy with the idea of talking about them very much. So they were left as a list. However, as time went on June did relate the stories of some events.

The list was to become the basis of the therapy.

Carrie came to the second meeting with two items that she wanted to add to the list. They were:

4. Trying and wanting to pay attention in class.
5. Going all around inside the school.

In subsequent meetings Carrie and June added more items to the list. Virginia asked Carrie what the list should be called, suggesting "bravery" as one of several possibilities. Carrie liked "bravery," so "Carrie's Bravery Project" was born.

At one point, after about 20 items were listed, Virginia asked, "How many things do you think we need on this list for you to know you have finished the "Bravery Project?" To Virginia's amazement, Carrie said, "I think it would take 100."

This is "Carrie's Bravery Project" list, recorded during 19 therapy meetings:

CARRIE'S BRAVERY PROJECT

1. Speaking up for yourself when someone yells at you.
2. Sitting with a grown-up and talking about the sneakiness of fears.
3. Going to school each day.
4. Trying and wanting to pay attention in class.
5. Going all around inside the school.
6. Going to specials and other meetings by yourself.
7. Going to the lunch room where it is VERY noisy and crowded.
8. Going on your own to see other teachers you like, like Ms. Whitehouse [the kindergarten teacher].
9. Going to the bathroom alone.
10. Doing your work in class.
11. Cooperating with others.
12. Going to the playground with Ms. Brown.
13. Going to get milk at lunch with someone.
14. Helping Eva with tasks in class.
15. Working on assignments in class and out all the time.
16. Going to get lunch when you want it.
17. Going to the school playground before school by yourself.
18. Going to the playground at lunch sometimes.
19. Running in gym class by yourself, without the teacher.

20. Leaving with the reading teacher by yourself.
21. Going with Ms. Lakely on the playground.
22. Going to get milk by yourself at lunch.
23. Trying something new at a party.
24. Going to a party and staying by yourself, even if you get nervous.
25. Telling the teacher when you forget money for something.
26. Taking ski lessons more by yourself and not crying.
27. Talking to Santa about what you wanted.
28. After time off from school, returning without crying.
29. After time off from school, going to school by yourself.
30. Going sledding with a friend and her parents.
31. Going outside at Monday lunch.
32. Going outside at Tuesday lunch.
33. Went to a friend's house with a new sitter.
34. At the friend's house ENJOYED yourself.
35. At school you can walk away if you need to and know everything will be okay.
36. You can tell grown-ups you know what you want, like, and don't like.
37. You can ask grown-ups questions you need answers to.
38. You did not get upset when the drain didn't work and there was no water at the cabin.
39. You did not get scared or cry when your mom got a bloody nose in the van on the way home.
40. At the basketball game, you went out and got a drink by yourself.
41. You were interested in flute and kept asking.
42. You went to flute lessons alone.
43. You practiced your flute regularly, and you know what you like.
44.-54. You went sledding with a friend on the BIG BIG hill, and you were not afraid.[7]
55. You went to Anna's house with a sitter who only speaks Spanish.[8]
56.-76. You got home and no one was there yet. You did think smart and went to Liza's house to wait.
77.-83. At Grandma's you accidentally got locked out and rang the doorbell on both sides BEFORE you got upset. (10–15 minutes!!)
84. Took swimming classes.

---

[7]June was quite astounded when Carrie came home from a friend's house, grinning, and reported that the friend's father had taken the two of them sledding. This sledding did not occur on a small hill or even a big hill, but on a big, big hill. Virginia knew the hill in question and both she and June had been quite sure that only big kids went on that particular hill. Not knowing what to make of this Virginia wondered if this event was worth more than one place on the list. Carrie decided it was worth ten. This initiated the practice of evaluating events for how many places on the list they were worth.

[8]Carrie only speaks English.

85. Mom leaves and you are okay, more than okay, you correct, you are FINE.
86. You sat through the entire *Joseph and the Technicolor Dream Coat* performance.
87. You stayed home with the timer while Mom took sister to lessons, and called the neighbor for a chat.
88. Stayed home by yourself while Mom picked up sister and watched TV.
89. You went to play with a brand-new friend at the cabin, and had fun.
90. When your sister babysits you it's fine (no crying).
91. You let Monica babysit you.
92. You are raising your hand in school and answering a question in front of the class.
93. At Indian Princesses you have been raising your hand and talking.
94. You read a story out loud with Dad at Indian Princesses.
95. At dance you took a lead role in front of everyone.

At the point that there were 83 items on the list Carrie, June, and Virginia agreed that what they were now sometimes calling the "Bravery Project" and other times the "Growing Up Project" was well underway. Virginia asked about Carrie's interest in a celebration and Carrie agreed. She wanted her mother, father, sister, and Virginia to attend and suggested balloons, cake, and pretzels.

Carrie and June set the celebration date for two months after the meeting in which the list reached 83, which would be two weeks before school ended for the year.

Before the celebration, Virginia sent Carrie this letter:

Dear Carrie:

Hello there! I've been wondering how you have been doing. I was wondering especially about your "growing up" project, and if you would have more things to add to your list of things you are doing that lets you and everyone else know how you are growing up. So far, I have it that you have got 83 ways you have grown up, into your age and older than your age. How many more things could we add to the list now? Would I have to get out more paper? I guess I'll have to wait to find out until the celebration.

Are you ready to celebrate? Sometimes the "growing down" or "backing up" feelings sneak back in kids' lives once in a while, at least that is what other children have told me. Has that happened to you too? Do you think you can outsmart them, if they show back up in your life?

I heard from your mom how very very well you practice and play the flute!! You could bring it when you come so I could hear a song or two if you would like. I would enjoy that if you want to.

Best regards,
Virginia Simons

At the celebration, at Carrie's request, her sister read the list to everyone assembled. After the reading, family members suggested the additions of items 84 through 95.

Then Virginia presented Carrie with this Certificate of Bravery (Figure 8.4).

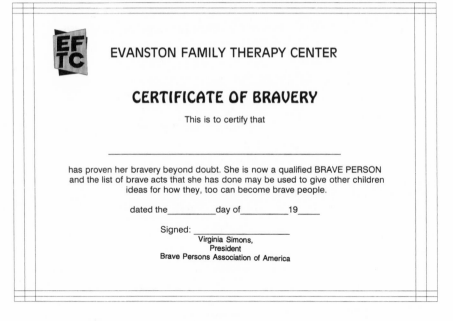

Figure 8.4

Spreading the News

As "self" is a performed self, the survival of alternative knowledges is enhanced if the new ideas and new meanings that they bring forth are put into circulation.

—Michael White, 1988b, p. 10

The hard-won meanings should be said, painted, danced, dramatised, put into circulation.

— Victor Turner, 1986, p. 37

If people constitute their preferred selves by performing their preferred stories, then it is important that there be audiences for those stories. Once they exist, such audiences make up local subcultures which construct and circulate alternative knowledge — knowledge that provides new lenses through which to interpret experience. As preferred stories are circulated and shared in a subculture, *all* the participants in that subculture construct each other according to the values, beliefs, and ideas carried in that subculture's preferred stories. This whole process constitutes the kind of "insurrection of subjugated knowledges" about which Foucault (1980) wrote. Madigan and Epston (1995) propose the term "communities of concern" for such participant audience subcultures.

Although in the dominant culture therapy tends to be a secret enterprise, in the narrative subculture the people who consult with us are usually enthusiastic about the idea of letting other people in on the process. We think that externalizing and antipathologizing practices offer people a different kind of experience in therapy. When therapy becomes a context in which people constitute preferred selves, they have nothing to hide and much to show. David Epston (O'Hanlon, 1994, p. 28) puts it this way,

. . . in this therapy, people emerge as heroes and they often want that heroism acknowledged in some social way. They are usually quite happy to communicate with others and tell their stories.

Ideas about ways to recruit a participant audience or local subculture are currently burgeoning. In this chapter we describe some possibilities for how to foster such communities of concern. Some involve using ideas we've already described, such as reflecting processes and letters. Others, such as "leagues," we haven't touched on yet.

QUESTIONS TO IDENTIFY
AND RECRUIT AN AUDIENCE

Asking questions is probably the easiest way for therapists to encourage the people they work with to identify and recruit an audience. The following are examples of questions that encourage people to name candidates and consider recruiting them:

- Who would be most interested to learn of this step you've taken? Why would that interest her so? How could you let her know?
- Who in your current life would have predicted that you would make this kind of commitment? What do they know about you that would have led them to make this prediction? How would knowing about this step support this knowledge about you? Would that be helpful to you? How? How could you let them know?
- Who would most appreciate this event we've been talking about? What might he learn about you if you let him in on it that would be of interest to him? What might he say to you about this? How could you initiate such a conversation?

These questions all presuppose that the person might actually initiate a conversation. Such conversations, when they occur, are very valuable. They constitute lived experiences that can become important incidents in people's life narratives. Simply entertaining the idea of such conversations often motivates people to initiate them.

We've found that even if the conversations do not actually happen, an audience still develops in people's thinking or imagination. Even an imaginary conversation can constitute real experience of a supportive audience. It is not unusual for someone to name a particular person who would be interested in their story and then, without ever letting that person in on it, assume support and appreciation from her. This assumption makes it more likely that the person will perform preferred versions of himself when he is around the unknowing audience. In this way, the unknowing audience becomes an actual audience!

Questions that don't go as far as suggesting conversations with other people can also be useful — either in creating audiences in imagination or simply in reminding the person that she is a member of a supportive community.

- Who will be most pleased to discover that you have taken this step? How might she discover it?
- Who will be most affected by this development? What will he notice that will let him know?

Even if a particular person is not available in the current situation, it can be helpful to name her as a potential audience member.

- Who from your past would have predicted this development? What did she know about you that would have led to that prediction? Was there a particular incident that let her in on this about you? How was that incident like this development?
- Who would you like to talk with about this that you have not yet talked with?[1] It could be anyone, living or dead, here or far away. What might they say?

INVITING AN AUDIENCE
TO THERAPY MEETINGS

Harlene Anderson and Harry Goolishian, among others (Anderson & Goolishian, 1988; Anderson, Goolishian, & Winderman, 1986; Goolishian & Anderson, 1981, 1987; Hoffman, 1988; Levin, Raser, Niles, & Reese, 1986) have emphasized the idea that problems are maintained through language and social interaction. In accordance with their emphasis, they have invited members of the "problem-determined system" — those who are in language about a problem — into the therapy room.

The Brattleboro team members (Lax, 1991) routinely ask, "Who is involved with this situation?" when someone calls to set up therapy. During that first phone call they introduce the possibility of everyone involved coming to the meeting.

We appreciate the language "introduce the possibility" because a direct request for the presence of friends, relatives, co-workers, or representatives of involved agencies can be an occasion for distress. When

---

[1]Tom Andersen (1991b) has suggested this question.

most people originally seek therapy, the dominant discourses lead them to assume that something is wrong with them. If we suggest including other people in the process, they may imagine experiences of embarassment, shame, and possibly of social control. As their assumptions about therapy are deconstructed in the course of our work together (including the initial phone conversation), people tend to be more open and even enthusiastic about inviting others to join in. The final choice about who should attend therapy meetings is, of course, always in the hands of the people who consult with us.

An experience I (JF) had years ago was helpful in showing us how useful the option of including others can be. At that time I was working with Donna, who had been sexually abused by a number of family members throughout her childhood. In her late thirties, the abuse affected her by coaching fear and distrust of others. The fear and distrust not only made Donna withdraw from social situations, but also paved the way for anger and bitterness to take over, often with little current provocation. Social isolation characterized most of Donna's life. She told me that other people thought she was difficult to get along with, suspicious, and touchy.

In our work together I felt very honored to witness her perseverence and integrity. She made meticulous distinctions in judging what was important to her in relationships and how she could recognize if someone was trustworthy. These distinctions gradually made it possible to be more open to people. As she began to constitute herself as someone who could be connected to others, we were both disappointed that there was seemingly no recognition of her change outside of the therapy room. It seemed that her reputation was blinding others to the current developments in her life.

She suggested that she would like to bring the principal of the school where she taught to therapy with her. At the time, the idea was somewhat threatening to me. Before that time, I had had conversations with employers *about* someone I was working with, but Donna was proposing something different. She wanted someone from work to see her the way she was when we interacted in therapy. She thought that having someone experience that view of her would help her to keep the person she was becoming alive. Since I wanted that to happen too, how could I refuse?

I faced the interview with some trepidation. Would the principal discredit the therapy? Or try to convince me of what Donna was "really" like? This idea of including someone else who was not a family member flew in the face of ideas I had been taught about confidentiality. Even though I was already abandoning many of the therapy ideas I learned, this idea was difficult to let go of. Nonetheless, Dan, the principal at Donna's school, attended a meeting.

We invited Dan to listen to our conversation, saying we would ask him at points for his thoughts, then we proceeded to have the kind of conversation we had been having together. At one point Donna glimpsed the possibility of being a person who could have conversations with ease. We considered it a step in that direction that she could have such conversations with me. A second step was that she could imagine it happening with certain other people. "If you continue in this direction, who do you think you might be able to talk with? In what contexts might this begin to happen?" I asked.

Donna was silent for what seemed like a long time. "I just don't know," she said, shaking her head in discouragement.

Dan cleared his throat and blurted out, emphatically, "But that's been happening already! At the last faculty meeting you participated in a way I had never seen before. It seemed natural; you were at ease. I've also seen you in the teachers' lounge talking to people. It might be just about the weather, but before, you'd scurry in, get some coffee, and scurry out. Now, you're there. You're sitting down for a minute and not startling if someone sits next to you."

Donna looked at him dumbfounded.

"Did you know that others were seeing you this way?" I asked.

"No," she said and began to weep.

"This might seem like a strange question," I said to Dan, "but before this conversation had you recognized the steps Donna had taken to connect with people?"

"No. I hadn't thought about it," he said. "But now I see."

Dan's "seeing" made a difference in how he subsequently responded to Donna at school. His different responses helped Donna maintain her new vision of herself and supported her in taking risks to be in relationship with others.

We learned from Donna's idea. Now we often ask whether it might be useful to invite other people to join in our meetings.

When Wayne first called me (GC) he requested individual therapy. At that time, playing games on the computer was about the only thing depression would allow him to do besides sleep and worry. Soon after therapy began, we invited Doris, Wayne's partner, to come to meetings. The depression had come between them and coated their relationship with hopelessness. The only other person Wayne seemed very involved with was their next-door neighbor, Don, who ambled over some afternoons to play computer games. With therapy at a near standstill, we invited Don to join us, too.

What follows is a brief transcript of one of my meetings with Wayne, Don, and Doris. Wayne had been saying that he was stuck. He felt like depression had him in a corner again, and he was losing ground. He was talking as if he was convinced that he had made no progress whatsoever. Doris and Don began to list evidence to the contrary, and as they did, I remembered that I had forgotten to turn on the videotape equipment. Wanting to be sure we all had a record of this, I excused myself for a moment. Here's what happened when I came back:

GENE You were making a list there — and that's part of what I wanted to get on the tape — of things that you were seeing, that you think are . . . are evidence to you that Wayne's doing better.

DORIS Right.

GENE What's. . . . So let's go back and get that list.

DORIS Being alert. And being focused. And I can think of numerous times over the last few years where, you know, you'd ask Wayne a question and you'd just get kind of a blank look, and you knew . . . for one thing, he was probably trying real hard to understand what you were saying. And processing it internally. And then later, maybe coming out with a response. But often not. Um. That's . . . that's the type of thing I don't see anymore. I mean, when we talk or anything, he comments on stuff. He's right there and he understands what I'm saying. The alertness. The being able to focus on a task. And complete it. Um . . . and have the interest in doing it. Um . . .

GENE So he's . . . would the word "responsive" make sense? I mean, it sounds like he's responding more to you, or to . . . to the tasks at hand.

DORIS Yeah, definitely. Umm hmm. That's a good word. So . . . but not just responding. I mean, but also taking responsibility to do it.

GENE Taking initiative?

DORIS Yeah, initiative. Exactly. Follow . . . start it and follow through on his own.

DON Would you say that you're not dealing with so much confusion because there's not . . . there's . . . rarely is there a period of time where. . . . It used to be you would be in the middle of saying something and then you would lose the word. Or actually the whole thought. It would be like, "I have no idea what it was I was trying to tell you." Or, "I can't think of the right word." And you're not coming up with that kind of a response.

WAYNE Yeah, that's not happening so much. And, and just let me see . . .

GENE So that . . . that fog that you used to talk about . . .

WAYNE Yes.

GENE . . . is eased? Is somewhat lifted?

WAYNE Diminished, yeah.

DON And the sudden confusion.

GENE Does that fit, too?

WAYNE Umm-hmm. Um . . . and a lot of the feeling of . . . of reluctance to do anything, uh, is kind of lifted. It's quite a bit more comfortable in that respect.

GENE Reluctance?

WAYNE Living in this body.

GENE How do you notice the reluctance being gone? I mean, what. . . . How do you . . . ?

WAYNE Oh, just in . . . um, just in sitting down and working at the computer . . . or anything. I used to have to just force myself to do those things. And I'm finding less and less of that. I still have days that aren't as good as the next, or previous, but I think I've moved up on the scale some.

DORIS I think you're having fun at what you're doing, too. You know. Like some of the graphics that you've attached to the bottom of the faxes, and stuff like that. You know?

WAYNE Umm-hmm.

DORIS I mean, you're . . . in some respects I think that's pride in your work as well? Hm? (to Gene) I also see impatience in him, Gene, believe it or not. Which is something I haven't seen for a while either. We were working on a spreadsheet last night. You know, "Well, I want to do this." "Well," you know, "I don't want to do this." You know, really, hounding me for an answer. For — in some cases for things I wasn't even aware of how to do. You know? And that type of impatience you don't see. I haven't seen.

GENE I would almost call that more . . . I would call that "eagerness," almost.

DORIS Exactly. Exactly, yeah.

GENE So, Wayne, do these things that Doris, and Don, too, are noticing, do they fit for you? I mean, do you think you're feeling more alert? More focused on tasks? More responsive? That you're taking initiative? That you're following through on things?

WAYNE (jokingly) More impatient.

DON But . . .

GENE Is that a good or a bad thing? I mean . . .

WAYNE Which?

GENE The impatience. I mean, is that a . . .

WAYNE Um. I think it's like anything. It depends. It depends on the outcome.

GENE Well, if you think about it in terms of, um, your relationship with depression, in terms of where you stand, in terms of how big a grip depression's got on you. Is it impatience . . .

WAYNE I think . . .

GENE Is the impatience a good sign, or a bad sign in terms of that?

WAYNE Well, it's a valid indicator, because, like I said before, I would just ignore it. You know. Just not even take the energy to respond to it. So, I think that the fact that I'm responding to it is an indicator of, you know, having a little more energy, or moving up the scale some. Whatever.

DON Yeah, cause . . .

WAYNE (to Doris) I think you're making more progress than I am.

DORIS I think we're all making progress, which is pretty exciting. (Laughter)

WAYNE Uh-huh.

(We skip ahead here to the end of the conversation. As I sense that it is nearly time to stop, I reflect out loud about the list.)

GENE This was a pretty . . . this was an interesting list to me, you know, all that stuff that you rattled off in the beginning. It's different. I don't know if it feels like progress to you or not, but can you see how it sounds like progress to me? To hear this whole list of stuff?

WAYNE Oh, it does to me, too. Yeah. I was just measuring hers against the progress I've made.

GENE Well, maybe next time we should start by me getting a list from you of all the changes you're seeing in Doris.

WAYNE Okay. I'll make a list.

(Laughter)

DORIS It will be a bible by the time we get together.

DON   That's what happens when people live together for years and years. (Laughter)

GENE   And I would be. . . . If we made such a list, I'd be curious to know what the effect of those changes is on you. You know. Because when one person in a relationship changes it does have real effects on others.

WAYNE   Oh, definitely.

People may be invited to be an ongoing part of the therapy, as Don and Doris were, or they may be invited for a single meeting, as Dan was. We've also found that it can be helpful to invite people to attend an occasional meeting, expressly to fill them in. We've done this with parents when a teenager has been seen alone or with relationship partners. These meetings often take the form of a summary of the developing alternative story or of a celebration of accomplishments. Although people may or may not contribute to the therapy conversation, their bearing witness to alternative stories and preferred versions of selves is often important to the people we are working with. Also, this witnessing almost always makes a difference in the witnesses' perceptions of the people they witness. This difference then becomes a part of subsequent interactions.

TEAMS

With the notion of "nurturing teams," Michael White (1995) has taken the idea of inviting people to attend meetings in a different direction. He says that "nurturing teams" can serve as a counterweight to the "abuse teams" that have typically been at work in the lives of some people. White notes that many people who have been subjected to severe abuse come to see themselves as having "dependent natures," and to criticize and pathologize themselves for having such natures. He wonders if people are persuaded of this view of themselves by dominant cultural stories about "independence," "self-possession," "self-reliance," and the like—stories of "separation and individuation."

To deconstruct these dominant stories, White inquires about the presence of an abuse team. Has there been such a team? Who are its members? Over how many years, at what level of intensity was each member active? He then calculates the "weightiness" of the abuse by multiplying the number of team members by the number of years per member by the level of intensity per year. He then wonders aloud what might serve as a "counterweight" to the abuse, and proposes the idea of a "nurturing team," wondering how big a team it would take, over what amount of time, to balance the effects of the abuse team. White suggests that people can actually invite those they believe they have been dependent on, as well as other people they think would accept the invitation, to join such a nurturing team. Therapists might suggest other people for the team. He (White, 1995, p. 106) describes what might happen at a nurturing team meeting:

First, the person who has issued the invitations provides some account of the abuse team's membership, its activities, the duration of these activities, and the long-term effects of these activities. Second, the notion of the nurturing team is introduced, along with some thoughts about the part that this team could have to play in undoing the work of the abuse team. Third, the work that has already been done in this direction by prospective nurturing team members is acknowledged, along with the effects of this work. Fourth, prospective team members then talk about the sort of ongoing contribution to nurturing work that they believe might challenge the work of the abuse team, and that might fit with the necessities of their own lives in a way that would not be burdensome to them. Fifth, the person who called the meeting responds to these proposals, and makes further suggestions about what might work best for them. Sixth, all of these proposals and suggestions are negotiated, and plans are made for their introduction. At this time, these plans are worked through in their particularities.

White suggests that therapists should attend at least the first meetings and be available to support and clarify the process.

In structuring support systems in this way, people are not so much being asked to respond to crises, but instead, are being filled in on the story and given the opportunity to play a role in creating a new culture in which a preferred story has a chance to flourish.

When I (JF) heard Michael White talk about such teams I thought of a dear friend of mine whose life has been dragged down and severely limited by chronic fatigue syndrome. She has lost her livelihood and her professional identity, as well as the energy and the ability to participate in many of the activities that have brought her pleasure for most of her life. I know this about her, and I have watched her valiant struggle to keep hold of as much of her life as she can. Yet, when she calls me in a state of misery, needing some support, I am often rushing from one thing to another, with an overabundance of work commitments and, seemingly, no time. Too often, I respond by cutting her short. I would willingly join a nurturing team for her and would gladly schedule in my contribution. If I were to think of myself as having a role in creating a subculture to support her in keeping her life for herself and to appreciate her efforts on her own behalf, I would make the time. If this was agreed on in advance instead of at the whim of chronic fatigue syndrome, I could make it part of my life. I know others would, too, for all of the people that they care about.

In addition to the idea of teams that meet and share responsibilities, we have found that proposing the idea of a team to hold close in one's thoughts and heart has been quite helpful. After a project is named, we can ask questions to help a person identify who is on the team for that project. Here is an abbreviated set of such questions:

- We've talked quite a bit about where the idea that you'll never accomplish anything comes from. I understand how messages and comments feed the stuck lifestyle. That makes me wonder if messages and comments from others would feed the taking-your-life-back lifestyle. Who would be on the team that supports the taking-your-life-back lifestyle? They could be from your present, your past, a teacher, maybe, who saw something in you a long time ago, or someone who doesn't personally know you but would support what you're beginning to accomplish here.
- If you were to have the team with you in your heart and thoughts as you move ahead on this project, how would that make a difference?

These questions give people the opportunity to decide who they want to be in their community, on their team. All of us hold people in our hearts and minds. This idea invites people to choose who. We've discovered that often there is a grade-school teacher who has been a lifesaver and can continue to play an important role even if we don't know her physical whereabouts or even if she is no longer living. Since we are from Chicago, it should come as no surprise that in our practice Michael Jordan and Phil Jackson, the Bulls' coach, are on many teams. We are sure that they would be honored.

For those team members who know the people we work with, we can ask questions to develop the story of the relationship and their knowledge of our clients:

- If I were to interview your cousin Sheila, what would she tell me she most appreciates about you?
- What has she noticed about you that led to that appreciation?
- Is there a particular event she would tell me about?

- How does this knowledge she has of you qualify her to be on the team?

Or we can consider the possibility of inviting available team members to a therapy meeting and interviewing them.

If there has been no prior relationship with team members, we can ask hypothetical questions:

- Knowing what you do about Phil Jackson, what do you think he would most appreciate in you if he knew you?
- What that you've done might stand out to him?
- Why would that stand out?
- How would he support even more developments along those lines?

Additionally, people often have creative ideas for making team members present in their lives. One person framed pictures of his team members that he put in a prominent place in his apartment. Since he couldn't locate a picture of his sixth-grade guidance counselor, an important team member, he framed her name.

Once a team is named, we can help keep its members active by asking questions about them in therapy:

- How can the team help as you prepare for the job interview?
- Now that you have the team with you, how is facing this project different?
- Who on the team can you count on if terror sneaks into your dreams? What might she do or say?

REFLECTING PROCESSES

In Chapter 7 we describe how when we work with couples, families, or groups, we generally talk to one person at a time while inviting the others to take up a reflecting position.

If a problem is affecting one person in particular, it is obvious how those in a reflecting position can serve as an audience. For example, a family came to therapy because night fears had been terrorizing seven-year-old Bruce, waking him, drenching him with sweat, and sending him to his parents' bed. Although the fears affected everyone, their influence on Bruce was by far the strongest. At the second meeting I (GC) discovered that on the previous Tuesday night Bruce had put the fears in their place when they tried to send him to wake up his parents. As Bruce and I had a conversation about how he did this, his parents and younger brother listened. When a robust story of Bruce's accomplishment had come forth, I asked the "audience" a number of questions: What did they think this new development meant about the fate of the relationship between Bruce and the fears? What did it say about Bruce that he had taken matters into his own hands this way? Had they known him to take matters into his own hands this way before? And so on.

During this conversation, it was clear that the story about Bruce was spreading. Now it was not just self-knowledge; it was family knowledge. There was an audience for Bruce's victory.

Even if two people are in therapy to work on "relationship problems" each can serve as an audience to the other. In fact, when a partner witnesses the other partner's telling of the story of the relationship (which is always different in some way for each partner) his or her ideas both about the relationship and about the partner can change. Such is the nature of an audience.

The structuring of conversations so that one person talks while others listen to his story, and the listeners then reflect on the talker's story, maximizes the possibility that each will serve as a witness or audience to the others and minimizes the chances that people will dispute or contradict each other's stories.

"Formal" reflecting teams, of the sort that we use in consultation and supervision, offer a different kind of participant audience. Although the members typically do not, like friends and family members, continue to show up in the lives of the people whose stories they reflect on, they embody a new local subculture during therapy meetings. This can be very powerful, and people do tell us that they carry "the team" with them in their hearts and minds.

A reflecting team provides an "insurrection of subjugated knowledges." The diverse people who constitute a reflecting team introduce themselves and situate their comments so that people hear them speaking as specific people with specific personal experiences, ideas, and intentions (White, 1991). Often, in the part of the meeting when people reflect on the team's reflections, they talk about team members by name or description ("the guy with a beard" or "that woman sitting over there — is her name Ann?"). In therapy conversations people often mention doing something between meetings and wondering what a particular team member or the team as a whole would have thought about it. Instead of a "blind panel" of experts, a team is a participant audience of individuals for people's emerging stories.

CIRCULATING THE STORY THROUGH
TAPES, LETTERS, DOCUMENTS,
AND CEREMONIES

Witnessing can happen anywhere, not just in therapy rooms. In Chapter 8 we wrote about tapes, letters, and documents as ways to continue and thicken stories. They can also be used to spread the news of an alternative story, as a way of recruiting an audience.

The following is an example of how a document can be used to invite others into a community of concern:

Stuart is a 30-year-old man who tested HIV-positive a year before he came to therapy. The test results were an entry-point for depression and relentless thoughts about dying. As a single, heterosexual man working as a high school teacher, Stuart was not part of a community skilled or experienced in dealing with HIV. He did have a small group of family members, friends, and co-workers whom he told about the HIV status. One of these co-workers, concerned about the depression, convinced Stuart to come to therapy.

In therapy, Stuart named depression as the problem and recognized that it had taken away his life before full-blown AIDS had even entered the picture. His decision to live with HIV for the rest of his life, rather than spend the rest of his life dying of AIDS was a turning point of enormous importance. It was one that was not easy to arrive at. Once Stuart did arrive at this turning point, the trouble was that it was hard to go about living his life surrounded by friends and family looking stricken and mournful whenever they encountered him, and offering to do things for him instead of having fun with him. Stuart decided that he could distribute a document to people that would both let them in on his turning point and let them know the kind of audience he thought would be most helpful. We created the following document.

A PLEDGE TO LIFE

1. You may not have faced this yet, but we are all in the same predicament. With each breath we are closer to dying. In the face of this predicament, we can focus on death or focus on life.
2. I HEREBY CHOOSE TO FOCUS ON LIFE.
3. Since I *may* have a shorter life than most, I intend to play harder, work harder, talk more intensely, and get closer to people than I have ever done before.
4. If you really want to help me, don't try to stop me with concern and fear.

5. If you really want to help me, feel joy for my life and if you can, join me!
6. This does not mean I am unwilling to talk about my health, my fears, and my death. I am willing, but I ask you to remember, until my last breath, I do this in the context of my life.
7. As a living person I may choose to join you in your life and struggles, too.

Stuart gave the document, which originally consisted of the first six points, to friends, co-workers, and family members who knew about his HIV status and who wanted to be supportive. He distributed the document over a period of several months, each time in the context of a conversation in which he told people that he appreciated their care for him but that their expressions of care did not fit with the direction that he wanted for his life. Uniformly, people expressed relief at being given information about how to respond to Stuart's HIV status. In one instance, a friend's career was becoming unravelled but she had not turned to Stuart for support because, with his own problems, she didn't think he needed any of hers. She used the presentation of the document as an opportunity to ask Stuart whether hearing her problems would feel like a burden. Stuart realized that part of what had made him feel as if he were dying was a lack of reciprocity in relationships. People were helpful to him but asked nothing in return. He wanted two-way relationships. He added the seventh point to his document as a result of this realization.

Although the "pitying looks" have not completely stopped, Stuart thinks that the document has let his community in on his perspective on life, which does make it easier to live the life he wants to live. He has noticed that since he gave people the document, they seem freer to talk with him about their relationship with him, which gives him the opportunity to ask for more of what he wants.

Just as documents can be used to recruit an audience, so can letters. In a recent paper, Stephen Madigan and David Epston (1995) describe several letter writing campaigns, each of which originated as Madigan realized that a willing and appreciative audience was available, but at some distance. He joined with the people he was working with to send letters to these distant friends, asking them to remind the people he was working with of things the friends knew about them, their accomplishments, and so on. Like a reincarnated and elongated version of "Queen for a Day," memories and testimonials poured in.

There are a number of examples in Chapter 8 of stories being circulated, including "Susan's Declaration of Standing Tall," which she read to her family at a holiday meal, the therapy conversations with Erica's family in which we unveiled her picture, read her list of friends, and had cookies, and the celebration in which Carrie's Bravery Project was read out loud and Carrie's certificate was awarded to her.

In each of these situations something new about a person's story was made public to a participant audience. In some instances, participant audiences are invited to join in ceremonies and celebrations in the context of therapy. In others, audiences are considered in therapy and then recruited outside of therapy meetings. For example, we've experimented with creating videotapes recording people's preferred stories that they can share in spreading the news. For several teenagers we've seen, who, with their parents' agreement, wanted therapy to be "private," making videotapes was a way of letting their parents in on important aspects of preferred stories while maintaining the privacy of the therapy relationship.

LEAGUES

The idea of "leagues" (variously called clubs, associations, teams, or guilds, but usually leagues) has been mentioned by Michael White and David Epston (1990), and others (Freeman & Lobovitz, 1993; Zimmerman & Dickerson, 1994b) but it has rarely been the focus of articles.

In the earliest applications of this idea in the narrative community, people were awarded certificates that proclaimed them members of the "Monster Taming and Fear Catching Association of Australia," the "Monster and Worm Catchers' and Tamers' Guild," "The Australian and New Zealand Fear Bashers' and Ghost Busters' Club," and other associations. When leagues are used in this way, there is often discussion of what would qualify a person to become a member of such a league, but usually no mention of any league activities following membership. These leagues are "virtual" communities of concern; they serve the same purpose that membership in a professional organization does for many people. Joining a league signifies that a person has reached competence in a particular arena. Her membership certificate recognizes her achievement of a new status!

David Epston has taken the role of leagues quite a bit further. For more than a decade he has served as the archivist for a number of leagues, collecting tapes, artwork, and letters that offer ideas about how people are escaping from problems such as temper tantrums, night fears, school refusing, and asthma (Madigan, 1994). The league that seems to be most active in recent times is the Anti-Anorexia/Anti-Bulimia League of New Zealand.

Before his days as an archivist, Epston was known as a storyteller, publishing his work in the "Story Corner" of the *Australian and New Zealand Journal of Family Therapy*. In the conversation in which we first heard of the archives, Epston said that he was no longer very interested in telling stories. He went on to describe his work with members of the Anti-Anorexia/Anti-Bulimia League, saying something like, "As I'm talking with Carla about a dilemma she faces I ask, 'Would you like to know how Barbara faced a similar dilemma?' If Carla is interested I tell her what Barbara has said and then also what Renee found made a difference."

We looked at each other when we heard this description and thought, "he *does* still tell stories." We were dead wrong.

David Epston and the people who are fighting to take their lives back from anorexia and bulimia have created a large archive of letters, tapes, transcripts, journal entries, artwork, notes, and various other contributions. The collection is available for members to use in their fight against anorexia and bulimia.

When I (JF) read some of the materials of the league to Leanne, who I have joined with in her battle for her life, Leanne found hearing the words of someone else facing a similar enemy compelling. Passages that I would have thought were not particularly relevant moved her to tears. "Can we ask her she took that step?" Leanne entreated when hearing of an accomplishment one of the members had achieved. We wrote and in this way an anti-anorexic, anti-bulimic sisterhood and correspondence began.

We say we were dead wrong when we thought this work was the same as therapeutic storytelling because, even though we are tremendous fans of storytelling, we can see that this work is in a whole different league. It unites and circulates the voices of people involved in a common struggle. Their voices, not therapists', are privileged. When Leanne reads the words of her anti-anorexic, anti-bulimic correspondent from New Zealand, she considers them very seriously, as real and relevant experiences. No therapist's retelling could hold the same validity for her. After we read the most recent letter together, Leanne looked at me and said, "When I hear her experience I realize that I've been planning to lose and I begin to wonder what it would be like to plan to win."

As I have talked with colleagues about the experience that I share with Leanne as she participates in the Anti-Anorexia/Anti-Bulimia League, an unexpected opportunity has come my way. People keep giving me journal entries, notes, letters, and the like. Upon hearing about what is happening in New Zealand, people here have become so enthusiastic about starting a local league that it seems to have started of its own accord!

As we have argued, the dominant culture often constructs people as problematic. Especially when it comes to anorexia and bulimia, but with many other problems as well, this leads many people to isolate themselves in shame and self-revulsion. When combined with the externalization of problems, a community such as a league not only provides an audience for the circulation of stories of resistance and accomplishment, but also changes the context of people's lives. "I don't feel so alone," Leanne tells me. Although I (JF) experience myself as being in her struggle with her, it is not the same as a connection with others who experientially understand what she is up against.

The Vancouver Anti-Anorexia/Anti-Bulimia League, born from an inpatient anti-anorexia/anti-bulimia group led by Stephen Madigan (1994), has established itself as a grass-roots organization that meets regularly, has membership committees and responsibilities, and produces a newsletter. Besides personal stories and tapes, the Vancouver League also has collected anti-anorexia reading materials and a referral list. The League not only extends its benefits to members — people struggling with anorexia and bulimia, therapists, family members, lovers, and friends — but also includes an outreach component that offers consultation and education to community and professional groups.

As recipients of a consultation with members of the Vancouver League, we can tell you that they knock the wind out of traditional therapy stories about "anorexics." They are not only circulating stories of hope and possibility; as their membership swells well beyond 300 people, they are turning the tables on anorexia's isolating and silencing effects.

They intend not only to create a subculture, but to change the dominant culture as well. Stephen Madigan (1994, p. 27) recently described some of the League's activities:

> The League's media watch committee publicly denounces pro-anorexic/bulimic activities against women's bodies such as department store use of waif-figured mannequins or gymnasium advertising designed to induce body-guilt. The membership writes letters to company presidents and newspaper and magazine editors, and gives media interviews. League stickers with slogans like "Starvation kills your appetite for Life" and "YOU are not just a body," are placed over billboard advertising designed to encourage women to view emaciation as a physical ideal. Diet centers are also favorite targets for the stickers campaign. . . .
>
> Because of the alarming fact that dieting is being discussed among toddlers as young as four, our school action committee has developed an anti-anorexic/anti-bulimic program for primary and

secondary school students. These programs provide students with the graphic and gory details that accompany anorexic and bulimic lifestyles, along with strategies and information on how to resist the growing trend of "eating disorders."

A fascinating aspect of leagues is that they allow members not only to have an audience to the performance of new stories and new constitutions of self but also to be an audience to others' new stories and constitutions of self.

Groups

Another way that people struggling with similar problems can become audiences to each other is through therapy groups. Janet Adams-Westcott and Deanna Isenbart (1995, p. 335) offer this description of their work with people who have experienced child sexual abuse:

We invite group members to develop connections and create a community that supports each participant's personal journey of change. This "community" provides an audience for members to: (1) develop their own self-knowledge, (2) practice more validating stories about self and (3) incorporate preferred narratives into their lived experience.

Janet Laube and Stephen Trefz (1994) have used a narrative framework in working with people struggling with depression. They (p. 33) identify "audience" as one of the "curative factors" and explain:

The group participants are the initial audience for the telling of stories in a safe setting where there is validation, commonality, affirmation about how depression has become a dominant influence. The members help each other transform their tales by being an audience for discovering exceptions and noticing differences.

Other Ideas

There are all sorts of ways to create audiences and subcultures for the sharing of knowledge. Jenny Freeman (Freeman, Loptson, & Stacey, 1995) has been using audiences in her work with children. She writes:

We are developing "public practices" in which communities of children are connected with each other's support and knowledge. When their ideas are gathered for circulation to audiences through hand-books, tapes, letters or verbal communication by the therapist, children enjoy being respected for these ideas and have the added satisfaction of making a contribution to others.

The handbooks, which take the form of anthologies, include, "The Temper Tamer's Handbook" and "The Fear Facer's Handbook." Children contribute poems, notes, and drawings within the pages of these handbooks or dictate their contributions to the therapist. Freeman (Lobovits, Maisel, & Freeman, 1995) adds pictures and cartoons. The handbooks are available for other children facing similar problems or as " . . . accounts for inspiration and reference in case the authors themselves experience a setback" (Freeman, Loptson, & Stacey, 1995). Freeman has begun circulating the handbooks among other therapists. The children they work with add their own entries before the books are returned.

Another innovation, still in the planning stage, is the idea of a public information board. Paul, who is changing his relationship with depression so that he manages it instead of it managing him, is at work on creating a public information board for people affected by depression. Family members, friends, and therapists will be invited to participate along with people who are directly affected. Although Paul has discovered 17 databases dealing with depression on the Internet, he is aware that people struggling with depression frequently lose jobs and are therefore beset with financial concerns. This has led him to take on the project of creating a public information board, with an 800 number. (The other databases all have fees.)

The idea grew gradually as Paul asked himself this question: "Since depression can be a barrier to so-called 'ordinary social environments,' then what environment would it not be a barrier to?" He realized that boards are a supportive yet anonymous context. They can also be set up to have separate categories. For example, if depression is torturing a person with thoughts of suicide, the person can make an entry in a "suicidal thoughts" category. Another person might enter the "suicidal thoughts" category from a position of strength and confidence, offering stories of what made a difference in her struggles. The choice involved in entering categories is an advantage over support groups in which people may be flooded with depressive stories.

Founding this information board is an important step in Paul's project of changing his relationship with depression. "This is something not everybody can do, but I can," he told us. And because of Paul's efforts, it will be something that many others can join.

RECRUITING AND COORDINATING A
PROFESSIONAL AUDIENCE

Sometimes a therapist is in an ideal position to circulate an emerging story to people in other professions, institutions, or organizations. Such people can serve as audience members only if someone makes the story accessible to them. With Misha, for instance, it seems to have made a big difference that I (GC) went to talk with his school's staff on their own turf.

Misha had beautiful eyes—big, dark, shiny, interested-in-everything eyes with long, black lashes. He was intelligent, poised, and talkative all the way through my first meeting with him. This puzzled me. According to his parents, the people at Misha's school saw him as shy, surly, and slow. They thought he needed to be placed in a special track for developmentally and behaviorally disordered children. How could I be seeing such a different person?

I learned from Misha and his parents that they, along with Misha's two younger sisters, had emigrated from Russia to Chicago two years previously. They had moved in with Misha's mother's sister, and Misha had started attending the local Chicago public school. Most of the students at the school were Hispanic, and Misha, ten years old at the time, had picked up both Spanish and English rapidly. His teacher there liked him and thought he did amazingly well considering that he was learning a whole new culture in addition to the usual fifth-grade curriculum.

But Misha's parents were worried about the school. There had been incidents of gang violence, including a drive-by shooting that involved a sixth-grader. Both parents had found good jobs through relatives and friends, so in their second summer here they decided to move to the suburbs where all their friends told them Misha and his sisters could attend a safer, better school.

In the second meeting, which was with Misha alone, he told me how things had gone wrong for him from the first day at the new school. He didn't know anybody, and no one seemed interested in knowing him. The kids at this new school dressed differently than at his old school. He had a different teacher for every class, and he had to go to a different room every time a new class started. All this was very confusing and a little scary.

As the year went on, all Misha's teachers treated him like he was dumb; all of them except his English teacher, that is. She noticed that he liked to read, and she began to suggest books that he might like to check out of the library. When they read a play out loud in class, she complimented him on how well he read.

He didn't make any close friends. In gym class the kids laughed at him because he didn't know the rules for basketball. He began spending more and more time alone. He hated this new school.

As the year drew to a close, Misha was flunking math and just barely passing all his other classes except English. Even there he was having trouble with essay-type writing assignments. This was when the suggestion was made that he should be placed in the B.D./D.D. track. The school psychologist suggested that maybe Misha's problem was depression. Misha's parents were very alarmed at this suggestion, and followed through on it immediately. That's how they ended up at my office, as Misha's uncle had consulted with me a few years back and recommended me for the evaluation.

Inquiring further, I learned that at home, except for bouts of sadness and frustration when the subject of school came up, Misha continued to be the intelligent, funny, charming kid his family had always known. He still had two good friends from his old school whom he often visited on weekends. It seemed to me that, if depression was the problem, it was a highly contextualized form of depression. The same held true for any major sort of learning disability or behavioral disorder. These things just weren't in evidence when Misha was away from school.

Over the course of my third meeting with Misha, which his parents and sisters also attended, we brought forth the story of all that he had accomplished since moving to the U.S. He had learned two new languages. (He still spoke Spanish fairly often with one of his friends from the old school.) He knew how to operate a VCR, cable TV, Nintendo, and his dad's personal computer. In addition to soccer, which he already knew, he was becoming proficient at baseball and, finally, with the help of his inner-city friends, basketball. Everyone agreed that at home Misha was doing just fine. The problem was how to circulate this story of Misha at school.

With Misha and his parent's permission, I called the school psychologist. She was a little surprised and very interested to hear how well Misha had done at his old school and how differently he acted at home. She said that she had been under the impression that Misha had immigrated when he was quite young. She hadn't really been aware that he had learned all his English in the last two years. She was glad to hear that I didn't think he was suffering from major depression, but she wasn't sure how the school could best help him get back on track.

Several of the teachers seemed to have given up on him. His math teacher saw him as "incorrigible." It certainly wasn't going to work if he were just placed in the usual seventh-grade curriculum. The end-of-the-year staffing for Misha was coming up, and she was not sure what she should recommend there. I wasn't either. I asked her if outside consultants such as myself could attend staffings, and she said that it didn't happen often, but yes, she was sure I would be welcome.

I checked with Misha and his family to see if they thought it would be useful for me to attend Misha's staffing. I explained that my role there, as I saw it, would be to let everyone know about the Misha that had existed at his old school and still existed at home—to tell the story of what he had accomplished in the last two years. I said that I hoped that I could get people to wonder how they might make the new school a place where Misha could flourish. They thought that might help a lot, and encouraged me to go.

At the staffing, which included the principal and all of Misha's teachers as well as myself and the psychologist, the initial talk was all about how poorly Misha was doing. The math teacher seemed to see him as a thug from the inner city who had somehow wandered into the wrong school. The other teachers saw him more as shy, uncertain, and confused. The English teacher thought he showed promise if only he could be coaxed out of his shell. The psychologist, to my surprise, went into great detail about how depressed, negativistic, and asocial Misha looked on the battery of tests she had administered—it was as if our telephone conversation had never happppened.

When I was offered a turn to speak, I told Misha's story as I understood it, asking the staff members to put themselves in his place as much as they could while they listened. I understood that these people were witnessing a different story of Misha than the one I believed, but I hoped that, if they could put his experience into a wider context, they would begin to recognize different possibilities. If they began serving as an audience to Misha's preferred story, their performance of that story would keep it alive.

I wondered aloud what it might be like to come from a smallish city in Russia to the streets of Chicago. I asked them to imagine being placed in a huge public school where most of the students spoke Spanish while the teachers in class spoke English. I told how Misha had quickly learned both languages well enough to get around. I told how he had made friends, learned new games, new social customs, new styles of dress—a whole new culture. It would probably be more accurate to say two whole new cultures.

I asked them to imagine what it might be like, just as you were beginning to do really well in this strange new environment, to be whisked into yet another setting—one where difference was less tolerated than it had been at the inner-city school. At this new school, things were smaller, more personalized, and more homogeneous. What stood out for Misha was how he didn't fit in. Could they see how he might feel that the students had ostracized him? That the teachers seemed to have him under a microscope? When they considered his accomplishments at the old school and at home, could they believe that he was actually an intelligent and capable person who was struggling with loneliness and confusion?

"Yes," the math teacher said, "but he's still not keeping up, and no matter what the cause, things will only get worse if we promote him to seventh grade."

The English teacher said that she was doing a special drama project in summer school, and she would be willing to see that Misha had a prominent place in it. She thought she could arrange things so that Misha had more opportunities to make friendships if he were enrolled in the project. The psychologist, who now seemed to be back in the world of Misha's preferred story, asked if it would be possible to get special tutoring for Misha in math, and the math teacher, who seemed to be warming to the project, said he could arrange for that. Another teacher volunteered to help Misha catch up in his other classes over the summer. By the end of the meeting, people were talking about Misha's problems as though they were an interesting challenge for their creativity rather than a drain on their time and energy.

As the staffing ended, I asked the psychologist if we could talk for a few more minutes. She invited me into her office, and we spent a few more minutes in which I did the best I could to keep the story of Misha as a bright and more-successful-than-not navigator of new cultures alive in her mind. We agreed to stay in touch by telephone over the summer so that she could fill me in on how the new plan for Misha was progressing.

I met with Misha and his family once more, three weeks after the summer session had started. They were pleased with how he was doing in school. They believed that the people at school were pleased too. Misha said that he was beginning to like some things about the new school. He especially liked it that several people seemed to want to be friends with him.

The psychologist called me twice during the summer and one last time in the fall, and each time she let me know that the staff was proud of the plan they had put together for Misha. Everyone, even the math teacher, thought that he was doing just fine.

Once the staff became an audience to the preferred story, their participation changed dramatically. They created a plan that I couldn't have anticipated or put in place myself, one that worked well for Misha and furthered his story.

I believe that things might have gone quite differently for Misha if I had not been able to attend the staffing at his school. Going there in person allowed me to share his preferred story in a more compelling way than I ever could have done over the telephone or in a letter. With all the staff present in one place, they could become involved as a group in

Misha's story and discover their interest in being members of Misha's team.

As useful as it can be to meet potential audience members on their own turf, it is not always possible. Sometimes other helping professionals involved are so far away or spread out in so many locations that a face-to-face meeting is impractical. In these cases telephone calls, letters, faxes, and the like can be used. Hayley's story illustrates one way this can happen.

Hayley was stricken with a very rare disease that made her blood clot too easily. The disease announced itself in Hayley's life by causing a clot that cut off the blood flow to her liver and caused it to die. Soon after her sixteenth birthday, Hayley underwent a liver transplant which didn't take. It was completely rejected within two months. She then received a second transplant which her body accepted, and it was still working quite well when I (GC) first saw her two years later.

Hayley had been started on an experimental drug that was doing a great job of controlling the clotting disorder. The problem now was pain. Over the course of her two liver transplants, the surgeons had opened and closed Hayley's belly at least ten times — twice for the transplants themselves and eight other times to correct abscesses, smaller blood clots, and bowel obstructions. She had a chronic, dull, throbbing ache in one location in her abdomen and an intermittent, incapacitatingly intense, stabbing pain in another spot.

Initially, the surgeons had been glad to treat the pain with opioid drugs, but as time wore on they became more and more reluctant to continue those drugs, even though nothing else relieved Hayley's pain. According to Hayley and her mother, the doctors were afraid she would become addicted to the pain medications. As the pain continued to plague Hayley, the various professionals involved in her care (a gastrointestinal surgeon, a hepatologist, a hematologist, a social worker, the nurse practitioner who headed the surgeon's office staff, and an anesthesiologist who specialized in chronic pain, to name a few of them) disagreed about its meaning and the proper way of treating it. More and more of them began to doubt that the pain was "real." These people saw Hayley as either weak-willed or manipulative. They began to talk about attention-seeking, drug-seeking, and overly dependent behaviors in Hayley.

As people began to view Hayley's actions through lenses colored with ideas of drug-seeking and overdependence, her actions came to be storied in ways that supported those labels. As these stories circulated among the people who were charged with her care, they created a reputation that began to precede Hayley at her clinic visits. When Hayley's mom, Simone, stood up for her daughter and pushed to have her complaints taken seriously, she was storied as a pushy and demanding person. Hayley and Simone began to feel more and more cut off and misunderstood. Depression began to be a frequent visitor in Hayley's life, and Simone was often consumed with anger. The anger and depression were seen by treatment team members as further evidence that Hayley and Simone were not nice people, and more stories circulated about how unpleasant, uncooperative, and demanding they were.

As I listened to their story, I was moved by the courage and determination that both Hayley and Simone showed. Hayley had fought her way back from the very threshold of death's door at least twice in the previous two years. Although she had spent more days in the hospital than out of it over that time, even with a very uncertain future, she was making plans to enter college in the fall. Simone was fiercely determined to see that her daughter received good care. She was willing to ask hard questions, read technical medical journals, and seek second and third opinions if that was what it took for her daughter to have a meaningful life. In spite of the distancing effect it had with the people who were supposed to be helping them, they were determined that Hayley be treated as a deserving person with real problems, not as a "crock" or a drug addict.

Immediately after our first meeting, with Hayley's consent, I called the nurse practitioner, who was the "gatekeeper" for the treatment team. It was this nurse who was most concerned about "attention-seeking and drug-seeking behaviors." I told him that I had just met with Hayley and her mother, and (resisting my impulse to tell him he had the story all wrong) I wondered how he thought I might be helpful. He talked about his increasing frustration with what felt like insatiable demands from Hayley and Simone. He recounted several incidents in which some member of the treatment team had tried to help with Hayley's pain and/or discouragement only to meet with failure. It seemed like nothing that anyone did was good enough for Hayley and her mother. In the most recent multidisciplinary staffing on Hayley, someone had pointed out the high doses of opioid drugs she was taking and how long she had been on them. The nurse felt personally responsible for "turning Hayley into a drug addict."

Again resisting my impulse to "correct" the story, I asked some questions that I hoped might bring forth a different reality. I asked about Hayley's prognosis. The nurse said Hayley could possibly live a long time—some people with liver transplants were going strong fifteen years after the operation—or she could suffer any one of a number of possible complications and die very soon. I asked the nurse to review for me (and, I hoped, for himself) the various surgeries Hayley had been through. I asked if he thought any of Hayley's pain could be from old scars, adhesions, or nerve damage from the many surgeries. He said it certainly could. I asked about his opinion about the use of powerful and possibly addictive pain relievers immediately after surgery. He said he favored their use in high enough doses to completely alleviate the pain. I asked about his philosophy about giving opioids for pain relief in cases of terminal illness. He favored their use there, as well. My hope with these latter questions was to bring forth different contexts in which he could restory the use of pain relievers for Hayley.

I asked what he thought about sending Hayley for a consultation with another specialist in chronic pain. He thought it would be a good idea. I asked if, in the interim, until the consultation was obtained, he would feel comfortable treating Hayley's complaints of pain as if they were real and reporting them as such to the surgeon, who was currently in charge of prescribing the pain medication. He said he would be very comfortable doing that. A second phone call, to the surgeon, took much the same shape. I also spoke with Hayley's hepatologist and hematologist within the next few days. In each of these cases, my main intention was to invite the person to entertain a story of Hayley as the brave and determined survivor that I believed her to be. Once Hayley had made an appointment with the pain specialist, I called him to tell Hayley's story as I knew it. I acknowledged the concern about drug addiction, and affirmed my commitment to work with Hayley and Simone to help them control the worry, fear, and discouragement that were coached by her medical problems. I wondered if he would work with me to find the best strategy that we could to keep Hayley free of severe pain and in control of her life. He said he would. This different attitude helped Hayley's preferred story flourish, whereas the previous pain specialist's ideas had undercut it.

It is now two years since I first met Hayley. She is still on opioid drugs much of the time. She still struggles with pain, and, thanks to the efforts of her treatment team, we now know that one cause of the pain is chronic pancreatitis — yet another complication of her many surgeries. Much of my role in her care has been that of message bearer and facilitator of communication. In that role, I have tried to keep the story of her brave struggle in the face of a nearly overwhelming illness alive, and more often that not — largely due to the continuing strength and courage of Hayley and Simone — I have succeeded. Hayley and Simone are much better at telling that story themselves now, and it is only in their most overwhelmed or overworked moments that other members of the treatment team give in to the old story of manipulation and drug-seeking. For the most part they are a participant-audience to the new, preferred story of how everyone is working together to help Hayley live the best life she can for as long as she can. I'm delighted to report that this story has a life of its own now.

Relationships and Ethics

Far from despair, the idea that each of us recreates reality with each encounter fills me with wondrous hope, empowerment and community connection. If there is no absolute truth "out there" to create pristine "expert systems" that can somehow solve our problems mathematically . . . [i]f we accept that when we enter into dialogue we *both* change; if it is true that we *co-create* reality, which in turn creates us—then we are called to a new kind of community. If I can only ever be part of the creation I must act humbly. I'd take that over being a goddess. . . .

— *Maureen O'Hara, 1995, p. 155*

Therapeutic interaction is a two-way phenomenon. We get together with people for a period of time over a range of issues, and all of our lives are changed for this.

— *Michael White, 1995, p. 7*

We've heard Karl Tomm say that he came to this work through falling in love with Michael White's ideas. We too have fallen in love with White's ideas (and those of other people working in this realm), but in stages, a little at a time. At first we didn't really recognize the significance of the ideas or the shift in worldview they reflected. What we fell in love with first were the relationships we saw Michael White, and then David Epston, and the people they worked with, creating with each other. We witnessed how people could transform themselves and their lives in preferred ways within those relationships.[1]

---

[1] We don't mean to suggest that the relationships that Michael White and David Epston engage in are better than relationships that anyone else engages in or that others in the narrative community do not engage in relationships that might be attractive in similar ways. We refer to the relationships that Epston and White have because they have been the most visible demonstration of these ideas and because we have been very moved by watching them at work with people.

As we have taken on this way of working as our own, we have discovered that it facilitates different kinds of therapeutic relationships than we had had before—relationships that are decidedly two-way in fostering membership in new communities and new life stories for both therapists and the people who consult with them. We think that much of the unique character of these therapeutic relationships has to do with the ethical practices that shape their construction.

There are differences in postmodern and modern approaches to ethics. Since the modernist project centers on sweeping meta-narratives and perfectible scientific theories, modernist ethics tend to be based in rules that can be prescribed and enforced in a "top down" way, as in the codes of ethics of the American Psychological Association, the American Association of Marriage and Family Therapy, and most any other professional organizations.

In the postmodern world, ethics focus on particular people in particular experiences, and there is considerable skepticism about the applicability of any kind of sweeping, universal, one-size-fits-all truth claims. Sheila McNamee (1994), discussing the differing ethics of different discursive communities, points out that any discourse is a story and that any story is always told from a perspective. She (1994, p. 74) writes,

> This has bold implications for . . . the issue of ethics because we at once realize that there are varying and competing perspectives and that any evaluation or judgement of a story is also a story and thus is similarly situated within a perspective.

Some (Doherty, 1991; Minuchin, 1991) have worried that narrative/social constructionist ethics imply that one story is as good as another.[2] We disagree. Instead, we see the idea that ethics should not be based in monolithic truth claims as supporting a number of important shifts—a shift to making room for marginalized voices and marginalized cultures, a shift to people in the client position choosing what fits for them, a shift to therapists being clear about where we stand so that people know how to take our ideas, and a shift to considering both the local, interpersonal, moment-by-moment effects of our stands and practices and the ripples that those effects send into the world at large.

---

[2]Vicki Dickerson and Jeff Zimmerman (in press) think that this idea results, at least in part, from a confusion between "constructivism" and "social constructionism." They write that " . . . a constructivist perspective can be relativistic, seeing all constructions and techniques as equally useful. . . . In this perspective, any one person's frame is as true as any other, and whatever works in any situation becomes what matters." Much of this chapter, and, we hope, the book, describes how a social constructionist perspective is quite different.

Rather than leading us to treat all stories as equal, these ideas lead us to scrutinize our ethical stands from more than a single, Olympian perspective, and to consider the effects of particular practices in particular local cultures. We can think of this as a "margin-in" approach to ethics — one which values the experience of people at the margins of any dominant culture or at the bottom of any culture's hierarchies and takes a strong ethical stance in favor of making space for such people's voices to be heard, understood, and responded to.

A recent article in the *Journal of the American Medical Association* (Carrese & Rhodes, 1995) illustrates the differences in modernist and postmodernist ethics in the domain of medicine, and we think it also illuminates the differences in our field. Carrese and Rhodes studied the meaning within traditional Navajo culture of certain practices based on Western biomedical and bioethical concepts. They (p. 826) lay out one aspect of the modernist position quite clearly:

In the culture of Western biomedicine and bioethics, the principles of autonomy and patient self-determination are centrally important. Consequently, explicit and direct discussion of negative information between health care providers and patients is the current standard of care. For example, informed consent requires disclosing the risks of medical treatment, truth telling requires disclosure of bad news, and advance care planning requires patients to consider the possibility of a serious future illness.

The authors (pp. 826–827) then describe some aspects of traditional Navajo culture:

. . . it is held that thought and language have the power to shape reality and to control events. . . . In the Navajo view, language does not merely describe reality, language shapes reality. For these reasons traditional Navajo patients may regard the discussion of negative information as potentially harmful.

They also descibe *hózhó*, a central concept in Navajo culture, whose meaning encompasses everything positive, including beauty, goodness, blessedness, order, and harmony.

Carrese and Rhodes' ethnographic field work taught them that the Navajo people have their own ways of responding to health concerns and life-threatening situations that reflect *hózhó* and the idea that language and thought shape reality. They draw the conclusion that practicing the dominant morality with people such as the Navajo people, who view it as not fitting, is ethically problematic. They point out that the United States is made up of people from diverse cultural backgrounds and that the moral perspectives of the dominant society do not fit for many other cultures. Carrese and Rhodes end with a declaration that is very much in tune with our intentions in this chapter, asserting that they are challenged to consider other cultures for whom the application of the dominant morality may be problematic.

This chapter is about some of the ways different therapists in the narrative community have begun to articulate ethics that consider people in their local cultures and to put those ethics into practice. It is also about the interrelationship of ethics and therapeutic relationships, about how each shapes the other.

THE CONSTITUTION OF SELF
AS AN ETHICAL PRACTICE

We'll start by getting back to the relationships we have witnessed Michael White and David Epston and the people they work with forging together, because these relationships were what first excited us about narrative ideas in practice. Obviously, every interpersonal relationship is different; also, White and Epston work very differently from each other in many respects. Here we want to focus on something that their work has in common.

Both White's and Epston's interviews are composed mainly of questions. In their therapy conversations, experientially compelling and meaningful stories are brought forth. These stories seem to be both already there and not-before-developed. Once they are developed, the stories speak important "truths" about people—about their lives, relationships, and possibilities. People who observe these conversations generally see the people in client positions in a new light. They usually think that White or Epston had something to do with the new light.

Modernist explanations of how the new stories come into being would focus on either (1) certain personality traits of White and Epston, perhaps concluding (as has been done about Carl Whitaker and Milton Erickson) that their success is based on charisma and personal power, or (2) certain quantifiable techniques that they use, perhaps suggesting that certain questions, asked in certain ways, will result in certain kinds of stories.

From a constitutionalist and social constructionist perspective, we are not so much interested in the personality styles or exact question choices of White and Epston as we are in how they constitute themselves in relationships with other people. That is, rather than hypothesizing that

White and Epston have some built-in characteristic of personhood or some fail-safe technique, we are interested in how they actively participate in forming their identies so as to contribute to a special kind of relationship.

Remember that, as social constructionists, we view "self" not as a core or essential or preordained entity, but as something that we constitute in relationship with other people. We believe that White and Epston intentionally situate themselves in discourses and in communities that support them in constituting themselves according to certain ethical principles and values. Then, when they enter a new situation they can carry those communities and discourses — and, therefore, the values they support — with them in their hearts. To the extent that we have choice in the matter, the choice of a community or a discourse is an ethical act.

We are not proposing that each of us act according to White's or Epston's ethics. For us, though, since we find their work and the relationships it is based in so attractive and effective, it is useful to think about how they constitute themselves and how they participate in the development of certain kinds of relationships.

We asked Epston and White some questions about their ethics, particularly in terms of the choices they make in constituting themselves in relationship with others. We wondered if there were particular ideas they kept in mind or certain ways of orienting themselves that enabled them to enter into their preferred working relationships. In response, they offered the following questions, saying that they have long guided them in their choices of models, theories, and practices.

1. How does this model/theory/practice "see" persons?
2. How does it press you to conduct yourself with people who seek your help?
3. How does it press them to conduct themselves with you who offer your help?
4. How does it have them "treat" themselves? "See" themselves?
5. How is this person being redescribed/redefined by it?
6. Does it invite people to see the therapist or themselves as experts on themselves?
7. Does it divide and isolate people or give them a sense of community and collaboration?
8. Do the questions asked lead in generative or normative directions (e.g., propose alternative or conserve dominant social practices)?
9. Does the model require the person to enter the therapist's "expert" knowledge or does it require the therapist to enter the "world" of the client?

10. What is its definition of "professionalism"? Does its idea of "professionalism" have more to do with the therapist's presentation of self to colleagues and others or with the therapist's presentation of self to the person(s) seeking their assistance?

These questions cover a lot of ground. They offer several ways to reflect on the effects of the models, theories, and practices that constitute both our "selves" and our work. Three things particularly impress us about these questions.

First, they are questions. Just as this is not a therapy that dictates to people, but rather poses questions to people, these ethical guidelines are expressed not as rules or formulas, but rather as questions that invite therapists to examine their practices and revise them in terms of the values and relationships that those practices bring forth. This is very different from the kind of "just do it and don't think about it" compliance that top-down rules may invite.

Second, these ethics are about people and relationships. They do not propose truths, but concern themselves with people, particularly questioning whose voices are dominant in therapy relationships.

Third, the questions focus largely on the *effects* of practices, so that what therapists do is not evaluated by how well their actions follow rules but by the actual effects of those actions on people's lives.

We agree with Tom Andersen (1991b, p. 13) who has said

For me, the time has come to ask the questions: If I want to apply a method in my work with clients will it demand a relationship I don't want to have? Maybe time has come to let our ethics and aesthetics form our relationships, and let those relationships allow for possible activities (of which methods make up some).

ETHICAL POSTURES

Karl Tomm (Bernstein, 1990) has described a set of ethical postures and situated himself within them. His work in this area speaks to some of the points we've been addressing. Tomm identifies how he uses his schema in constituting himself in relation to the people who consult with him, and he outlines other possibilities for how people might constitute different kinds of relationships than those he prefers. He uses a series of cross-shaped diagrams to explain his ideas. (See Figure 10.1 for an example.)

On the horizontal axis of the basic diagram, he plots the way knowledge is shared in the change process. The left end of this axis represents

Figure 10.1 Diagram of Karl Tomm's model.

change that is based in totally "secret" (professional) knowledge. The right end represents change that is based in shared knowledge, so that all parties are informed and collaborating in the process. Both hypnosis and medication, for example, would be plotted on the left (secret, noncon-scious) end of the line, while advice with accompanying explanations would be plotted somewhere close to the right end.

The vertical axis represents the intended means through which thera-peutic change is to occur. This second axis is comprised of a continuum that goes from reducing options or closing space at the top to increasing options or opening space at the bottom. For example, if a person is considering suicide, a plan to block that option through hospitalization and constant observation would close space. At the other end of the continuum, questions that allow a person immobilized by self-doubt to see herself in a new light that in turn makes new job opportunities seem possible could be plotted as opening space.

With these two dimensions in mind, Tomm labels the four quadrants that they demarcate (starting with the top left and going clockwise) "manipulation" (based on secret knowledge and closing down options), "confrontation" (based on shared knowledge and limited options), "em-powerment" (based on shared knowledge and many options), and "succorance" (based on professional knowledge and open options), stipulating that all models of psychotherapy include all of these postures while relying on a primary one. He also notes that each posture disposes therapists toward a different kind of relationship.

Tomm is interested in constituting himself as a therapist who primarily engages in empowering relationships and secondarily in succorant ones. He has identified three things that he does to support and remind himself of his preferences. The first is to relabel the ends of the vertical axis "therapeutic violence" (closing space) and "therapeutic loving" (opening space), using Maturana's definitions of violence as "any imposition of one's will upon another" and love as "opening space for the existence of the other." Since Tomm is drawn to loving and repelled by violence, this naming helps him choose to act in ways that he believes will aid in the cocreation of empowerment and succorance.

In Chapter 5 we mention what Tomm calls "bifurcation questions"— questions that juxtapose two contrasting options, inviting people to pick one. The opposing labels of the two ends of this axis serve much the same purpose, mobilizing emotional responses in a particular direction. Tomm purposely picked labels that would attract and repel him.

Tomm's second method for ethically constituting himself in relation to others is to examine how he sees the people with whom he works. Since seeing people with problems as subjugated, oppressed, or restrained (as opposed to, say, uneducated, ill, or stubborn) helps him choose empowering methods, he endeavors to see people in these ways.

Third, Tomm has articulated four guidelines that he follows in empowering himself and others: *grounding* (being sensitive), *recursioning* (being mindful), *coherencing* (being congruent), and *authenticating* (being honest). Each of these guidelines—you might note that the "ing" conjures a degree of "verbness"—implies particular actions for Tomm. For example, grounding includes attending to the context and conditions of others, listening carefully, and sharing descriptions rather than keeping them private. Recursioning includes listening to others' listening and assuming that one is assuming. Examples of coherencing include identifying inconsistencies between intent and effect and privileging emotional dynamics in order to seek intuitive consistency. Authenticating includes privileging direct experiences over explanations, performing one's own explanations, and being open to seeing oneself through others' eyes.

What is particularly attractive to us about Tomm's ethical postures schema is his thoughtful description of possible therapeutic and ethical stances. He has delineated certain postures through which he wants to constitute himself in relation to others and invented language that will support and remind him to make the ethical choices he wants to make in an ongoing way. The schema provides distinctions that can be used in a generative and loving kind of continual deconstruction and reconstruction of self-in-process.

ASSUMPTIONS ABOUT
PEOPLE AND THERAPY

James and Melissa Griffith (1992a, 1994) have written accounts of how they seek to participate in therapeutic relationships characterized by an atmosphere of curiosity, openness, and respect. Their 1992a paper on this subject was inspired by the experience of attempting to teach narrative approaches to psychiatry residents. Investigating numerous instances in which families dropped out of therapy after one interview, the Griffiths learned that the residents involved had asked a memorized series of "narrative questions" as though they were standard protocol, with no effort to establish a context in which families could freely tell their stories and be heard. The following quote from one of the psychiatric residents in their program is illustrative:

> What originally drew me to seek supervision with you was wanting to better connect with my clients as I had seen you do, but I was so intent on organizing the next question that I didn't even flinch when the father revealed he had been diagnosed with cancer. That is not like me. (Griffith & Griffith, 1992a, p. 5)

In reflecting on such comments, the Griffiths decided that they had not sufficiently emphasized relationships and emotional postures in their teaching. To rectify the situation, they revised their supervision course so that the first ten weeks (out of 30) were spent developing skills in creating a therapeutic relationship, teaching no specific questions or procedures until the later weeks of the course.

In their course, the Griffiths began to stress attitudes and beliefs that are conducive to the curious, open, and respectful atmosphere they desire in therapeutic conversations. They remind us that the language and assumptions that we choose will contribute to the cocreation of particular emotional postures in the therapy room. In their article, they (Griffith & Griffith, 1992a, p. 9) share the following assumptions as ones that they value:

- "These family members and I share more similarities than differences as human beings."
- "Family members are ordinary people leading everyday lives who unfortunately have encountered unusual and difficult life experiences."

- "When a person or a family with a problem requests psychotherapy, it is because they are struggling with a dilemma for which the kind of conversation needed for its resolution cannot occur."
- "Persons and families always possess more lived experience as a resource than can be contained by the available narratives about the problem."
- "Persons and family members in their deepest desires do not wish to harm self or others."
- "I cannot understand the meaning of the language a person uses until we talk together about it."
- "Change is always possible."
- "A person or a family with a problem wishes to be free of the problem."
- "I cannot know for sure what actions family members need to take for the problem to be resolved."

Like Karl Tomm's decision to see people with problems as subjugated, oppressed, or restrained, these assumptions about individuals and families play a significant role in how the Griffiths see the people who consult them and how they hear the stories people tell them. Can you imagine how these assumptions might influence the moment-to-moment choices the Griffiths make in the course of their work? How do these assumptions fit with your own assumptions about people and the problems that bring them into therapy?

THE ROLE OF COMMUNITY

So far, we have been discussing ethics in terms of the ways in which different therapists constitute themselves in relationship with the people who consult them. Dean Lobovits and Jennifer Freeman (1993) look at some of the larger contexts that influence the constitution of lives and relationships in therapy.

Their inquiry stems from an examination of sexual exploitation by therapists. They start by focusing on the cultural norm that privileges personal gratification over relatedness. They think that to behave ethically in terms of sexual exploitation therapists must embody principles that do not fit with this norm. Asking themselves what processes instill such principles, they (1993, p. 34) find answers that have to do with experiences of belonging and being accountable to "communities that support power-with, collaborative relationships, rather than power-over expert relationships."

In Chapter 9 we write about how teams and communities can help in developing and maintaining new narratives. Narrative therapy communities,[3] both international and local, are beginning to serve as participant audiences that can hold each other accountable for the kind of selves and relationships each is bringing forth in its members. Sheila McNamee (1994, p. 72) writes,

> If particular ways of talking *construct* our worlds, then the discursive forms that emerge and gain viability within particular communities construct the ethical standards by which we live.

Narrative communities, like any other communities, over time will privilege certain stances over others, and, of course, different narrative communities will privilege different stances. The questions Epston and White ask themselves, Tomm's ethical postures, and Griffith and Griffith's assumptions have contributed to the current ethical discourses in "the narrative community." The writing, teaching, demonstrations, videotapes, and the like of others who align themselves with these ideas, as well as the practices and stories that circulate among us, also contribute to which discourses and ethics are being privileged.

The ethics that are being privileged in turn attract members to the community. For example, recently there was a three-page article about narrative therapy in *Newsweek* (Cowley & Springen, 1995). People called from all over the country to ask for referrals to a narrative therapist or for information about a program where they could study narrative therapy in their area. At first, we found this surprising. After all, very little can be said in three pages.

When we began interviewing the people who called, we found that they were attracted to the idea of seeing people as separate from problems. They told us stories of the awful effects of confusing people with problems in their lives and in the lives of people they loved. They seemed to hunger for a community whose ethical stance was to separate people from problems. When we couldn't locate a referral for one woman, she asked if we would collaborate in developing a list of questions she could ask local therapists. "Maybe," she said, "they're doing narrative therapy without knowing it."

We are very excited about the development of narrative communities. However, the fervor with which people are responding to these ideas also raises a dilemma: How do we stop narrative communities from becoming

---

[3]Participating in narrative therapy communities can take many forms, such as working together with others using these ideas, perhaps on a reflecting team or in talking about therapy, participating in therapy in the client position, participating in workshops or conferences in which these ideas are discussed, and reading books and articles that use narrative ideas and letting those books and articles or their authors be on your team.

monolithic movements or cults that no longer reflect the ethics they were built on?

If narrative practices are taken up as "techniques" and used in a worldview that does not encourage collaboration, openness, and ongoing examination of the effects of its practices, they can have undesirable effects. It is vital that practices that have become part of the work not be used out of the context of the reflective, deconstructionist, nonpathologizing worldview in which they were developed. Also, we must continue to modify our practices according to the preferences of the people who consult us and the "real effects" of those practices in their local cultures.

ETHICS IN PRACTICE

In a recent issue of the newsletter *News of the Difference*, Dvorah Simon (1995) repeats a story that Jay Haley told at a conference held in New Orleans to honor John Weakland. Haley said that on a visit to Japan he was interested when he saw family members bow to the father of the family. He interpreted the bows as an expression of respect, and mentioned this in talking to the family. They corrected him, saying (p. 3), "Oh no. We bow to *practice* respect."

Simon goes on to suggest that the therapeutic practices she has learned are not presciptions that must be adhered to; instead, they are ways of practicing attitudes. In this light, and keeping in mind that they are always changing, we'd like to look at some of our therapeutic practices.

Situating Ourselves

When we say "situating ourselves" we refer to the practice of clearly and publicly identifying those aspects of our own experience, imagination, and intentions (White, 1991) that we believe guide our work. In so doing, we enter therapeutic relationships as fallible human beings, rather than as experts. We present ourselves as particular people who have been shaped and affected by particular experiences. We hope that this gives people an idea of how they might want to take what we say and do.

In describing this practice in his work with heterosexual couples, John Neal (1995, p. 10) writes:

> . . . it is useful for the therapist to begin by acknowledging his or her own context in some way. With heterosexual couples, particularly, the acknowledgment of the effects of the therapist's gender is important (since the therapist can only match the gender of one of the partners). In my case as a man, I routinely announce that it will be helpful if we remain attentive to the fact that as a man I am likely

to misunderstand or not notice some of the woman's experience; that
I know that I "do not know" and will make the effort to frequently
check with her to ascertain if there are things I am "missing."

Along with finding out something about people outside of the problem
at the initial meeting, we also typically ask if they would like to ask us
any questions. The responses we've received have been quite diverse. Some
people decline to ask questions. Others ask about our training and ideas
about therapy. Others have asked all sorts of questions. Two of our favor-
ites are, "Do you believe in God?" and "What do you like to read?"

Situating is an ongoing process. As we introduce new ideas we situate
them in our experience, at the same time taking care not to dominate
the conversation by talking overly much about ourselves. David Epston
(White, 1991) has introduced the term *transparency* to refer to this process of deconstructing and situating therapists' contributions to the therapy process.

In Chapter 7 we have described how reflecting team members situate
themselves and ask each other questions to facilitate transparency. Additionally, whenever circumstances permit it, we include a *post session* in
which reflecting team and family members are invited to interview the
therapist about his experience of the therapy process and why he did
what he did when in the session. (We ask family members to listen to
orient themselves to the kinds of questions we are posing before we invite
them to join in.) In this process we ask questions such as these:

- What stands out about the interview to you? How is that meaningful
  for you as a therapist?
- What was your experience of working with this family?
- Early in the interview, when John named two different areas of concern, it seemed to me you could have gone in two different directions.
  How did you decide which direction to take? What made that direction seem important?
- (From a family member) You asked Susie lots of questions about how
  depression was affecting her. Why didn't you ask how it was affecting me?
- I would have asked more about the conversation they had on Tuesday
  night. Did you notice some cue that led you away from that subject?

At times we have similar conversations asking reflecting team members to deconstruct their comments and questions. As Stephen Madigan
(1993, p. 223) notes,

Therapeutic curiosity that directs itself only to narrative accounts
of client restraints, without publicizing and recognizing therapist
restraints, continues to perpetuate modern myths of expert knowledge.

Although not everyone is interested in contributing to these conversations inviting therapist transparency, those who are interested usually find this process extremely meaningful. One man commented after his first post-session discussion, "You guys really mean it!" We took this as referring to what Karl Tomm calls "coherencing"—striving for consistency between intent and effect. Therapist transparency offers a way for us to practice horizontal, collaborative relationships (or at least to begin flattening the hierarchy).

Listening and Asking Questions

At one point in our work we would structure interviews with particular, goal-oriented questions. Our rationale was that if we allowed people to just talk they would become immersed in their problems, which would not be helpful. Now, we begin by *listening deconstructively* to people's stories (see Chapter 3). In so doing we hope to gain some understanding of people's local culture and their particular dilemmas, while at the same time opening at least a little space in problem-saturated stories. Instead of inviting them to become further immersed and isolated in their problems, we seek to *join them* in their experience of the world. For us, this initial listening sets an ethical tone in which we commit to joining people in their struggles (provided they are open to that kind of relationship).

In our interactions as therapists, we seek to ask *questions* rather than to interpret, instruct, or more directly intervene. We do this for several reasons having to do with ethics. First, although questions are not neutral, they are more open-ended than statements. People can choose how to respond to a question, and when we genuinely listen to and value people's responses, *their* ideas, not ours, stay at the center of therapy. Penn and Sheinberg (1991, p. 32) write:

> For the therapists to resist declarative language and to stay in a questioning and speculative mode . . . acts as a counterweight to the inherent properties of language that represent reality as though it were independent of our construction of it. . . . Maintaining this position also protects the therapists from assuming a hierarchical posture and reconfigures the idea of the therapist as an expert.

How we receive people's answers to questions is very important. In this work we are interested and often delighted when people come up with expansive answers in which they recount events and tell stories, particularly if the events and stories reflect preferred paths in their lives. In the evolution of our own work, we have moved from thinking about ourselves primarily as storytellers to thinking of ourselves as audience members (or, at times, co-authors).

At least two of the questions that Epston and White have suggested for evaluating our clinical practices seem relevant to this shift in who is the privileged storyteller:

- Does this model/theory/practice invite people to see the therapist or themselves as experts on themselves?
- Does it require the person to enter the therapist's "expert" knowledge or does it require the therapist to enter the "world" of the client?

We frequently ask questions such as "Is this what you want to be talking about?" and "Is it okay if I ask about this?" These and other *preference questions* (which we discuss in Chapter 5) ask people to decide which directions, alternatives, and narratives they prefer. In deciding, people become experts about their own lives and actively tailor their therapy to their own desires.

Another important area of inquiry is *asking about effects*. We regularly ask about the effects of particular interviews and of the therapy process as a whole. The answers to these questions help us revise our work so that it fits different people in different situations. Tailoring therapy in response to people's preferred effects demonstrates our accountability for the effects of our work. This practice fits with Tomm's guideline of "coherencing," as we strive to make the effects consistent with our intentions. The following are examples of questions we might ask in inquiring about effects:

- Has this meeting been helpful? How has it been helpful?
- I'm curious about the effect the therapy is having in your life. Can you tell me what some of the effects have been so far? Have these been positive effects or negative effects?
- What thoughts and ideas have you had that relate to what we talked about last time? How have those made a difference in your life? Is that a difference that you find useful?

Accountability Practices

A problem that is built into relationships between therapists and clients is that therapists are in a privileged position[4] in the context of

---

[4]A friend of ours disagrees with this analysis, saying that some people view therapists as "hired hacks" who can be fired at the drop of a hat. While this attitude may characterize some therapeutic relationships some of the time, the relationship still typically takes place in the therapist's space, in time increments determined by the therapist, and in a structure suggested by the therapist. Furthermore, the therapist is usually thought of as having expertise in this kind of relationship and the client is defined as needing help. All of these factors in a therapist-client relationship, as it is characterized in Western culture, suggest that the therapist is in a dominant position.

therapy. Particularly when we work with people from marginalized cultures, to be in an expert position inadvertently reinforces cultural dominance (Hall & Greene, 1994). In a therapy where we strive to deconstruct problems and unmask cultural discourses that support them, we certainly want to avoid replicating the oppression that contributes to problematic narratives (Kazan, 1994). Yet, as members of the dominant culture, we do participate in cultural dominance. Carmel Tapping and her colleagues (1993, p. 8) write,

> Our secularised concepts of mental health, of individualism and identity, of nuclear family structure and dynamics, of generational boundaries, of "welfare" and child rearing practices, can, to people whose cultures and spirituality are very different from ours, be every bit as unjust and harmful as the shotguns and poisoned waterholes of our ancestors.

Because of the process of reification that we discuss in Chapter 2, we easily lose sight of the constructed nature of reality and assume that our realities are shared. This assumption closes space for the possibilities of other realities and contributes to domination and oppression. In therapy, when a man begins to tell us about his relationship and, assuming it to be a heterosexual one, we ask about "her," or when we schedule an initial appointment and, assuming the person has a car, we give directions on how to drive to our office, or when, in conversation with a heterosexual couple, assuming that they married because of love, we ask them to tell us about what first appealed to each about the other—in all these situations we are shaping the therapy relationship in terms of our own culture and crowding out other possible cultures. When we assume that people's responses to our questions are candid reflections of their experience, we are assuming that they feel free to talk openly with us. This may not be so.

There are many, many other examples of mistaken assumptions that we can't give because, as members of a dominant culture, we are not aware of them.

We can respond to these assumptions in a variety of ways. First, we can commit to scrutinizing our own work and, as assumptions become apparent, stop imposing them on others. Second, we can intentionally raise the issue of false assumptions with all the people who come to see us, letting them know that we take responsibility for any misunderstandings that may occur. When they do occur, we can examine false assumptions with the presupposition that they relate to our privilege. Third, we can build in accountability structures and practices.

Accountability practices, we believe, were first introduced to this work through the example and inspiration of the Just Therapy team from The Family Centre of Lower Hutt, New Zealand. At their center, they have structured practices to reverse the sociocultural bias against women and people from marginalized cultures (see Tamasese & Waldegrave, 1993). To do this, they have established gender and cultural caucuses. Within their center, they have agreed that the caucuses composed of people from dominated groups can initiate meetings whenever they experience an injustice in staff relationships, in models of therapy, or in practice. The caucuses of people of the dominant cultures are responsible for consulting with the other caucuses about projects and direction. Policy decisions are made only through this process of consultation, and no policy is implemented until it is approved by all concerned caucuses.

Kiwi Tamasese and Charles Waldegrave (1993) point out that through caucusing, individual people can be heard as members of a collective, which may be vital to their willingness to speak out in situations where they are outnumbered or in positions of low status.

Christopher McLean (1994, pp. 2–3) writes,

> [Accountability structures] offer a practical way forward. They start from the recognition of the centrality of structured power differences in our society, and develop means of addressing them, so that groups that have been marginalised and oppressed can have their voices heard. . . . accountability . . . is primarily concerned with addressing injustice. It provides members of the dominant group with the information necessary for them to stand against the oppressive practices implicit within their own culture, of which they will often be totally unaware.

When members of marginalized groups provide this type of information to culturally dominant groups, there is a certain injustice in their having to take their time and energy to teach people who are already more privileged than they. The beauty of accountability practices like those of the Just Therapy team is that they privilege the voices of people from groups that have been marginalized. Their ideas are allotted more space. The practice itself is a counter-practice, constructed to turn practices of marginalization on their heads. When they take part in these sorts of accountability practices, people from marginalized groups are not just teaching us; they are also participating in a more equitable context — one in which members of the dominant culture take the responsibility for acting in accordance with the information we are given.

Rob Hall (1994) suggests "partnership accountability" as a name for these practices, which are so different from the hierarchical practices so often associated with accountability. He emphasizes that goodwill, including a commitment to constructing ethical solutions that promote social justice, critical self-appraisal, and responsibility, are necessary components of partnership accountability.

Accountability practices speak to several of the principles on which Epston and White's ethics questions rest:

- They bring people together in community and collaboration.
- They lead in generative directions and encourage alternative social practices.
- They turn the tables on whose knowledge is considered expert and whose "world" is privileged.

In our own work, we have begun applying these ideas in a number of ways. We think of this book, which makes our work very public, as a way of being accountable. Showing videotapes of our work and doing live interviews are also accountability practices, especially when the presentations occur in contexts that support an open and honest critique. We have used gender caucusing in our teaching as a way of incorporating a counter-practice into our training and to privilege women's voices.

The accountability structure we developed was probably the most significant aspect of one couple's therapy. Kevin initiated therapy because it was clear to him that Yvette was preparing to leave the relationship. He had beaten her a number of times, and she was no longer willing to live with him. She did agree to join him for one meeting of couple therapy. In that meeting, she indicated that if she believed that Kevin would never touch her in violence again, and that he would not treat her with disrespect in other ways, she would be interested in having a relationship with him.

However, she made it very clear that he had to be the one to take responsibility for the abuse. She wanted evidence that things had changed, but she did not want to be a part of therapy with him, as she believed that the problem would then be defined as a shared problem, rather than as Kevin's problem.

Together, we worked out an agreement that I (JF) would see Kevin individually, that the therapy would be videotaped, and that the tapes would be available for Yvette's review. Initially, because of concerns about danger and manipulation, Yvette and I reviewed the tapes together, without Kevin. Her impressions of the therapy and her thoughts and desires about how to proceed were paramount in my work.

Although Kevin agreed to this plan, the first time he became aware that Yvette had actually reviewed a tape anger took over, prompting him to speak harshly to me about confidentiality. We used this as an occasion to deconstruct the way invisibility and lack of accountability had supported violence in the relationship.

As the therapy proceeded, we deconstructed some of the sociocultural contexts and attitudes that supported the abuse. Kevin named and took responsibility for the effects of the abuse, and he began to put himself in Yvette's place and understand the devastation she had experienced.[5] At this point, Yvette decided that Kevin could join her in watching the tapes and hearing her responses. In that way, he became directly accountable to her, in person.

We continued meeting until Yvette, based on what she had witnessed in reviewing Kevin's work, judged that she was willing to re-enter the relationship. I met together with the couple twice in the month following their reunion. I talked with Yvette on the telephone a year later. She told me that Kevin had never hit her again or treated her abusively, and that his changes in attitude had affected the relationship in ways she couldn't have predicted. She said that she experienced herself as an equal partner with an equal voice in the relationship.

Externalizing Conversations

Every time we engage in an externalizing conversation with someone we practice seeing her as separate from and in a relationship with the problem. This practice has a snowballing effect. In order to frame a question in externalizing language, we must see the problem as a distinct and separate entity. This perception can alert us to new areas of inquiry, which can sharpen our perception of the problem as separate from the person. At the same time, we offer the person a different view of herself, one that is not obscured by the problem.

Externalizing conversations help us align ourselves with the Griffiths' assumption that family members are ordinary people leading everyday lives who unfortunately have encountered unusual and difficult life experiences.

When we join people in a perceptual mode that allows everyone involved to see them as separate from their problems, we inevitably forge a different relationship than we would if we saw them as problematic people or as containing problems. Seeing problems and people as separate allows us to enter a collaborative relationship with each other and against the problem. In this collaborative relationship, we recognize that the person and the family have more direct experience with the problem than we do. We acknowledge their expertise[6] in this area and follow their lead.

---

[5]See Alan Jenkins' (1990) book, *Invitations to Responsibility: The Therapeutic Engagement of Men Who Are Violent and Abusive*, for a thorough description of working to engage men in taking responsibility for violent and abusive behavior.

[6]We recognize that we also have relevant experience and knowledge of therapeutic practices that we bring to this enterprise. Most of this book is about those things. We find that keeping our focus on the often unrecognized, but vital, role of people's own experience and expertise helps forge the kind of relationships in which we want to participate.

People new to narrative practices often perceive an ethical dilemma concerning responsibility when they consider externalizing conversations. They wonder if seeing problems as separate from people lets people off the hook. We do not think that this is what happens. We believe that separating people from problems makes it *more* likely that they will be able to act responsibly in relation to the problem.

As David Epston and Sallyann Roth (in press) emphasize, once the problem is seen as separate from a person, the person is in a position to see the relationship she has with the problem and to see the possibility of resisting, protesting, or renegotiating that relationship. When people see themselves as problematic, they often feel helpless to do anything about their plight. Perhaps they can "control themselves"; however, when this idea is taken to the logical extreme, short of suicide, there is little room to get free of a problem when that problem is oneself.

When we see ourselves as separate from problems, we can take responsibility for our relationships with them and decide what to do in relation to them. Much of narrative therapy has to do with bringing forth descriptions of people's preferred ways of relating to particular problems and documenting the preferred identities they construct once separated from problem-saturated self-descriptions.

Just as seeing the problem as separate from the person opens space for people to recognize, evaluate, and renegotiate their relationships with problems, this perceptual position opens space for therapists to *consider and ask about the larger sociopolitical contexts and discourses that support problems*. When we engage in these kinds of considerations and make them a part of the process of therapy, our views about people and problems are forever changed.

For example, I (JF) currently see a family of five adults who live in a four-room apartment. Although the referral information, based on a recent psychiatric hospitalization, focuses on Jean, the 23-year-old daughter, as being "violent, having poor impulse control, and paranoid ideation," I see the effects of poverty, racism, and related inequities as having created a context in which hopelessness and desperation have flourished.

The idealized images of what constitutes "success" in our capitalist society, through contrast with this family's actual situation, have encouraged them to internalize feelings of failure and shame. These feelings have inhibited Jean from making friends or getting a job. In our culture (especially for women), much of one's worth outside of financial success is tied up in one's relationships. This means that the lack of friends or co-workers has intensified Jean's feelings of failure and shame, leading her to be overcome by desperation.

In Jean's local culture, which is infested with gangs, violence is enacted daily as an appropriate response to difficulties. When we consider this, it should come as no surprise that, after being fired at a minimum-wage job, Jean came home, trashed the apartment, and repeatedly slapped Marina, her mother, when Marina tried to stop her. It was this act that resulted in her hospitalization and subsequent labeling as "violent, having poor impulse control, and paranoid ideation."

As we've named the problem "desperation" and begun to deconstruct it, Jean has decided to protest the feelings of failure and shame and hold people and experiences having to do with appreciation close in her heart. Keeping these experiences close helps her choose to turn away from violence and take steps that she judges will create more satisfaction in her life. She is developing her own ideas and images of success rather than comparing herself to the dominant society's images.

From the vantage point of Jean's current narrative, the description of her as "violent, having poor impulse control, and paranoid ideation" seems unfair and perhaps even unethical, especially when it is not accompanied by a description of the financial and intrapersonal hardships that oppress her every day and that are maintained by racism and classism. The practice of asking about the sociopolitical context paves the way for us to see people with problems as subjugated, oppressed, or restrained, a perspective that, in Tomm's schema, aids in the cocreation of empowerment.

Reflecting Practices

Reflecting practices, in all the forms that we have already discussed in Chapter 7, are a particularly clear example of postmodern ethics in action. The move from invisible, behind-the-mirror teams to reflecting teams is based in ethical postures that value openness, transparency, multiple viewpoints, and decentering of the therapist. By opening space and sharing knowledge, reflecting teams support "empowerment," Karl Tomm's preferred style of relating in therapy. Griffith and Griffith (1994) remind us that the practice of reflecting in front of the mirror while family members observe and listen is a *political* act, the purpose of which is to share power among all the participants in therapy.

In the reflecting team process, we are inviting people to listen evaluatively to our various understandings of their story and to comment on which of those understandings they find useful and fitting. This is what David Epston would call a "counter-practice" in that it turns the dominant story about who should be doing the evaluating on its head.

Reflecting team work fits with several of the principles implied by White and Epston's list of questions from earlier in this chapter:

- It invites people to see themselves as experts on themselves.
- It offers people a sense of community and collaboration.

- It requires therapists to enter the "world" of the client.
- Its idea of "professionalism" has to do with the therapist's presentation of self to the persons seeking assistance.

There is nothing as effective as public reflection in training therapists to think and talk in respectful, nonpathologizing terms about the people they work with. As we mentioned in Chapter 7, in our first attempts at talking about people while they watched and listened from behind the mirror, we were nearly paralyzed by our awareness of their presence. We could sense that our accustomed ways of talking behind the mirror were not always as respectful as we might wish. This meant that our thoughts were also less than fully respectful.

We like to think that years of experience with reflecting teams has shaped both our thinking and our talking so that they reflect a more respectful attitude toward people. Nowadays, even when the people we are working with aren't actually present, we strive to talk, think, and act as if they were. This, to us, is a central practice in constituting the kinds of relationships that bring forth our preferred ways of being.

When we invite people involved in the process of therapy to reflect on a therapy meeting (as we do formally at the end of many sessions involving a reflecting team), we engage in both an ongoing research project and a deconstruction of the work and its effects. We have already discussed this in some detail under "situating ourselves."

Even when we do it without a team, reflecting is a basic way that we continually question the effects of our actions. Every time we inquire about the effect of a belief or the meaning of an action, we are asking people to evaluate some aspect of the therapeutic process and to choose whether to make that belief or action a part of their preferred direction in life.

We believe that it is useful to reflect at regular intervals on our own continuing development as therapists—questioning the effects of our current beliefs and behaviors, not just on the lives and relationships of the people who consult us, but on our local culture as well.

As we reflect on reflecting practices, what stands out for us is the importance of switching roles with those who consult us—being in front of the mirror while they listen, being behind the mirror while they comment on our comments, hearing their reflections and questions about our work. This switching of positions is done in the spirit of solidarity. Michael White (1993, p. 132) writes,

I am thinking of a solidarity that is constructed by therapists who refuse to draw a sharp distinction between their lives and the lives of others, who refuse to marginalize those persons who seek help;

by therapists who are prepared to constantly confront the fact that if faced with circunstances such that provide the context of the troubles of others, they just might not be doing nearly as well themselves.

Relationship Practices That Counteract Hierarchy

When we "situate" ourselves, we do so in part so that people will view us as particular people rather than as generic professionals. When we emphasize listening and asking questions over talking, giving advice, or making pronouncements, we are again advocating practices that counteract the hierarchy implied by our professional position. Reflecting practices and accountability practices are both anti-practices that intentionally invert the dominant discourse about whose voice is most important in therapeutic relationships.

David Epston and Michael White (1992) have developed a therapeutic practice called "consulting your consultants" that, in their words,

> . . . encourages persons to document the solution knowledges, and the alternative knowledges about their lives and relationships, that have been resurrected and/or generated in therapy. (p. 12)

The knowledge that people document in this process is their own. Once documented, the knowledge is available for use by other people struggling with similar problems and by therapists who want to learn from others' lived experience.

Epston and White describe a process in which, as people decide that they have sufficiently enough revised their relationship with a problem that they no longer find therapy necessary, a celebration is planned. As part of this celebration, they are consulted about the knowledge they have gained in overcoming the problem. This knowledge is documented in letters, certificates, videotapes, and the like, and, with appropriate permission, the knowledge is eventually shared with other people struggling with similar problems.

When we appreciate, utilize, and circulate the hard-won knowledge of the people who consult us, we participate in the creation of communities of concern in which problem conquerors' wisdom is at least as important as therapists' wisdom. (The archives of the Anti-Anorexia League of New Zealand are a particularly well-known and extensive collection of such knowledge.[7]) We can decenter ourselves even more in this process

---

[7]The archives include notes, letters, artwork, tapes, and the like that were made as part of the therapy process as well as documents produced through consultations.

by paying for consultations when people share their time and wisdom with us, and (with their consent) publicly acknowledging them as the source of that knowledge and wisdom.

In this same vein, we can enter into co-research projects with people, formally consulting with them about the effects of particular practices on particular problems. I (GC) am currently engaged in a project with one person in which she evaluates and reflects on one hour of videotape of my earlier work with her in return for each hour of consultation with me in the present.

In a very real sense, all narrative therapy is co-research. When we listen carefully to people's stories we are doing research. When we ask meaning questions and preference questions we are asking people to join us in research. When we reflect — with or without a team — on unique outcomes, on the effects of various practices, on preferred directions in life, or on any other aspect of therapy, we are doing co-research.

One particular purpose of this co-research is that of evaluating the ethics of the beliefs, attitudes, and practices that constitute our work. In the light of such evaluation, the work is always changing.

Acknowledging the Effects of Relationships on Us

In December, Sancho, our beloved cat, died. I (JF) grew up in an anti-pet household, and sharing the whole life of another being — and he was a very special being, a cat of peace who purred whenever I even *looked* at him — was an experience I treasured. When Sancho died, I was devastated. The greatest comfort to me was a very clear memory of the words of 11-year-old Jane, who had come to therapy because, in the course of changing schools, she had been tricked into thinking she wasn't smart. I had asked Jane whether she had any pets, and I struck a veritable gold mine. It turned out she had Fluffy (a cat), Fred and Ted (two goldfish), Babbit (a rabbit), and Rusty. Rusty, she told me, was a golden retriever, who had died when she was eight. "He's still my favorite pet. We talk about him all the time. We have pictures of him. And I have him in my heart." The wisdom of this 11-year-old girl, who, along with her family, was consulting me, guided me through the early part of my grief.

Every day that we go to work, people entrust us with stories of heart-felt pain, life-and-death struggle, and finding the courage to fight back. What an honor it is to be let in, not just on another's life, but as a partner in another's struggle. As we, through this work, redefine the roles and relationships of people in therapeutic endeavors, we find that their voices, their pain, and their wisdom penetrate more deeply into our lives.

We tell people about their effects on us. When we hear people's stories of pain and injustice, we cry with them. And when they recognize that self-hatred or despair is not them, but a problem that had become internalized, we rejoice. When Madeline told me (GC), in a trembling voice, that, for the first time, she understood that she deserved to have a say in her life, that the internalized "voice of torture" no longer determined her every move, and told of treating herself to dinner at a local restaurant to celebrate, a tremendous pleasure stayed with me for days. I feel that pleasure again whenever I pass the restaurant or revisit the memory. I've told Madeline what this has meant to me and our combined tellings have become an experience that helps her fight the voice of torture and helps me in authoring my story as a therapist. Knowing that we can be on such teams makes work and life very rich, indeed.

Bibliography

Adams-Westcott, J. (1993). Commentary on J. L. Zimmerman & V. C. Dickerson, Bringing forth the restraining influence of pattern in couples therapy). In S. Gilligan & R. Price (Eds.), *Therapeutic conversations* (pp. 215–217). New York: Norton.

Adams-Westcott, J., Combs, G., Dickerson, V., Freedman, J., Neal, J., & Zimmerman, J. (1994, November 3). *Narrative therapy and supervision: A postmodern experience.* A pre-conference Institute presented at the 52nd Annual Conference of the American Association for Marriage and Family Therapy, Chicago.

Adams-Westcott, J., Dafforn, T., & Sterne, P. (1993). Escaping victim life stories and co-constructing personal agency. In S. Gilligan & R. Price (Eds.), *Therapeutic conversations* (pp. 258–271). New York: Norton.

Adams-Westcott, J., & Isenbart, D. (1995). A journey of change through connection. In S. Friedman (Ed.), *The reflecting team in action.* New York: Guilford.

Adams-Westcott, J., & Isenbart, D. (in press). Creating preferred relationships: The politics of "recovery" from child sexual abuse. *Journal of Systemic Therapies.*

Andersen, T. (1987). The reflecting team: Dialogue and metadialogue in clinical work. *Family Process, 26,* 415–428.

Andersen, T. (1991a). Guidelines for practice. In T. Andersen (Ed.), *The reflecting team: Dialogues and dialogues about the dialogues.* New York: Norton.

Andersen, T. (1991b, May 10–12). *Relationship, language, and pre-understanding in the reflecting process.* Read at the Houston-Galveston Institute's Conference, "Narrative and Psychotherapy: New Directions in Theory and Practice for the 21st Century," Houston.

Andersen, T. (1993). See and hear, and be seen and heard. In S. Friedman (Ed.), *The new language of change: Constructive collaboration in psychotherapy* (pp. 303–322). New York: Guilford.

Anderson, H. (1990). Then and now: A journey from "knowing" to "not knowing." *Contemporary Family Therapy, 12*(3), 193–197.

Anderson, H., & Goolishian, H. (1988). Human systems as linguistic systems: Preliminary and evolving ideas about the implications for clinical theory. *Family Process, 27,* 371–393.

Anderson, H., & Goolishian, H. (1990a). Beyond cybernetics: Comments on

Atkinson and Heath's "Further thoughts on second-order family therapy." *Family Process, 29*, 157–163.

Anderson, H., & Goolishian, H. (1990b, November). *Changing thoughts on self agency, questions, narrative and therapy.* Paper read at the "Reflecting Process, Reflecting Team" Conference, Salzburg, Austria.

Anderson, H., & Goolishian, H. (1991). Supervision as collaborative conversation: Questions and reflections. In H. Brandau (Ed.), *Von der supervision zur systemischen vision.* Salzburg: Otto Muller Verlag.

Anderson, H., & Goolishian, H. (1992). The client is the expert: A not-knowing approach to therapy. In S. McNamee & K. J. Gergen (Eds.), *Therapy as social construction.* Newbury Park, CA: Sage.

Anderson, H., Goolishian, H., Pulliam, G., & Winderman, L. (1986). The Galveston Family Institute: Some personal and historical Perspectives. In D. Efron (Ed.), *Journeys: Expansion of the strategic-systemic therapies* (pp. 97–122). New York: Bruner/Mazel.

Anderson, H., Goolishian, H., & Winderman, L. (1986). Problem-determined systems: Towards transformation in family therapy. *Journal of Strategic and Systemic Therapies, 5*(4), 1–13.

Anderson, W. T. (1990). *Reality isn't what it used to be: Theatrical politics, ready-to-wear religion, global myths, primitive chic, and other wonders of the postmodern world.* San Francisco: Harper & Row.

Auerswald, E. H. (1987). Epistemological confusion in family therapy and research. *Family Process, 26*(3), 317–330.

Avis, J. M. (1985). The politics of functional family therapy: A feminist critique. *Journal of Marital and Family Therapy, 11*, 127–138.

Bateson, G. (1972). *Steps to an ecology of mind.* New York: Ballantine.

Bateson, G. (1979). *Mind and nature: A necessary unity.* New York: Dutton.

Bell, M. S. (1987). *The year of silence.* New York: Ticknor & Fields.

Berger, P., & Luckmann, T. (1966). *The social construction of reality.* New York: Doubleday.

Bernstein, A. (1990). Ethical postures that orient one's clinical decision making. *AFTA Newsletter, 41*, 13–15.

Bogdan, J. L. (1984). Family organization as an ecology of ideas: An alternative to the reification of family systems. *Family Process, 23*, 375–388.

Boscolo, L., Cecchin, G., Hoffman, L., & Penn, P. (1987). *Milan systemic family therapy: Conversations in theory and practice.* New York: Basic Books.

Bourdieu, P. (1988). *Homo academicus.* Stanford, CA: Stanford University Press.

Bruner, E. M. (1986a). Experience and its expression. In V. W. Turner & E. M. Bruner (Eds.), *The anthropology of experience* (pp. 3–20). Chicago: University of Illinois Press.

Bruner, E. M. (1986b). Ethnography as narrative. In V. W. Turner & E. M. Bruner (Eds.), *The anthropology of experience* (pp. 139–155). Chicago: University of Illinois Press.

Bruner, J. (1986). *Actual minds/possible worlds.* Cambridge: Harvard University Press.

Bruner, J. (1990). *Acts of meaning.* Cambridge: Harvard University Press.

Bruner, J. (1991). The narrative construction of reality. *Critical Inquiry, 18*, 1–21.

Burke, K. (1969). *A grammar of motives.* Berkeley: University of California Press.

Campbell, D., Draper, R., & Huffington, C. (1988). *Teaching systemic thinking.* London: D.C. Associates.

Carrese, J. A., & Rhodes, L. A. (1995). Western bioethics on the Navajo reservation. *Journal of the American Medical Association. 274*(10), 826–829.

Carter, E., Papp, P., Silverstein, O., & Walters, M. (1984). *Mothers and sons, fathers and daughters.* Monograph Series *2*(1). Washington: The Women's Project in Family Therapy.

Cecchin, G. (1987). Hypothesizing, circularity, and neutrality revisited: An invitation to curiosity. *Family Process, 26*, 405–413.

Chang, J., & Phillips, M. (1993). Michael White and Steve de Shazer: New directions in family therapy. In S. Gilligan & R. Price (Eds.), *Therapeutic conversations* (pp. 95–111). New York: Norton.

Combs, G., & Freedman, J. (1990). *Symbol, story, and ceremony: Using metaphor in individual and family therapy.* New York: Norton.

Combs, G., & Freedman, J. (1994a). Milton Erickson: Early postmodernist. In J. Zeig (Ed.), *Ericksonian methods: The essence of the story* (pp. 267–281). New York: Brunner/Mazel.

Combs, G., & Freedman, J. (1994b). Narrative intentions. In M. F. Hoyt (Ed.), *Constructive therapies.* New York: Guilford.

Cowley, G., & Springen, K. (1995, April 17). Rewriting life stories. *Newsweek,* 70–74.

Davidson, J., Lax, W., Lussardi, D., Miller, D., & Ratheau, M. (1988). The reflecting team. *Family Therapy Networker, 12*(5).

Davis, J., & Lax, W. (1991). Introduction to special section: Expanding the reflecting position in family therapy. *Journal of Strategic and Systemic Therapies, 10*(3 & 4), 1–3.

Dell, P. (1980). Researching the family theories of schizophrenia. *Family Process, 10*, 321–326.

Dell, P. (1985a). Understanding Bateson and Maturana. *Journal of Marital and Family Therapy, 11*, 1–20.

Dell, P. (1985b). Book review of *The invented reality: How do we know what we believe we know? Family Process, 24*, 290–294.

Derrida, J. (1988). *Limited, inc.* Evanston, IL: University of Illinois Press.

de Shazer, S. (1991). *Putting difference to work.* New York: Norton.

de Shazer, S. (1994). *Words were originally magic.* New York: Norton.

Dickerson, V. C., & Zimmerman, J. L. (1993). A narrative approach to families with adolescents. In S. Friedman (Ed.), *The new language of change: Constructive collaboration in psychotherapy* (pp. 226–250). New York: Guilford.

Dickerson, V. C., & Zimmerman, J. L. (in press). Myths, misconceptions, and a word or two about politics. *Journal of Systemic Therapies.*

Doherty, W. J. (1991). Family therapy goes postmodern. *Family Therapy Networker, 15*(5), 36–42.

Dolan, Y. (1985). *A path with a heart: Ericksonian utilization with resistant and chronic clients.* New York: Brunner/Mazel.

Durrant, M., & Kowalski, K. (1990). Overcoming the effects of sexual abuse: Developing a self-perception of competence. In M. Durrant & C. White (Eds.), *Ideas for therapy with sexual abuse.* Adelaide, Australia: Dulwich Centre Publications.

Efran, J. S., & Clarfield, L. E. (1992). Constructionist therapy: Sense and nonsense. In S. McNamee & K. Gergen (Eds.), *Therapy as social construction* (pp. 200–217). London: Sage.

Elkaim, M. (1985). From general laws to singularities. *Family Process, 24*, 151–164.

Emerson, R. W. (1830). *Journals.*

Epston, D. (1989a). Temper tantrum parties: Saving face, losing face, or going off your face. *Dulwich Centre Newsletter*, autumn, 12-26.

Epston, D. (1989). *Collected papers.* Adelaide, Australia: Dulwich Centre Publications.

Epston, D. (1991). I am a bear: Discovering discoveries. *Family Therapy Case Studies, 6*(1).

Epston, D. (1993a). Internalizing discourses versus externalizing discourses. In S. Gilligan & R. Price (Eds.), *Therapeutic conversations* (pp. 161-177). New York: Norton.

Epston, D. (1993b). Internalized other questioning with couples: The New Zealand version. In S. Gilligan & R. Price (Eds.), *Therapeutic conversations* (pp. 183-189). New York: Norton.

Epston, D. (1994). Extending the conversation. *Family Therapy Networker, 18*(6), 30-37, 62-63.

Epston, D., & Roth, S. (1994). Framework for a White/Epston type interview. Handout.

Epston, D., & Roth, S. (in press). Consulting the problem about the problematic relationship: An exercise for experiencing a relationship with an externalized problem. In M. Hoyt (Ed.), *Constructive therapies II: Expanding and building effective practices.* New York: Guilford.

Epston, D., & White, M. (1992). *Experience, contradiction, narrative, and imagination: Selected papers of David Epston and Michael White, 1989-1991.* Adelaide, Australia: Dulwich Centre Publications.

Erickson, M. H. (1965/1980). The use of symptoms as an integral part of hypnotherapy. In E. L. Rossi (Ed.), *The collected papers of Milton H. Erickson on hypnosis. IV. Innovative hypnotherapy* (pp. 212-223). New York: Irvington.

Erickson, M. H., & Rossi, E. L. (1979). *Hypnotherapy: An exploratory casebook.* New York: Irvington.

Erickson, M. H., & Rossi, E. L. (1980). The february man: Facilitating new identity in hypnotherapy. In E. Rossi (Ed.), *The collected papers of Milton H. Erickson on hypnosis. IV. Innovative hypnotherapy.* New York: Irvington.

Erickson, M. H., & Rossi, E. L. (1981). *Experiencing hypnosis: Therapeutic approaches to altered states.* New York: Irvington.

Erickson, M. H. & Rossi, E. L. (1989). *The february man.* New York: Brunner/Mazel.

Erickson, M. H., Rossi, E. L., & Rossi, S. I. (1976). *Hypnotic realities: The induction of clinical hypnosis and forms of indirect suggestion.* New York: Irvington.

Fleuridas, C., Nelson, T. S., & Rosenthal, D. M. (1986). The evolution of circular questions: Training family therapists. *Journal of Marital and Family Therapy, 12*(2), 113-127.

Foucault, M. (1965). *Madness and civilization: A history of insanity in the age of reason* (R. Howard, Trans.). New York: Random House.

Foucault, M. (1975). *The birth of the clinic: An archeology of medical perception* (A. M. Sheridan Smith, Trans.). New York: Random House.

Foucault, M. (1977). *Discipline and punish: The birth of the prison* (A. Sheridan, Trans.). New York: Pantheon Books.

Foucault, M. (1980). *Power/knowledge: Selected interviews and other writings, 1972-1977.* New York: Pantheon Books.

Foucault, M. (1985). *The history of sexuality, vol. 2: The use of pleasure* (R. Hurley, Trans.). New York: Pantheon Books.

Freedman, J., & Combs, G. (1993). Invitations to new stories: Using questions to explore alternative possibilities. In S. Gilligan & R. Price (Eds.), *Therapeutic conversations* (pp. 291-303). New York: Norton.

Freedman, J., & Combs, G. (in press). Gender stories. *Journal of Systemic Therapies.*

Freeman, J., & Lobovits, D. (1993). The turtle with wings. In S. Friedman (Ed.), *The new language of change: Constructive collaboration on psychotherapy.* New York: Guilford.

Freeman, J., Loptson, C., & Stacey, K. (1995, March 1-4). *Collaboration and possibility: Appreciating the privilege of entering children's narrative world.* Handout from workshop presented at "Narrative Ideas and Therapeutic Practice," Third International Conference, Vancouver, BC.

Furman, B., & Ahola, T. (1992). *Solution talk: Hosting therapeutic conversations.* New York: Norton.

Geertz, C. (1978). *The interpretation of cultures.* New York: Basic Books

Geertz, C. (1983). *Local knowledge: Further essays in interpretive anthropology.* New York: Basic Books.

Geertz, C. (1986). Making experiences, authoring selves. In V. W. Turner & E. M. Bruner (Eds.), *The anthropology of experience* (pp. 373-380). Chicago: University of Illinois Press.

Gergen, K. (1985). The social constructionist movement in modern psychology. *American Psychologist, 40,* 266-275.

Gergen, K. (1991a). *The saturated self: Dilemmas of identity in contemporary life.* New York: Basic Books.

Gergen, K. (1991b). Therapeutic professions and the diffusion of deficit. *Journal of Mind and Behavior, 11,* 353-368.

Gergen, K. (1992). The postmodern adventure. *Family Therapy Networker,* Nov./Dec., 52 & 56-57.

Gilligan, S. (1987). *Therapeutic trances: The cooperation principle in Ericksonian hypnotherapy.* New York: Brunner/Mazel.

Goldner, V. (1985a). Feminism and family therapy. *Family Process, 24,* 31-47.

Goldner, V. (1985b). Warning: Family therapy may be dangerous to your health. *Family Therapy Networker, 9*(6), 18-23.

Goolishian, H. (1990). Therapy as a linguistic system: Hermeneutics, narrative and meaning. *The Family Psychologist, 6,* 44-45.

Goolishian, H., & Anderson, H. (1981) Including non-blood related persons in family therapy. In A. Gurman (Ed.), *Questions and answers in family therapy.* New York: Brunner/Mazel.

Goolishian, H., & Anderson, H. (1987). Language systems and therapy: An evolving idea. *Journal of Psychotherapy, 23*(3S), 529-538.

Goolishian, H., & Anderson, H. (1990). Understanding the therapeutic process: From individuals and families to systems in language. In F. Kaslow (Ed.), *Voices in family psychology.* Newbury Park, CA: Sage.

Griffith, J. L. (1986). Employing the God-family relationship in therapy with religious families. *Family Process, 4,* 609-618.

Griffith, J. L., & Griffith, M. E. (1992a). Owning one's epistemological stance in therapy. *Dulwich Centre Newsletter, 1,* 5-11.

Griffith, J. L., & Griffith, M. E. (1992b). Speaking the unspeakable: Use of the reflecting position in therapies for somatic symptoms. *Family Systems Medicine, 10*, 41–51.

Griffith, J. L., & Griffith, M. E. (1994). *The body speaks: Therapeutic dialogues for mind-body problems.* New York: Basic Books.

Griffith, M. E. (1995). On not trampling pearls. *AFTA Newsletter, 59*(spring), 17–20.

Haley, J. (1963). *Strategies of psychotherapy.* New York: Grune & Stratton. (Reissued 1990 by Triangle Press, Rockville, MD).

Haley, J. (1973). *Uncommon therapy: The psychiatric techniques of Milton H. Erickson, M.D.* New York: Norton.

Haley, J. (1976). *Problem-solving therapy: New strategies for effective family therapy.* San Francisco: Jossey-Bass.

Hall, R. L., & Greene, B. (1994). Cultural competence in feminist family therapy: An ethicial mandate. *Journal of Feminist Family Therapy, 6*(3), 5–28.

Hare-Mustin, R. (1978). A feminist approach to family therapy. *Family Process, 17*, 181–194.

Hare-Mustin, R. (1994). Discourses in the mirrored room: A postmodern analysis of therapy. *Family Process, 33*, 19–35.

Hoffman, L. (1981). *Foundations of family therapy.* New York: Basic Books.

Hoffman, L. (1985). Beyond power and control: Toward a "second order" family systems therapy. *Family Systems Medicine, 3*, 381–396.

Hoffman, L. (1988). A constructivist position for family therapy. *The Irish Journal of Psychology, 9*, 110–129.

Hoffman, L. (1990). Constructing realities: An art of lenses. *Family Process, 29*, 1–12.

Hoffman, L. (1991). Foreword. In T. Andersen (Ed.), *The reflecting team: Dialogues and dialogues about the dialogues* (pp. ix–xiv). New York: Norton.

Hoffman, L. (1992). A reflexive stance for family therapy. In S. McNamee & K. J. Gergen (Eds.), *Therapy as social construction* (pp. 7–24). London: Sage.

Howard, G. S. (1991). Culture tales: A narrative approach to thinking, cross-cultural psychology, and psychotherapy. *American Psychologist, 46*(3), 187–197.

Jenkins, A. (1990). *Invitations to responsibility: The therapeutic engagement of men who are violent and abusive.* Adelaide, Australia: Dulwich Centre Publications.

Kazan, Z. (1994). Power: A multi-dimensional perspective. *Dulwich Centre Newsletter, 1*, 28–31.

Keeney, B. (1983). *The aesthetics of change.* New York: Guilford.

Keeney, B., & Sprenkle, D. (1982). Ecosystemic epistemology. *Family Process, 21*, 1–22.

Kuhn, T. (1970). *The structure of scientific revolution.* Chicago: University of Chicago Press.

Kvale, S. (Ed.). (1992). *Psychology and postmodernism.* London: Sage.

Laird, J. (1989). Women and stories: Restorying women's self-constructions. In M. McGoldrick, C. Anderson, & F. Walsh (Eds.), *Women in families: A framework for family therapy* (pp. 427–450). New York: Norton.

Laube, J., & Trefz, S. (1994). Group therapy using a narrative theory framework: Application to treatment of depression. *Journal of Systemic Therapies, 13*(2), 29–37.

Law, I. (1994). A conversation with Kiwi Tamasese and Charles Waldegrave. *Dulwich Centre Newsletter, 1*, 20–27.

Lax, W. D. (1991). The reflecting team and the initial consultation. In T. Andersen, *The reflecting team: Dialogues and dialogues about the dialogues* (pp. 127–144). New York: Norton.

Levin, S., Raser, J., Niles, C., & Reese, A. (1986). Beyond family systems-toward problem systems: Some clinical implications. *Journal of Strategic and Systemic Therapies, 5*(4), 62–69.

Lipchik, E. (1988). Interviewing with a constructive ear. *Dulwich Centre Newsletter*, winter, 3–7.

Lipchik, E., & de Shazer, S. (1986). The purposeful interview. *Journal of Strategic and Systemic Therapies, 5*(1), 88–99.

Lobovits, D., & Freeman, J. C. (1993). Toward collaboration and accountability: Alternatives to the dominant discourse for understanding sexual exploitation by professionals. *Dulwich Centre Newsletter, 3 & 4*, 33–46.

Lobovitz, D., Maisel, R., & Freeman, J. (1995). Public practices: An ethic of circulation. In S. Friedman (Ed.), *The reflecting team in action.* New York: Guilford.

Lowe, R. (1991). Postmodern themes and therapeutic practices: Notes towards the definition of "family therapy": Part 2. *Dulwich Centre Newsletter, 3*, 41–52.

Madanes, C. (1981). *Strategic Family Therapy.* San Francisco: Jossey-Bass.

Madanes, C. (1984). *Behind the one-way mirror: Advances in the practice of strategic therapy.* San Francisco: Jossey-Bass.

Madigan, S. (1991). Discursive restraints in therapist practice: Situating therapist questions in the presence of the family. *Dulwich Centre Newsletter, 3*, 13–20.

Madigan, S. P. (1993). Questions about questions: Situating the therapist's curiosity in front of the family. In S. Gilligan & R. Price (Eds.), *Therapeutic conversations* (pp. 219–230). New York: Norton.

Madigan, S. (1994). Body politics. *Family Therapy Networker, 18*(6), 27.

Madigan, S. (in press). Undermining the problem in the privatization of problems in persons: Considering the socio-political and cultural context in the externalizing of internalized problem conversations. *Journal of Systemic Therapies.*

Madigan, S., & Epston, D. (1995). From "spy-chiatric gaze" to communities of concern: From professional monologue to dialogue. In S. Friedman (Ed.), *The reflecting team in action.* New York: Guilford.

Madigan, S., & Law, I. (1992). Discourse not language: The shift from a modernist view of language to the postmodern analysis of discourse in family therapy. *Dulwich Centre Newsletter, 1*, 31–36.

Mair, M. (1988). Psychology as storytelling. *International Journal of Personal Construct Psychology, 1*, 125–137.

Maisel, R. (1994). *Engaging men in a re-evaluation of practices and definitions of masculinity.* Paper presented at "Narrative Ideas and Therapeutic Practice," Third International Conference, Vancouver, BC.

Maturana, H., & Varela, F. (1980). *Autopoesis and cognition: The realization of living.* Boston: D. Reidel.

Maturana, H., & Varela, F. (1987). *The tree of knowledge: The biological roots of human understanding.* Boston: Shambhala.

McLean, C. (1994). Editorial. *Dulwich Centre Newsletter, 2 & 3*, 2–5.

McNamee, S. (1994). Research as relationally situated activity: Ethical implications. In M. Snyder (Ed.), *Ethical issues in feminist family therapy* (pp. 69–83). New York: Haworth.

Myerhoff, B. (1986). "Life not death in Venice": Its second life. In V. W. Turner & E. M. Bruner (Eds.), *The anthropology of experience* (pp. 261–286). Chicago: University of Illinois Press.

Minuchin, S. (1991). The seductions of constructivism. *Family Therapy Networker, 15*(5), 47–50.

Morrison, T. (1992). *Playing in the dark: Whiteness and the literary imagination.* Cambridge: Harvard University Press.

Neal, J. H. (1995). *Gender and men in narrative couples therapy.* Presented at "Narrative Ideas and Therapeutic Practice," Third International Conference, Vancouver, BC.

Neal, J. H. (in press). Consultation and training from a narrative perspective. *Journal of Systemic Therapies.*

Nylund, D., & Thomas, J. (1994). The economics of narrative. *Family Therapy Networker, 18*(6), 38–39.

O'Hanlon, B. (1994). The third wave. *Family Therapy Networker, 18*(6), 18–26, 28–29.

O'Hanlon, W., & Weiner-Davis, M. (1989). *In search of solutions: A new direction for family therapy.* New York: Norton.

O'Hara, M. (1995). Constructing emancipatory realities. In W. T. Anderson (Ed.), *The truth about the truth: De-confusing and re-constructing the postmodern world.* New York: G. P. Putnam.

Paré, D. A. (1995). Of families and other cultures: The shifting paradigm of family therapy. *Family Process, 34*, 1–19.

Parry, A. (1991). A universe of stories. *Family Process, 30*, 37–54.

Pearson, L. (1965). Introduction. In L. Pearson (Ed.), *Written communications in psychotherapy* (pp. xi–xii). Springfield, IL: Charles C Thomas.

Penn, P. (1982). Circular questioning. *Family Process, 21*, 267–280.

Penn, P. (1985). Feed-forward: Future questions, future maps. *Family Process, 24*, 299–310.

Penn, P., & Frankfurt, M. (1994). Creating a participant text: Writing, multiple voices, narrative multiplicity. *Family Process, 33*, 217–31.

Penn, P., & Sheinberg, M. (1991). Stories and conversations, *Journal of Strategic and Systemic Therapies, 10*(3&4), 30–37.

Rambo, A. H., Heath, A., & Chenail, R. J. (1993). *Practicing therapy: Exercises for growing therapists.* New York: Norton.

Reiss, D. (1985). Commentary: The social construction of reality—the passion within us all. *Family Process, 24*, 254–257.

Roberts, J. (1994). *Tales and transformations: Stories in families and family therapy.* New York: Norton.

Rorty, R. (1989). *Contingency, irony, and solidarity.* New York: Cambridge University Press.

Rorty, R. (1991a). *Objectivity, relativism, and truth: Philosophical papers, vol. 1.* New York: Cambridge University Press.

Rorty, R. (1991b). *Essays on Heidegger and others: Philosophical papers, vol. 2.* New York: Cambridge University Press.

Rosaldo, R. (1986). Ilongot hunting as story and experience. In V. Turner & E. Bruner (Eds.), *The anthropology of experience.* Chicago: University of Chicago Press.

Rosen, S. (1982). *My voice with go with you: The teaching tales of Milton H. Erickson.* New York: Norton.

Rosenblatt, P. C. (1994). *Metaphors of family systems theory: Toward new constructions.* New York: Guilford.

Rossi, E. L. (Ed.). (1980a). *The collected papers of Milton H. Erickson on hypnosis. I. The nature of hypnosis and suggestion.* New York: Irvington.

Rossi, E. L. (Ed.). (1980b). *The collected papers of Milton H. Erickson on hypnosis. IV. Innovative hypnotherapy.* New York: Irvington.

Roth, S., & Epston, D. (in press). Developing externalizing conversations: An introductory exercise. *Journal of Systemic Therapies.*

Roth, S., & Chasin, R. (1994). Entering one another's worlds of meaning and imagination: Dramatic enactment and narrative couple therapy. In M. F. Hoyt (Ed.), *Constructive therapies* (pp. 189–216). New York: Guilford.

Salinger, J. D. (1955/61). *Franny and Zooey.* Harmondsworth, Middlesex, England: Penguin Books, Ltd.

Schmidt, G., & Trenkle, B. (1985) An integration of Ericksonian techniques with concepts of family therapy. In J. Zeig (Ed.), *Ericksonian psychotherapy, vol. II: Clinical applications* (pp. 132–154). New York: Brunner/Mazel.

Schultz, A. (1962). *Collected papers, vol. 1: The problem of social reality* (M. Natanson, Ed.). Nijhoff: The Hague.

Selvini Palazzoli, M., Boscolo, L., Cecchin, G., & Prata, G., (1978). *Paradox and counterparadox.* New York: Aronson.

Selvini Palazzoli, M., Boscolo, L., Cecchin, G., & Prata, G., (1980). Hypothesizing-circularity-neutrality: Three guidelines for the conductor of the session. *Family Process, 19,* 3–12.

Shilts, L. G., & Ray, W. A. (1991). Therapeutic letters: Pacing with the system. *Journal of Strategic and Systemic Therapies, 10*(3 & 4), 92–99.

Simon, D. (1995). Doing therapy as a spiritual path. *News of the Difference, IV*(1), 1–5.

Taggart, M. (1985). The feminist critique in epistemological perspective: Questions of context in family therapy. *Journal of Marital and Family Therapy, 11,* 113–126.

Tamasese, K., & Waldegrave, C. (1993). Cultural and gender accountability in the "Just Therapy" approach. *Journal of Feminist Family Therapy, 5*(2), 29–45.

Tapping, C. et al. (1993). Other wisdoms other worlds: Colonisation and family therapy. *Dulwich Centre Newsletter, 1,* 3–40.

Tomm, K. (1987a). Interventive interviewing: Part I. Strategizing as a fourth guidline for the therapist. *Family Process, 26,* 3–13.

Tomm, K. (1987b). Interventive interviewing: Part II. Reflexive questioning as a means to enable self-healing. *Family Process, 26,* 167–183.

Tomm, K. (1988). Interventive interviewing: Part III. Intending to ask lineal, circular, strategic, or reflexive questions? *Family Process, 27,* 1–15.

Tomm, K. (1989). Externalizing the problem and internalizing personal agency. *Journal of Strategic and Systemic Therapy, 8*(1), 54–59.

Tomm, K. (1993). The courage to protest: A commentary on Michael White's work. In S. Gilligan & R. Price (Eds.), *Therapeutic Conversations* (pp. 62–80). New York: Norton.

Turner, V. (1986). Dewey, Dilthey, and drama: An essay in the anthropology of experience. In V. Turner & E. Bruner (Eds.), *The anthropology of experience* (pp. 33–44). Chicago: University of Illinois Press.

von Foerster, H. (1981). *Observing systems.* Seaside, CA: Intersystems Publications.

von Glasersfeld, E. (1987). *The construction of knowledge.* Salinas, CA: Intersystems Publications.

Wagner, V., Weeks, G., & L'Abate, L. (1980). Enrichment and written messages with couples. *American Journal of Family Therapy, 8,* 36–44.

Waldegrave, C. T. (1990). Just Therapy. *Dulwich Centre Newsletter, 1,* 5–46.

Wangberg F. (1991). Self reflection: Turning the mirror inward *Journal of Strategic and Systemic Therapies, 10*(3&4), 18–29.

Watzlawick, P. (Ed.). (1984). *The invented reality.* New York: Norton.

Watzlawick, P., Weakland, J., & Fisch, R. (1974). *Change: Principles of problem formation and problem resolution.* New York: Norton.

Weingarten, K. (1991). The discourses of intimacy: Adding a social constructionist and feminist view. *Family Process, 30,* 285–305.

Weingarten, K. (1992). A consideration of intimate and non-intimate interactions in therapy. *Family Process, 31,* 45–59.

White, M. (1986a). Family escape from trouble. *Case Studies, 1,* 1.

White, M. (1986b). Negative explanation, restraint and double description: A template for family therapy. *Family Process, 25,* 169–184.

White, M. (1987). Family therapy and schizophrenia: Addressing the "in-the-corner" lifestyle. *Dulwich Centre Newsletter*, spring, 14–21.

White, M. (1988a). The process of questioning: A therapy of literary merit? *Dulwich Centre Newsletter*, winter, 8–14.

White, M. (1988b). Saying hullo again: The incorporation of the lost relationship in the resolution of grief. *Dulwich Centre Newsletter*, spring, 7–11.

White, M. (1988/9). The externalizing of the problem and the re-authoring of lives and relationships. *Dulwich Centre Newsletter*, summer, 3–20.

White, M. (1989). *Selected papers.* Adelaide, Australia: Duwich Centre Publications.

White, M. (1991). Deconstruction and therapy. *Dulwich Centre Newsletter, 3,* 21–40.

White, M. (1993). Commentary: The histories of the present. In S. Gilligan & R. Price (Eds.), *Therapeutic conversations* (pp. 121–135). New York: Norton.

White, M. (1995). *Re-authoring lives: Interviews and essays.* Adelaide, Australia: Dulwich Centre Publications.

White, M., & Epston, D. (1990). *Narrative means to therapeutic ends.* New York: Norton.

Wiener, N. (1950). *The human use of human beings.* New York: Avon Books.

Wilcoxon, A., & Fenell, D. (1983). Engaging the non-attending spouse in marital therapy through the use of therapist-initiated written communication. *Journal of Marital and Family Therapy, 12,* 191–193.

Winch, P. (1958). *The idea of a social science and its relation to philosophy.* London: Routledge & Kegan Paul.

Wojcik, J., & Iverson, E. (1989). Therapeutic letters: The power of the printed word. *Journal of Strategic and Systemic Therapies, 8*(2 & 3), 77–81.

Wood, D., & Uhl, N. (1988). Postsession letters: Reverberations in the family treatment system. *Journal of Strategic and Systemic Therapies, 7*(3), 35–52.

Zeig, J. (1980). *A teaching seminar with Milton H. Erickson, M.D.* New York: Brunner/Mazel.

Zeig, J. (1985). *Experiencing Erickson: An introduction to the man and his work.* New York: Brunner/Mazel.

Zimmerman, J. L., & Dickerson, V. C. (1993). Bringing forth the restraining influence of pattern in couples therapy. In S. Gilligan & R. Price (Eds.), *Therapeutic conversations* (pp. 197–214). New York: Norton.

Zimmerman, J. L., & Dickerson, V. C. (1994a). Using a narrative metaphor: Implications for theory and clinical practice. *Family Process, 33,* 233–246.

Zimmerman, J. L., & Dickerson, V. C. (1994b). Tales of the body thief: Externalizing and deconstructing eating problems. In M. F. Hoyt (Ed.), *Constructive therapies* (pp. 295–318). New York: Guilford.

Index